Praise for Iain Gately's

'A pacy journey through a sw[...]
comparisons, tellings anecdotes [...]

'Whether smoked, chewed or snuff[...] ...en smoked,
tobacco always had ritual significance, at least until its real dangers
were discovered. Mr Gately, a smoker himself, adopts a nicely
detached attitude towards the passions which have surrounded it and
which he records so assiduously here' *Sunday Telegraph*

'Iain Gately paints an alluring picture of tobacco tracing its history –
from its humble beginnings in ancient South American civilisations to
its use today in rituals and as a universal stimulant' *Evening Standard*

'Excellent . . . Gately, his mind sharpened no doubt by his
own smoking habit, presents this eventful tale with lucid,
if partisan, prose' *The Times*

'Plenty to enjoy' *TLS*

'Constantly fascinating' *Independent*

'Fascinating . . . Gately's obvious passion for his subject and his
impressively exhaustive research make it challenging for any reader,
including the most fervent anti-smoker, to resist enjoying [*La Diva
Nicotina*] . . . Deeply engaging and witty' *New York Times*

'A book that cuts through the fug of anti-smoking rhetoric and horror
stories, *La Diva Nicotina* is a well-researched history of the evil weed . . .
Gately's book is an intelligent, balanced historical document charting
one of the most vilified plants on earth' *Big Issue*

'Iain Gately's trawl through the history of smoking is riveting' *Insight*

'With irreverent wit and uncommon grace, Gately shares his
enthusiasms with any reader brave enough to buy a book with the
demon weed on the cover' *Publishers Weekly*

'Follow his wonderful tale, which winds and wreathes like tobacco
smoke. Take a peaceable look at tobacco, perhaps in the company of a
well-stored Monte Cristo' *Business Week*

IAIN GATELY was born in 1963 and brought up in Hong Kong. He studied law at Cambridge University before working in London's financial markets. His previous books are *The Assessor*, a novel, and *La Diva Nicotina: The Story of How Tobacco Seduced the World*.

PLANET PARTY

A World of Celebration

Iain Gately

POCKET
BOOKS

LONDON • SYDNEY • NEW YORK • TORONTO

First published in Great Britain by Pocket, 2004
An imprint of Simon & Schuster UK Ltd
A Viacom Company

1 3 5 7 9 10 8 6 4 2

Simon & Schuster UK Ltd
Africa House
64–78 Kingsway
London WC2B 6AH

www.simonsays.co.uk

Simon & Schuster Australia
Sydney

A CIP catalogue record for this book is available
from the British Library

ISBN 0-7434-7860-6

Typeset by M Rules
Printed and bound in Great Britain by
Cox & Wyman Ltd, Reading, Berkshire

The publisher has made every reasonable effort to trace the copyright holders of all
material reproduced in this book. Where it has not been possible to trace copyright
holders, the publisher will be happy to credit them in all future editions.

Picture Credits

12, 27, 33 © ePicscotland.com; 15 © Charles Tait; 36, 51, 58 © Trinidad Express
Newspapers; 42, a drawing by Melton Prior, Courtesy of the *Illustrated London News*;
55 © Jalisco Tourist Board; 62 © Keith Lomas; 75, 81, 84: reproduced with permission
from Landmark Publishing Ltd, 2002; 78 © Dave Burgess, *Daily Telegraph*; 88, 103, 108
© R. Olid; 120: reproduced from Padhi, Jagabandhu, *Sri Jagannatha at Puri*, Manorama
Puspalak, 2000; 136, 149 © Paul Newton; 148, 154, 155 © Jim Hollander; 160, 275 ©
Camera Press; 171 © Painetworks; 174, 177, 178, 180 © Pete Martin, Martin and Elders
Photography; 182 © Thom van Os; 192, 206 © Tony Pletts; 203 © Gabe Kircheimer;
208, 223, 225, 228 © Carol Beckwith, Robert Estall Photo Library; 230 ©
Reuters/Michaela Rehle; 242, 256 © Munich Tourist Board; 246, 248, 250 © Ben
Gladstone; 258 © *Cronicas y Leyendas de esta Noble, Leal y Mefitica Ciudad de México*,
September 2002; 267 © José Guadalupe Posada

This book is dedicated to my father,
Charles Gately.

CONTENTS

ACKNOWLEDGEMENTS

To Simon Trewin and to James Johnstone, for their advice and practical support; to Keith Miller and Desire Baptiste, for revealing the soul of Trinidad; to Lindsay Porter for his invaluable comments on Ashbourne; in Seville, to Rocio Olid Fiances, to David, and to Marco and Ellie Nicolas Olega; to Asoka in Kandy, and to the staff of the Love and Life guesthouse in Puri; to Caspar Luard in Pamplona; my belated thanks to Anthony and Jennifer Peebles for their hospitality in Siena, and to Katharina Grafin Reuttner von Weyl for her hospitality in Swabia; at Burning Man, my compliments to the captain, his audacious first mate, to G-fire, to Liz, and to the good folks of Unicamp; in Munich to Ben Gladstone for his steady camera hand, to Astrid Ganssen and her colleagues of the Munich Tourist Board; and to Eva Rodriguez Najera, besos, and my gratitude for her accounts of the days of the dead.

PLANET PARTY

A World of Celebration

I

ANY EXCUSE
FOR A PARTY

*A man hath no better thing under the sun than to eat, and
to drink, and to be merry*

ECCLESIASTES [8:15]

We are natural born hedonists, fun-loving animals, fashioned by
evolution to live for pleasure. This sybaritic streak is apparent not
merely in our solitary diversions and vices, but also in our social
activities, and in particular in the formal encounters that we have
devised to entertain ourselves in numbers. The world is filled
with a plethora of festivals, commemorating an abundance of
matters, that allow us to gather together in self-indulgence and
celebration. On almost any given day of every year, at some point
on the globe, people will be meeting to stage parades, to venerate
their gods, to sing and to dance, to send fireworks into the night

sky, and to applaud as the sound of their detonations reverberates from the earth. Somewhere, right now, drums, gongs, bells, brass bands and bagpipes will be sending out messages, melodies and rhythms aiming to inspire their audiences with ecstasy or Holy Dread. And strangers will be kneeling shoulder to shoulder, or dancing thigh to thigh, tangling their arms about one another and pressing their lips against each other's flesh, while perhaps the air around them is filled with the odours of jasmine, sweat, incense, orange blossom, gunpowder, roses and alcohol, and the stars above compete with candlelight to illuminate their revels.

A selection of such public entertainments, ranging from the desert beauty contests of nomads, to extended bouts of gluttony held in major cities, and including examples of piety, spheroludomania, blood sacrifice and crossdressing, forms the subject of this book. Together, they illustrate the marvels of diversity within human civilisation. They also form a collective tribute to human invention, for each of the festivals that has been selected is, in its own way, a fantasy as much as a spectacle, which encourages its participants not only to behave strangely, but to justify such behaviour with the most unlikely excuses. Indeed, most festivals require faith as much as hedonism from their participants – they are temporary, self-contained worlds, subject to their own special rules and philosophies. For instance, the belief that the dead return to earth every year and expect to be entertained for the duration of their visit, is central to an event staged in Mexico each November; and the knowledge that a painted log is in fact Jagannath, the Lord of the Universe, is the key to understanding the ceremonies performed in an ancient temple on the coast of Bengal during the first bright fortnight of the month of Asadha.

The eccentric behaviour and states of mind that are encouraged at festivals, and the host of pretexts employed to justify them, have long been matters of fascination to me. The very first festival that I remember attending, at the age of five, had, as its raison d'être, a typically improbable alibi. It was the Mid-Autumn festival in Hong Kong, whose notional purpose was to honour Chang-Er, a beautiful princess, Wu-Kang, a shiftless woodcutter, and To-Jai, the Jade Rabbit, each of whom, for various reasons, had been exiled from the earth to live together for eternity on the moon. The festival was timed to coincide with the eighth full moon of the Chinese Year of the Iron Monkey. It was celebrated on Repulse Bay beach, and commenced at dusk. Every child arrived with a moon-lantern, made from translucent waxed paper wrapped on a wire frame, with a candle mounted inside, and shaped to resemble an animal, a fish, a castle, a car. Mine was a tank. Families brought picnics and moon-cakes (Chinese pastries filled with bean curd or vintage eggs) and sat in groups on the sands. Each marked out their territory with concentric rings of candles. The air was warm, the atmosphere was happy and relaxed. When the moon rose out of the sea it was a pale lemon yellow, but as it ascended its colour changed to that of white gold, and its light defined a silver road across the surface of the ocean. A few rockets were fired in its direction, tracing arcs into the sky. I remember these particularly as fireworks were banned by the British administration the following year, on the grounds that they made the Chinese 'excitable'. Whether the rockets did their work and the event degenerated into an orgy or debauch I do not know – my parents carried me home fast asleep. The impression that the festival left was nonetheless profound. This was not only because it had allowed me to indulge in otherwise forbidden pleasures, such as staying up late and playing with fire, but also because, when taken in conjunction with an event that occurred shortly afterwards, it showed me that adults were not the rational gods I had suspected them of being. They too were prepared to suspend their belief in absolutes – if they thought that doing so might give them pleasure.

A few months after the moon festival, I was once again given a special dispensation to stay up late, this time to watch the first moon landing take place on television. The black and white images of Americans named Buzz and Neil bouncing around a desert were a vast disappointment. Where, I asked, were Chang-Er, Wu-Kang, and my favourite, the Jade Rabbit? Were they hiding?

'Probably,' my father told me, and left it at that. We returned to the Mid-Autumn festival the next year, once again to celebrate the resident immortals of the moon, and to pretend, if only for the space of a single night, that their celestial home had never yet been visited by men.

I have willingly suspended my disbelief, and sacrificed reason on the altar of pleasure many times since. I have sought out festivals, the stranger the better, delighting in their mysteries, and becoming, in the process, a connoisseur of weak excuses for irregular behaviour. I have travelled to new countries, and enquired of their inhabitants, in the manner of visitors in times past, 'What are your customs?' and 'Who are your gods?' I have admired the moon not only as a haven for rabbits, but also as Gidja, The Creator and totemic ancestor of the Australian Dreamtime. I have danced under tropical and Nordic stars, I have painted the nipples of absolute strangers, I have dressed in lucky colours, I have worn out shoe leather on pilgrimages and all the time have sought to find a pattern in the chaos of justifications offered for celebration. Why, I wondered, in an age of reason, should people be so eager to honour lies and myths? Why elevate and venerate anachronisms and delusions? And why surrender, if only temporarily, a functional narrative of life for one that admits of wonders and of prodigies? Surely there had to be a pattern, that made us delinquent for predictable reasons?

I decided to turn from looking at the stated justifications for any festival – the excuses for holding a party – to analysing the way in which such events are, and have been celebrated. Just as buildings created to worship different gods might employ identical methods of construction and similar architectural devices, so festivals staged in the nominal honour of a host of fantasies might yet serve as camouflage for universal patterns of behaviour; and the strange rules that they exhibit be cover for the practice of certain necessary if irrational pleasures, whose denial might render society unstable.

Perhaps we need to overeat, to dress up in disguise, to pretend that fairies exist, in order to live together in peace in numbers. And perhaps, also, as our social organisation has become more complicated, we need to compensate for the loss of animal freedoms – and we need to be compensated for surrendering our liberty. We need substitutes, and allegories that enable us to express ourselves in a natural manner, and it is festivals that fulfil these needs.

I began to investigate the history of celebration, with the aim of discovering whether the activities permitted or encouraged at festivals displayed any constancy over time. Perhaps, and notwithstanding their wildly disparate official purposes, the entertainments that they offered might be similar. Perhaps, just as intimacy is the same the whole world over, so the ways in which we engage one another en masse might reveal a common inspiration. I was pleased to discover that this seemed to be the case. The pleasures, in the sense of the activities at festivals requiring justification, are few in comparison to the mob of excuses employed to sanction them. They are feasting, intoxication, mingling with the opposite sex, starting fires, wearing disguises, singing and dancing, worship, observing and participating in spectacles, making works of art, self-denial, facing danger, killing or sacrificing, and contest. They are permitted in every human society, although sometimes only during festivals. Most of them have been practised by our species since its earliest days, and could be said to be innate. Feasting, for example, especially on meat, can be traced as a festive exercise to our most distant ancestors. Archaeological evidence, in the form of bone pits filled with the remains of many animals slaughtered simultaneously, show that we have been gathering together to binge on flesh for many tens of thousands of years. Dressing up is similarly ancient: the first picture of a human by a human, painted on the rock wall of a French cave circa 35,000 years ago, is of a semi-clothed figure known by archaeologists as the 'Shaman'. The Shaman, for reasons that have yet to be determined, is depicted wearing a reindeer's head upon his own. He may have been a hunter, he may have been a priest, but although his motives for disguise remain unclear, the fact that he is wearing it is incontrovertible.

In contrast to such primal forms of hedonism, some of the activities pursued at festivals appear to date from later in our history, and to have been introduced when our ancestors took up the practice of agriculture and grouped together to build cities. The step change in social order these developments occasioned meant that people could not behave as freely as they had done in the wild, so formulas had to be developed in order to accommodate the more savage aspects of human nature. Take competition as an example: we are an aggressive species, ready to challenge each other for mates and food, and this potentially destructive instinct cannot be removed from us by the simple expedient of packing us together in cities. If, owing to the exigencies of society, competition may not be enjoyed at will, provision must at least be made for its occasional exercise. The solution was to allow its expression in a ritualised manner. Hence, for instance, the Ancient Greeks devised *Agonistes*, organised games disguised as religious ceremonies, of which the most important were the Olympics, at which people might exercise directly, or by proxy, their instinctual rivalry.

Spectating, too, was a latecomer as a festive activity. But once it was understood that people could satisfy their less civic urges via stand-ins, that watching men fight one another, or kill animals was nearly as emotionally satisfying as doing so in person, a new host of festivals sprang up that featured such entertainments, and armies of excuses were marshalled to justify their presentation. These events were found to be useful ways of controlling the hedonistic masses, who could be manipulated by allowing or denying them their pleasures. In Imperial Rome, for example, festivals were accepted ways of winning the favour of the populace – and were expected by the latter as indicative of an aspiring statesman's gravitas. Cicero (106–43 BC), consul and orator, advised that the first consideration of any would-be politician should be to put on a *pompae plena*, i.e. a 'good show', which should be 'brilliant, resplendent and popular, with the utmost display and dignitas', for 'The Roman plebs should not be prevented from enjoying games, or gladiatorial contests, or banquets – all these our ancestors established – nor should candidates be restrained from showing that generosity which indicates liberality, rather than bribery.' Festivals were the key to power in Rome. As Juvenal observed, a century after Cicero, 'Limit the anxieties of the Romans to two things – bread and circuses.'

The example of Imperial Rome has been repeated many times over the intervening millennia. Festivals have been sponsored by tyrants, republics and religious faiths, in the hope of associating their messages in the minds of the people with the pleasures that they paid for or permitted. And while these messages have been as varied as the bodies that formulated them, the pleasures have been more or less constant. As a consequence, many events have outlived their founders, indeed have served as vehicles for a variety of doctrines, and so have come to be decorated with raisons d'être that are not only ridiculous but anachronistic. For example, the largest festival celebrated in the world in the present day, which is to all intents and purposes a giant meat feast, has as its nominal purpose the commemoration of the wedding of a minor European monarch, who has been dead for well over a century, who broke his marriage vows in his lifetime, and who abdicated in scandalous circumstances. History, it seems, is largely to blame for the forest of alibis that has grown up all over the world to justify a handful of simple, pleasurable, communal activities.

Having glanced at the roots of celebration, it is time to turn to its fruits and flowers. The series of examples that follows has been chosen to illustrate the common forms of collective hedonism, and also to provide a sense of the extraordinary variety of ritual that has evolved around these over time and across the continents. I have drawn from history, from my own experiences, and from the accounts of other travellers in order to provide as complete a portrait as possible of each event.

Collectively, this series of festivals may be conceived of as comprising the itinerary for a single journey around the world and through the seasons – a voyage of celebration. There will be dirt, sweat and danger en route, as well as feasting and fancy dress. Moreover, not just the exotic, but also the shocking will be on parade. Present day festivals are not merely time capsules, preserving fragments of the rituals and philosophies of expired civilisations, but rather are vital events that license their participants for excess, and enable them to indulge in actions that are otherwise proscribed in their daily lives.

However, and in addition to dissipation and depravity, there will be joyful crowds, dancing as if it were their last day on earth; there will be mysterious ceremonies performed at sunset on palm-fringed or storm-bound coasts, and firework-displays, and full moons, and costumes, mud, seduction, animals and opportunities for glory. There will be encounters with ancient and admirable cultures, and above all the chance to join people who believe that they can influence their fates through the energy or devotion that they put into their traditional forms of celebration.

Our itinerary commences with an event staged in January in a northern archipelago, that is famed amongst meteorologists for its tempestuous winters, and where the excuse for celebration is that Leviathan of fabrications: time.

II

NORTHERN LIGHTS

The motion of the earth through space provides us with an astral measure of time, a year representing the period required for the planet to spin through a single cycle of seasons and perform an orbit around the sun. The completion of each lap and the beginning of a new year is an occasion that many cultures have defined and commemorated, although the timing of the event has varied widely, as has the significance attached to it. Whereas Pharaonic Egypt commemorated its arrival in their month of Thoth (corresponding to our July) with intricate religious ceremonies, in England until 1752, the new year was honoured on 23 March, and its celebrations consisted of paying taxes. Other cultures, however, have marked the conclusion of each successful voyage around the sun in a less prosaic manner, treating it as an opportunity to look forward with optimism, and to lay the disappointments of the past year to rest. Indeed, some civilisations have considered the beginning of a new year not so much as an excuse for celebration, but believed themselves to be duty bound to commemorate it. Just as vegetation grew and died each year, so – it was deduced, mistaking the effect for the cause – must the sun. The Aztecs tried to help the lamp of the world through its trickier patches with blood sacrifices, the Babylonians by dancing, and the inhabitants of northern Europe by lighting fires.

With the standardisation of calendars and the rise and fall of empires, many of these ceremonies have disappeared. However, in most nations the new year is still accorded a formal welcome, and perhaps the most vigorous contemporary celebrations of the event take place during a festival known as *Up Helly Aa*, which is celebrated on the last Tuesday of January in Lerwick, the capital of the Shetland Isles, the most northerly part of Great Britain. Up Helly Aa consists of an enchanting blend of superstition, pyromania and fancy dress. Its highlight is a torch-lit procession, which culminates in the incineration of a Viking longship in a raging inferno, whose flames seem to consume all the ill will and vexation of the year gone by, while the warmth and brilliance that they generate in the middle of a northern winter provide hope for the year ahead. Once the longship has been reduced to embers the festival's costumed celebrants make a tour of the bars and halls of Lerwick, where they are greeted with food, drink and the opportunity to dance, and in return they perform theatrical entertainments. The festival lasts throughout the long dark night, and has a handsome pedigree of riot and intoxication.

However, Up Helly Aa is more than just an imaginative celebration of the calendar, a chance to defy the winter with fire and whisky, for it has been adopted by the Shetlanders as a platform on which to commemorate their Viking origin. Although the islands have been part of first Scotland and then the United Kingdom for more than 500 years, they were once ruled by the sea-rovers, and their inhabitants consider themselves to be a breed apart from the British. As a consequence, Up Helly Aa has been decorated with Viking iconography, and the festival has been pressed into service to assist a community that lacks its own political identity to define itself.

Although the Viking aspect of the present day festival is recent, the commemoration of the new year in the Shetlands is ancient. The islands were first colonised from the Orkneys to the south in the third millennium BC, and the members of this initial civilisation have left a wealth of archaeological information as to their way of life. They were fishermen, farmers and brewers, who lived in neat stone villages, and who demonstrated a special veneration for the new year in the form of the winter solstice. At Maeshowe in the Orkneys, around 2750 BC, they constructed a time machine – a complicated stone building – whose purpose was to record when this event took place. On the shortest day of the year, and only on that day, the rays of the rising sun fall through an aperture in the machine, and travel the length of a subterranean passage to strike a marker stone at its heart. It is still in working order, and is testament to the importance accorded to knowing when the earth would begin to tilt back towards summer.

CHARLES TAIT

The original solstice-measuring culture of the Shetlands starts to show signs of a Scandinavian influx – with the appearance of novel technologies and cultural artefacts – from the first millennium BC onwards. It is surmised that the newcomers were peaceful settlers, attracted by the lush pastures and hot summers that the Shetlands offered in the warmer climate of that age. Links were also forged with Scotland and Ireland, and in due course the Shetlanders were converted to Christianity around AD 600. The missionaries who instructed them travelled with calendars, so that they would know when to venerate their saints, thus introducing the concept of linear time, of a past and a future both immediate and distant, to the archipelago.

The next wave of immigrants to arrive in the Shetlands were the Vikings, who did very little initially in the way of peaceful settlement. They burned the monasteries, slaughtered the monks, raped or murdered the lay people and abducted the children that they had spared to serve as slaves. However, seduced perhaps by the climate, they began to establish communities and to introduce their customs to the islands. Like the culture they had supplanted, the Vikings were enthusiastic about the new year which they commemorated with a series of feasts known as *Yule*, during the course of which they would give each other presents, burn a special piece of wood called the Yule-log, sacrifice a wild boar and decorate each other with its blood, and drink vast quantities of beer and mead out of cattle horns. In time, however, the Vikings themselves were converted to Christianity, the Kingdom of Norway, of which the Shetlands were a part, taking the plunge in the eleventh century AD. Their customs were dressed in Christian clothes, and Yule became Christmas, whose nativity theme was perfectly suited to the Viking celebrations of the birth of a new year.

When the climate cooled around AD 1300, and the weather deteriorated to something like its present state, the Shetlands went into a period of decline, and in 1495 they were handed over to Scotland together with the Orkneys as part of a marriage settlement, with a very low valuation attached. After fifty years or so of neglect, the Scottish began to exploit their new empire in the North Atlantic, replacing Nordic law with feudalism and organising some parts of the islands into estates. They brought their own style of new year celebrations with them, and their hogmanay rituals included 'the heathenish idolatrous custom of burning torches', and *guizing*, or dressing up in disguise. The special reverence of the Scottish for hogmanay was due in part to the fact that Christmas, that accretion of Christian and pagan rituals, had been banned throughout Scotland on the grounds that it was popish mummery. As a consequence, the only excuse that could be employed for the traditional winter festivities of the nation was the changeover of years in the calendar. This temporal event was free of any associations with the Roman Church, not least of all because the Scottish calendar ran eleven days behind that of Catholic nations, for as Voltaire was later to observe of the British Isles as a whole, their inhabitants 'preferred their calendar to disagree with the sun than to agree with the pope'. The Scots, therefore, were the third successive culture to populate the Shetlands who considered the birth of a new year to be a matter for celebration.

In the seventeenth century, the islands became of economic interest due to their proximity to the fishing, sealing and whaling grounds of the North Atlantic. Around 1620 a settlement was established at Lerwick, whose name means 'Shit Creek' in Norse – a reflection of its muddy bottom, as an anchorage for the vessels involved in the opulent annual harvest. Lerwick, the site of the present Up Helly Aa celebrations, was founded to serve as the gateway to the Arctic, that rich if frigid zone. It was a cosmopolitan place from the start, and vessels of several nations, in particular the Dutch, used it as a shore base during the summer fishing season. The settlement developed facilities to cater to their needs, including bars and naval stores, and the Shetlanders provided a pool of labour for the fleets.

Not only was Lerwick a cosmopolitan place, but also, by the standards of the times, a godless one. Its foundation had coincided with the growth of the 'Suppress Christmas' movement in Scotland, led by the Kirk (the Scottish Presbyterian Church), whose ministers appeared in the port around the turn of the eighteenth century, with the aim of containing the popery of the natives. In the rest of Scottish territory the Kirk exercised considerable influence over both the manners and morals of the faithful. Neighbours were encouraged to spy on one another, and to report any examples of ungodly behaviour to its ministers, who would mete out punishments accordingly. However, the Kirk found it uphill work in Lerwick. While the population of the town was small – 700 or so in 1700, rising to 903 by 1792 – it seems to have been not just godless, but proud of it. Records from the period indicate a high incidence of fornication, and unrepentant fornication at that. The summer population of Lerwick was augmented by up to 5,000 sailors of all nations, who left a smattering of their vocabularies and a number of pregnancies behind when they departed each September at the onset of winter. Despite the efforts of the Kirk to chastise unmarried mothers, who were sentenced to appear in church on twenty-six consecutive Sundays for public rebuke, more often than not the guilty failed to complete their punishments, or indeed to appear in church at all. This spirit of disobedience seems to have been contagious: in 1795 the minister of the Kirk in Lerwick was dismissed after appearing drunk in his pulpit once too often and molesting a serving girl.

The failure of the servants of the Kirk to eradicate Catholic practices was a blessing in disguise, for as Dr Johnson observed, 'popery is favourable to ceremony; and among ignorant nations, ceremony is the only preservative of traditions'. As a consequence, 'heathenish idolatrous customs' commemorating the winter solstice, including vestiges of Yule, survived the arrival of Presbyterianism in the Shetlands. These festivities were composed, according to the account of a disgusted Kirk missionary, of an amalgam of folk and Roman Catholic rituals. Shetlanders would sing Norse songs, say Christian prayers, drink a great deal of alcohol, and perform various ceremonies to ensure the goodwill of the fairies in the year ahead. Their celebrations terminated on the twenty-fourth day after Christmas, which was known as 'Antonsmas' or 'Up Helly Night'. When these were translated from the isolated crofts to the new town of Lerwick, they sparked a conflagration of celebration.

From 1806 onwards reports begin to emerge of a port giving itself over to mayhem each new year, of men dragging chariots of fire through its single narrow street, and launching home-made bombs at one another and against the houses of local worthies. The celebrants were heavily armed, although they concentrated their firepower on glass windows, which in those days were a rarity. They were accompanied by drummers and fiddlers. A participant in the new year's eve festivities of 1806 has left an account of the fun:

> Here we are, a troop of some sixty or seventy – men of all arms, assembled at the north end of the walk at three o'clock of a Shetland winter morning. Every man carries firearms, from the humble sheep leg gun up to him whose wealthy sire enables him to sport the proud blunderbuss . . . the word is given; off we go – rattle go the cannister drums – crack! crack! pop! go the guns, pistols and blunderbusses . . . for we have decreed that whoever of [Lerwick's] denizens hope to sleep on a Yule morning shall hope in vain.

The very excitability of the new year celebrations in Lerwick raised them above both the rustic revels of the Shetland crofters and the hogmanay rituals of mainland Scotland which had been tamed by a ban on weapons after the last of the Jacobite rebellions. Their exuberant hedonism was assisted by a growing population: Lerwick was booming, and by 1821 it had no fewer than 2,224 inhabitants. References to disturbances during the 'Old Yule' period become more and more frequent, and suggest that the anarchic revels were fast becoming a tradition. In 1824, for instance, a visiting Methodist missionary observed that 'the whole town was in an uproar: from twelve o'clock last night until late this night blowing of horns, beating of drums, tinkling of old tin kettles, firing of guns, shouting, bawling, fiddling, fifeing, drinking, fighting. This was the state of the town all the night – the street was as thronged with people as any fair I ever saw in England.'

However, little by little a degree of ritual, if not order, appeared in the celebrations. The residents of Lerwick began to ornament proceedings with *krates*, which consisted of large wooden platforms, loaded with tar barrels and other flammable material which would be set alight and dragged through the town, accompanied by bands of armed men in disguise. Once the krates had burned out, the guizers would travel from house to house, serenaded at every step by their musicians, seeking refreshment. If they were refused hospitality, they would set off a bomb on the doorstep of the offending residence, shoot out its windows, or daub its façade with tar.

This festive anarchy encountered little in the way of opposition. Lerwick had no police force to speak of – when Sir Walter Scott visited the Shetlands in 1814 he noted the general absence of law and order, and the prevalence of intoxication. Lerwick was a 'poor looking place', its streets 'full of drunken riotous sailors', and the efforts of the sheriff who had travelled to the islands with Scott to prosecute offenders were met with ridicule. Thirty-two years later, circumstances had not changed. The new year celebrations of the town continued as a free-for-all and attempts to suppress the disorder with citizens co-opted as special constables were failures. During the new year's eve celebrations of 1846, for example, 'upwards of 40 Special Constables were sworn in, but they had to cut and run, and take refuge in the town house, where they were followed by the crowd, who shut them in, burning tar barrels under their very noses'. The celebrants, meanwhile, were escalating their firepower – in 1855 they broke into the fort and fired off two cannon that had been loaded with dead cats.

Further, the townspeople, if not actively involved in the revelry, seem to have approved of it, at least to the extent that they were prepared to put up with the damage it occasioned. After all the hustle and excitement of the summer fishing season, when its harbour was filled with vessels and seamen of all nations, Lerwick appeared very dull during the winter months, especially in early January, the mid-point between the departure and return of the fleet, when the sun was in the sky for no more than a few hours each day, and usually obscured by storm clouds. In this context, the new year celebrations were an act of defiance against the filthy weather, and a type of sympathetic magic – the drinking and merrymaking performed to ensure the return of the sailors, the blazing fires to recall the sun.

The festivities went from strength to strength in the 1850s and 1860s, and were supported by an ever-larger number of participants. Lerwick was enjoying the next of its many booms on the back of the herring fishing industry. The exploding population of Europe needed feeding and the supply of herrings seemed limitless. These nutritious yet enigmatic fish were a source not only of food but also of fascination in Victorian Britain. When they were especially prolific, the sea did not seem large enough to contain them and their bodies coagulated in decomposing heaps along the shoreline. Herrings were fuel for the human element of the industrial revolution. They were captured, gutted, split and cured by the Shetland-based fleets, and the islanders spent the traditional Viking raiding season plundering the seas in the service of progress.

However, the herring boom carried with it a greater threat to the new year anarchy than the forces of law had ever been able to muster – respectability. Lerwick had grown from a shore base into an affluent little town, with an attractive promenade of shops and a suburb. Its residents had become civic minded and house proud, and the mess created by the new year celebrations was at first lamented, then frowned upon. Further, religion had made a belated impression upon the port and Lerwick boasted several new churches, some of evangelical sects that advocated temperance amongst their flocks, and which organised new year celebrations to rival the mayhem, such as hymn-singing and improving lectures. Indeed, by the late 1860s these events had become so numerous that there were clashes of fixtures, and the godly were forced to chose between tea dances, YMCA meetings and church services to usher in the new year. Finally, society in Lerwick was becoming stratified. Its wealthy inhabitants had developed pretensions to precedence and these were fed by a round of social events, including dances and parades held by the army garrison, so that by the 1870s there were three types of new year celebrations to choose from – traditional (debauched), religious (often dry), and the formal events staged by secular bodies.

As a consequence of this changing environment the wild and dangerous style of ringing in the new year that had made such a promising start in Lerwick looked as if it might be extinguished. Explosives, firearms and conflagrations were out of place in a respectable Victorian town. Men who in the past would have fought each other and the forces of the law for the privilege of dragging blazing tar barrels through its streets or bombarding the town with dead cats were seduced by comfort and sought instead the pleasures of a heated hall and a cup of tea to welcome the new year. Those who tried to maintain the old anarchy were a minority, easily identified and easily castigated. Furthermore, the festival suffered the indignity of having its roots cut out from under it when the Shetlands made a belated shift to the Gregorian calendar in 1880, thus leaving it nearly a fortnight adrift of new year's eve – its official raison d'être.

At the eleventh hour relief arrived in the form of the Shetland Literary and Scientific Society, amongst whose aims was the preservation of the islands' heritage. Its luminaries had observed the metamorphosis of the Scottish Highlands from a barren region overrun by cattle thieves into a scenic paradise inhabited by kilted poets through the revival, and invention, of various folk traditions; they had also noted the popularity in literary circles of myths and fairytales. Further, customs that had been condemned and suppressed over the past two centuries as paganism and popery were now accepted throughout the United Kingdom as harmless local colour, of interest to travellers and antiquarians. Finally, all over Europe, the past was being plundered in the service of nationalism. In new countries such as Italy and Germany rituals that had been extinct for millennia had been revived in order to instil a sense of belonging in their citizens. As d'Azeglio, an architect of Italian unity commented, 'we have made Italy, now we must make Italians'. It was an age when countries were defining themselves, and in each case a face had to be fixed to the body politic. Might not something similar be achieved in the Shetland Islands? Although the archipelago had little in its recent past from which to construct a dignified identity, its remote Viking history had sensational potential. The revivalists set to work, selecting the anarchic new year celebrations of Lerwick for a fairytale transformation.

The first evidence of their influence on the festivities appears in a change of name. Whereas previously these had been called simply the Old Yule, or new year celebrations, in 1878 they were christened Up Helly Aa after the rustic diversions of the crofters. Soon afterwards, signs of organisation appeared. Instead, as hitherto, of gathering in little groups at random the guizers assembled in an orderly manner to form a torchlight procession. This was thought impressive enough to re-enact when the Duke of Edinburgh visited Lerwick in 1882 to lay the foundation stone of its first town hall, whose interior design, thanks to the Shetland Literary and Scientific Society, was retro-Nordic. By 1885 Up Helly Aa had an organising committee, which within three years was controlling entry into the ranks of guizers. In 1889 the krates were revived in the form of a Nordic galley, that was incinerated with some ceremony, and in 1897 the festival was graced with a stirring Viking anthem, set to the tune of a popular hymn. By the beginning of the twentieth century the transformation of the riotous new year celebrations of the gateway to the Arctic into a folk pageant that commemorated the Nordic roots of the Shetland Islands was complete, and Up Helly Aa was reborn as a fancy-dress party.

The success of the makeover stems from the fortuitous decision to equip Up Helly Aa with Viking blood, and to decorate it with Norse iconography. Whereas previously the festival had been Viking only in the sense that many of its celebrants were descended from the sea-rovers and expressed their inheritance with archetypal excess, once the same men were encouraged to don Viking garb the festival changed from being a riot into a spectacle. Norse blood is an attractive substance to imagine running in one's veins, and merely dressing up as a Viking can be liberating, for it implies a savagery and an unpredictability of behaviour so powerfully that these traits are carried by the costume alone. The Viking link also provided the festival with a vast body of sagas that could be pillaged for inspiration, thus gracing it with the cultural resources necessary to ensure its perpetuation. While the iconography of the Norsemen is simple and evocative – a raven, a dragon, double-bladed axes, brimming horns of mead – their reputation is founded not just on violence but a love of poetry and, interestingly, of law, thus broadening their appeal. The common law of the greater part of the English speaking world descends from principles laid down by the Vikings. Ultimately, however, their reputation for hedonistic excellence and their primal allure derive from the clarity of their desires, and their use of force in satisfying them, and this uncomplicated philosophy is reflected in the motto that has been adopted by the celebrants of the festival today: 'We axe for what we get.'

The Up Helly Aa celebrations of the third millennium are a happy combination of various elements of its real and imaginary past. Its mongrel blood exhibits the contributions made to its pedigree by the folklorists, by the Scottish, and even by the hymn-singing of the Victorian evangelists. The hedonism of the early nineteenth-century event has been maintained, without the danger and the damage it occasioned, to which have been added pageantry, spectacle and split-second timing.

Up Helly Aa commences with the publication of the Bill, a painted wooden signboard the size of a door, that is erected in the centre of Lerwick at dawn on the day of the festival. The Bill announces the impending celebrations and also launches a number of bombs, in the form of defamatory comments painted in heraldic script on its face, against various citizens of Lerwick, especially its politicians. The Bill provides a summary of the local events and follies of the year gone past, and although it is at best cryptic to the outsider, it can be genuinely wounding to the people it names. If its contents were published in any other medium they would provoke a swarm of writs. Its function is to maintain the element of social protest that animated the early new year's eve celebrations of Lerwick, and to demonstrate that a licence to speak freely is in operation. It may be compared to a theatre bill advertising an imminent performance, with the difference that the people of Lerwick will be the actors in the forthcoming drama, as opposed to mere spectators.

The Bill is issued under the seal of the Guizer Jarl, an individual elected by the organising committee to oversee Up Helly Aa in that particular year. The Jarl is chosen from amongst the squads of registered guizers, and selection for the post is accounted a local honour, for in addition to officiating at the festival, he will perform a number of civic duties throughout the year. The Jarl assumes the name of a famous Viking hero for the duration of his tenure – in 1999, for example, Davie Mathewson, a 36-year-old Shetlander, became Sigurd Hlodvisson (AD 980–1014), Earl of Orkney, who plundered Scotland several times and died on a battlefield in Ireland. The Jarl also grows a Viking style beard. He and his squad of guizers commence work on their Viking costumes months before the festival, during which time they also arrange the construction of a 30-foot replica longship, complete with a dragon-beaked prow, a mast, and a sail displaying a Viking emblem. The boat is a technically accurate reproduction of the ships in which the ancestors of the guizers arrived in the Shetlands, albeit somewhat whimsically decorated. It serves as the symbol of the festival – it is an offering to tradition – and it too is graced with a Viking name – that of Davie Mathewson/Sigurd Hlodvisson for instance was called Asmundervag.

Once the Jarl has published his Bill, he and his squad display their boat for the admiration of the Shetlanders. The squad are dressed from head to toe as Vikings. Those who can have grown beards, and all are equipped with horned or winged helmets, shields, body armour and battle-axes. They climb aboard their longship and pose for a team photograph, then set off in a body through the streets of Lerwick, waving their axes and singing the Up Helly Aa song. They are received formally at the Shetland Islands Council building, which in addition to flying the Shetland flag, displays the black raven of the Vikings against a red background, and the Jarl is presented with the freedom of Lerwick for the next twenty-four hours – a symbolic act in which the town is effectively placed in the hands of the lord of misrule for the duration of the festival.

The black raven banner that flutters over Lerwick town hall was once, according to the Orkneyinga saga (c. AD 1200), the symbol of the Viking earls of Shetland. It was also, incidentally, linked to the demise of Davie Mathewson's alter ego, the real Sigurd Hlodvisson, who was given one such item by his mother, with the warning that although the banner would lead whoever owned it to victory, whoever carried it for them would die. The raven led Sigurd to many victories, at the cost of as many standard bearers, until these latter mutinied at the battle of Svoldir (1014), telling Sigurd to 'Bear thine own Devil thyself'. He did so and perished at the hands of King Brian of Ireland.

EPICSCOTLAND.COM

Once the Jarl and his Viking squad have taken lunch with the town councillors, they spend the remainder of the daylight hours visiting primary schools and old people's homes, at each of which, in the best traditions of Nordic Yule, they give presents, make speeches, brandish their battle-axes and sing their song. Thus far, the scurrilous nature of the Bill, and the menacing beards and costumes aside, the festival is closer to a municipal pageant than a Berserker spree.[1] This is because the various civic

---

1 Contemporary accounts of Viking atrocities note that some of their perpetrators were gloriously violent, far above the usual mould. These geniuses of excess were distinguished by the title of Berserkers amongst their companions. Berserkers would go into battle naked, chewing on the edges of their leather shields to work up a froth. In times of peace they would attack trees and boulders in order to vent their passion for violence and maintain its edge. Psychologists today would have no hesitation in terming them psychopaths: their brutality was unpredictable, and they did not know the meaning of regret.

duties that the Jarl and his squad undertake are the price of respectability, and reflect the totemic importance of the festival to Shetlanders. Any inconsistencies with the behaviour of real-life Viking heroes such as Thorfinn Skull-Splitter and Eric Blood-Axe who, as their names suggest, did little in the way of community service in the islands, are overlooked for, ever since its facelift, Up Helly Aa has served as a confirmation of Shetlandic identity, whose authenticity is not to be questioned. Many Shetland *émigrés* return to their homeland for the festival, from the United States, from Canada, and from New Zealand, and those that are unable to make the journey are sent the Shetlandic equivalent of Christmas cards: postcards with scenes of that year's Up Helly Aa.

After a long day of playing Norsemen to every generation of islanders, the Jarl and his men return to the docks where they are joined by the mass of people who are participating in the festival as guizers. These are organised into squads, only one of which, the Jarl's, is dressed in Viking costume, while the remainder wear a variety of disguises, ranging from Teletubbies to mermaids. Some of the squads have costumes that satirise an event of local importance which has occurred in the past year, thus preserving the element of protest that characterised the early performances of the festival. In 1999, for example, a guizer squad appeared as 'Da Cross Folk', whose costumes were intended to ridicule an inept attempt by the local council to repave Lerwick that had resulted in damage to the municipal sewers, and who registered their displeasure in song as they paraded:

> *Da aroma at da Market Cross*
> *Is just beyond all wirds*
> *Wi broken drains and sewer pipes*
> *An antrin peerie turds.*

The costumes of each squad of guizers are kept secret until they appear in public. No theme may ever be repeated at Up Helly

Aa, so that inspiration is kept fresh. All the guizers are men, even those disguised as mermaids. Interestingly, the worship of the Norse god Freyr incorporated new year ceremonies in which Viking men, Berserkers included, dressed themselves as women and imitated their behaviour, and therefore the crossdressing aspect of Up Helly Aa has a genuinely Nordic pedigree.

Statistically, the weather during the festival is bound to be ugly – the sun, if it is visible at all during the day, limps along the horizon and plunges below it at four o'clock, and the darkness during which the guizing takes place is often enlivened by gales or blizzards. At 7.30 p.m. prompt the guizers assemble in a double line a thousand strong, that presents an extraordinary variety of dress – dinosaurs succeeded by fairy queens by Mickey Mice and so on. Each guizer carries a 4-foot torch resembling a giant swab, whose tip has been soaked in kerosene to make it blaze, and on the signal fire is passed from torch to torch. Once all the torches are alight, the guizers set off on a procession through Lerwick, dragging with them the replica longship mounted on a trailer. As they march they sing the Up Helly Aa song (to the tune of 'Glory, Glory Hallelujah!')

From grand old Viking centuries Up-Helly-A' has come,
Then light the torch and form the march, and sound the rolling drum:
And wake the mighty memories of heroes that are dumb;
The waves are rolling on.

Grand old Vikings ruled upon the ocean vast,
Their brave battle-songs still thunder on the blast;
Their wild war-cry comes a-ringing from the past;
We answer it 'A-oi!'

Roll their glory down the ages,
Sons of warriors and sages,
When the fight for Freedom rages,
Be bold and strong as they!

Once the guizers and the longship have progressed around Lerwick, they direct their steps to the municipal recreation ground where they gather in a circle around their vessel. A signal rocket is fired off, and every guizer throws his torch into the centre of the boat with its raven sail and its dragon prow. As the fire takes hold, it eats its way through the hull, leaving only the keel and thwarts, like the backbone and ribcage of a dead animal. It is an awesome conflagration that provides the festival with a memorable centrepiece. It is, as we have seen, a Victorian innovation, but is also proof of the simple pleasure people derive from setting even beautiful things on fire.

Though there is no doubt that the Vikings burned their longboats from time to time, whether they did so to celebrate Yule is quite another matter. Viking chiefs were frequently buried with their ships, and even their poor were entombed with models or images of boats carved on a stone, for these were believed to be capable of carrying the dead to Asgard, or heaven, where they might fight all day and drink mead all night. Interestingly, there is an eye-witness account of the cremation of a dead Viking leader in his longboat, so vivid that it has a filmic intensity, and which may have been the inspiration for the introduction of the ritual to Up Helly Aa by nineteenth-century folklorists. The account survives in the journals of Ibn Faldan, an Arab merchant who witnessed the event in AD 921. He describes at length the preparation of the body of the dead Viking, and the vessel that was to serve as his pyre, together with the ritual sacrifice of a slave girl after she had had sex with six companions of the deceased. Once the funeral arrangements had been completed, a naked man set the ensemble alight with a torch, covering his anus all the while with his free hand, lest it be invaded by evil spirits. Our correspondent records that the instant the boat caught fire, 'A powerful, fearful wind began to blow so that the flames became fiercer and more intense.' The watching Vikings began to laugh in a wild and demented manner, as the wind streamed through their beards and hair, and when Ibn Faldan enquired as to why they laughed, he was told 'You Arabs are fools . . . You take the people who are most dear to you and whom you honour most and put them into the ground where insects and worms devour them. We burn them in a moment, so that they enter Paradise at once.' The sudden wind, so it was claimed, was heaven sent to hasten the cremation, and carry the dead man to Asgard 'in an hour'. Ibn Faldan felt duty bound to record the accuracy of the Vikings' prediction, 'and actually an hour had not passed before the ship, the wood, the girl, and her master were nothing but cinders and ashes'.[2]

The spectacle at Up Helly Aa is usually wind assisted, and although the galley lacks a human cargo, it is symbolically charged with the past year. As it is consumed in flames the guizers sing the 'Norseman's Home', whose lyrics are sentimental but evocative – a declaration of affinity with the past, and of resolve for the future:

> *Then let us all in harmony,*
> *Give honour to the brave*
> *The noble, hardy, northern men,*
> *Who ruled the stormy wave.*

The heat and light generated by the conflagration are made to seem more fierce by the darkness and the cold. Sparks fly heavenwards through the falling sleet, the firelight takes hold of faces and distorts their features, and the scene is elemental and inspiring. However, instead of gazing on in meditation the guizers make haste back into Lerwick, for once the centrepiece of Up Helly Aa is roaring with flames, the ritual part of the festival, in the sense of a fixed sequence of actions, is over, and the time

---

2 Interestingly, the folklorists responsible for giving the festival its Nordic theme did not revive many of the other Viking customs described by Ibn Faldan, which included public fornication, the forced consumption of alcohol, and an utter disregard for personal hygiene.

has arrived to commence a tour of the halls and bars of the town. The halls are a survival of Lerwick's flirtation with abstinence from strong drink. The town was officially alcohol free between 1920 and 1947, when the temperance movement enjoyed a late and somewhat vindictive triumph. Despite the fact that alcohol had been consumed in the Shetlands for nearly 5,000 years, indeed for as long as they had been inhabited by humans, it was felt that people could no longer be trusted with the traditional battle potion of the Vikings. As a consequence, for twenty-seven years the participants at Up Helly Aa were regaled with tea and cakes in community halls and the assembly rooms of schools. This institution has survived the re-legalisation of alcohol, and together the halls form a circuit around which the guizer squads pass during the course of the night.

The squads are expected to perform a sketch, or to give an entertainment upon arrival at each hall, for which they are rewarded with food, drink and dancing. The entertainments that they offer range from well-rehearsed satirical pieces to singing a song badly together. Some halls are 'wet', i.e. provide alcohol, whereas others are still teetotal, although celebrants are free to supplement their tea with any whisky that they might have about them. Dancing consists of energetic Scottish reels, the music is supplied by fiddles, pipes and drums, and the guizers swing their partners around with truly Norse vitality. Their exertions and the cold night air that greets them as they move between the halls brings out the flush in their cheeks, as if they carried inside them some of the blaze that raged through the timbers of the longship. Indeed, all Lerwick is full of colour, noise and motion as inhabitants assert themselves as loudly, as eyecatchingly and with as much vitality as possible. It is as though they wish to demonstrate their persistence, in a shattered rock archipelago, encircled by the pounding Atlantic, on the northern rim of civilisation.

The latter stages of the festivities owe as much to Scotland as to Norway for their style. The circuit of the halls, for instance, has parallels with the Scottish custom of 'first-footing', in which neighbours pass from house to house, bearing gifts of salt and coal, which are exchanged for embraces and drinks. The scene inside a typical 'wet' hall resembles an ideal Scottish hogmanay, whose participants have been animated with the laudable principle that a new year should be given a flying start. The whisky flows, and while the tongues of the dancers may suffer in elasticity, their legs maintain their spring as they spin through the figures of the reels. Celebrations continue until sunrise, which occurs at the conveniently late hour of nine o'clock. The following day is a public holiday in Lerwick, to enable the celebrants of Up Helly Aa to sleep off excess, and to enjoy dreams filled with blazing longships and raven banners.

Up Helly Aa is the highlight of the year for many Shetlanders. It enables them to defy the long biting winter, and simultaneously to commemorate an identity that was invented for them in the

EPICSCOTLAND.COM

nineteenth century. It is a testament to the vision of a handful of folklorists, whose romantic and nationalist fantasies, by appealing to the primitive urge to dress up and make-believe, have proved not only enduring, but also have retained their potency in a very different age. It seems that Viking garb never goes out of fashion, nor, with a little reworking, does Viking sentiment.

The pleasures of costume, especially when sanctioned by tradition are widely appreciated: every culture seems to have allowed its members occasions, usually during festivals, when they might come as someone else. At times disguise has served to make a man a god for the course of a religious ceremony, while on other occasions it has encouraged him to behave like a beast. The joy of disguise derives from its power to deceive, and the recognition and acceptance of this power emboldens the wearer to act with a freedom that they would not risk without the camouflage of a costume to protect them.

The twenty-first century Vikings of Up Helly Aa are only mild fantasists in comparison to the inhabitants of other nations, some of whose festivals are dedicated to carrying the art of assuming an alter ego to far greater lengths. Less than a month after Up Helly Aa, on the other side of the Atlantic Ocean, an event takes place in which the costumes are only limited by the imaginations and physical strength of their creators. Several thousand miles to the west, and 42° south of the Shetlands lies another archipelago, where the art of festive disguise has been raised to new heights. Furthermore, the nationalistic aspects of Up Helly Aa are repeated, so that the same excuses people have employed to gather and celebrate in the grip of a northern winter are held to be equally valid in a tropical island. In the latter case, however, instead of an identity being imposed upon the festival as the price of continuance, it has been developed over time by the participants, and rather than expressing a single cultural heritage, it reflects the dynamic intermingling of influences from Africa, Asia and Europe.

TRINIDAD EXPRESS NEWSPAPERS

III

WE KINDA PEOPLE

Can you hear a distant drum
Bouncing on the laughter of a melody
And does the rhythm tell you come come come come
Does your spirit do a dance to this symphony
Does it tell you that your heart is afire
Does it tell you that your pain is a liar
Does it wash away all the unlovely

DAVE RUDDER 'CALYPSO MUSIC'

It is rare that an entire country dances together, that more or less every one of its inhabitants who is able to overdresses or undresses and takes to the streets. However, in Trinidad, an island nation in the West Indies just north of Venezuela, this is an annual occurrence: *Carnival*, its principal festival, is celebrated in some way by most of its population. Indeed, in the weeks leading up to the event, Trinidad is dominated by Carnival, and those of its citizens who object to the festival on moral or other grounds often choose to flee the country for its duration.

Carnival consists of forty-eight hours of non-stop celebration. It is an explosion of sensuality, of pulsing music, of rum, sunshine and provocative dancing, and it is decorated by a fantasia of disguises, which are months in the making, worn while the festivities last, and then are flung into the gutter or given away. Its celebrations are based around musical contests – in which calypso songs and steel band tunes are performed and judged – and costumed processions of perhaps 100,000 Trinidadians through the streets of their capital, each one of whom is aiming to surprise and please their peers with the energy of their dancing or the daring of their disguises. It is an event where invention and expression are valued above all else, and one at which every Trinidadian hopes to titillate the imaginations of their fellow citizens with the shock of the new.

The festival is a matter of patriotic pride – Trinidadians refer to themselves as 'Carnival People', and view its celebrations as an essential part of their society. Indeed, many Trinidadians believe that carnival is the secret lubricant that has allowed so wide a variety of cultures to rub along so easily on a small island. In addition to standing as a symbol for the nation, Carnival is also considered to carry in its celebrations a faithful record of the progress of Trinidad from slave island, through colony, to independent republic, and to represent 'the history of a common people's struggle for freedom of expression from the misguided paternalism inherent in colonial rule'.

The evolution of Carnival and the entertainments that it offers certainly mirror the development of the nation, for Trinidad was something of a backwater until the festival was introduced. Although the island was spotted by Columbus on his third voyage in 1498, and named and claimed for the Catholic kings of

Spain, it was neglected by its new owners for the following three centuries. Its original inhabitants were all but wiped out by small-pox in the interim, and as the island had no gold, and no longer any native workforce, it was of little interest to the metropolitan power. By the middle of the eighteenth century Trinidad had become so poor that its residents were forced to petition the Spanish crown for money, claiming that they had been reduced to such penury that they only possessed a single pair of trousers between them, and hence could not attend mass in a decent state. In 1783 King Charles III decided to try to breathe some life into the place by offering free land to any good Catholics who might want to settle there with their slaves and establish plantations. His plan was a success, French planters from Santo Domingo and other Caribbean islands took up the call, and the population of Trinidad jumped from 2,700 on the eve of the invitation to 17,700 within six years.

The French brought their festivals with them as well as their slaves, and introduced Carnival to Trinidad in the year of their arrival. The festivities that they imported were modelled on those current throughout Europe at the time, where 'carnival' was not so much a festival, but a season, whose roots lay in the various celebrations which used to occupy the European winter prior to the industrial revolution. There was no agricultural work to be done, it was the close season for military campaigns, so people whiled away their hours by dressing up and dancing. While Christianity had attempted to limit these popular revels to a few days preceding Lent, and had baptised them with their present name, which means 'a farewell to meat', the tradition of general winter debauchery was too popular to be circumscribed by the pious. Carnival retained an extended timetable and many of its pagan traditions, including some derived from the Saturnalia, the great Roman winter festival, well into the age of enlightenment. Eighteenth-century European carnivals were occasions for social inversion, when masters served their servants and these were given licence to speak freely without fear of the consequences;

when beggars were elected kings for a day and their whims enacted by the people; and the carnival season was a time for disguises, infidelities and hedonism. Furthermore, it was a period of official tolerance for popular excess. Johann Wolfgang Goethe, writing of the carnival of Rome in 1789, noted that it was 'a festival in which, in point of fact, is not given to the people, but which the people give to themselves. The state makes little preparation, and but a small contribution to it. The merry round revolves by itself, and the police regulate the spontaneous movement with but a slack hand.'

No sooner did Spain have a flourishing Catholic dependency in Trinidad than in 1797, as part of a general global reshuffle of colonial possessions, Great Britain assumed control. The British busied themselves with constructing fortifications, and Carnival continued under their rule as by and large a planters' affair, for some of whom it had assumed a certain poignancy. The French Revolution had turned the *émigrés* into exiles, and had eliminated the parent celebrations of the festival in France on the grounds that masquerading was 'beneath the dignity of a citizen'. Orphaned far from its native land, Carnival was adopted and fostered by the slaves of the planters, who by tradition were permitted a very limited freedom for the duration of the festival, and so had come to associate it with their dreams of liberty. Like doting parents, the slaves shaped Carnival to reflect their own aspirations, and their ambitions for both themselves and their protégés received a tremendous boost in 1834, when slavery was banned in British possessions, and it was decreed that all existing slaves must be set free. Two-thirds of the population of Trinidad lived in bondage, so there was a certain impatience that this legislation was put into effect. However, emancipation was an unhurried affair. Slaves were required to serve a six-year 'apprenticeship' with their former masters, who had nothing to teach them but slavery, before they were actually free.

This probationary period, although reduced to four years, was distinguished by protests, and the protests were strongest during

Carnival. Nineteenth-century Carnivals were spirited events. The not-quite-free slaves used the festival as an opportunity to assert their presence in the society of which they were shortly to become full members. In addition to violent protests, the festival was characterised by brawling, dancing, drinking and adultery. Its celebrations were condemned by Trinidad's fledgling press as 'a wretched buffoonery [tending] to brutalise the faculty of the lower order of our population'. Indeed, by the 1840s, Carnival had become so exciting that the British paid it the compliment of imposing martial law for its duration. Despite the official sanctions, the festival continued to grow and the entertainment it provided began to change. Carnival celebrants introduced traditional African diversions such as stick-fighting, drumming and stilt-walking to their foster child. They composed themselves into masked *canboulay* bands and held processions by torchlight, which culminated in vigorous public dancing. The British administration tried to impose some restraint by banning the canboulay parades in 1880, and drums in 1883. The fruits of their oppression were the adoption of lengths of bamboo, which were thumped against the ground in unison in order to create the required rhythm, more riots, and a general increase in the level of debauchery. In 1884, for example, there were complaints in the press that female masqueraders were taking to the streets dressed in transparent gowns, or in no more than menstruation cloths stained with fake blood, and that those who did wear clothing were throwing their dresses open to reveal that they had nothing on underneath.

Carnival soon outgrew the traditional disguises it had inherited from the French, and its participants began to invent their own costume themes. These included Moko Jumbies (stilt-walkers in African tribal dress), Dame Lorraines (people dressed as busty French matrons – a satire on the planters), Burrokeets (half-donkey, half-human figures, believed to be Indian in origin), Midnight Robbers, Bats and Dragons. Not only did the costumes change, but also the spirit in which they were worn. Whereas in

ILLUSTRATED LONDON NEWS

Europe carnival-goers dressed to conceal their identities by hiding
their faces, in Trinidad revellers sought to bring the character or
animal implied by their costume to life, and expressed this deeper
commitment as a figure of speech. To dress up as a bat, for
example, was to 'play' bat, and those Trinidadians who elected to
play winged mammals during Carnival would lure fruitbats into
their shanties by night, in order that they might study their
movements, and perfect their impersonations.

The creative streak that had emerged in Carnival was not
limited to costume design and role playing. Trinidadians
developed a new class of music – calypso – with which to enliven
their festival. Calypso music evolved from the extemporisations of
a species of cheerleader known as Chantwells, who would sing the
praises of stick-fighters prior to a contest, in order to disenchant
the opposition. It also shows the influence of the Spanish *caliso*
tradition, under which satirical songs were composed for the
carnival season in Cadiz. By the opening decade of the twentieth
century, calypso had become the principal form of popular
entertainment in Trinidad, functioning as a form of social
commentary that could be danced to. Its practitioners wrote songs
in which topical themes were combined with eternal – British
administrative incompetence with sickness, politics with lust, and

so on – and performed them with such melody and rhythm that one could enjoy their message at the same time as moving one's feet. The topical nature of the genre is illustrated by the earliest surviving example (1898) of calypso lyrics in English, whose target was the then governor, Sir Hubert Jerningham, who had attempted to suspend the Port of Spain Council:

> *Jerningham the governor*
> *Is a fastness in-to you*
> *Is a rudeness in-to you*
> *To break up the laws of Borough Council*

As the twentieth century progressed, these songs were premièred at Carnival, which came to function as a formal contest for calypso, during which its singers would hold duels with one another, to determine who was the fastest and wittiest. Their weapons were their lyrics, their presence and their voices; their rewards were the respect of their peers and improved breeding prospects. Like boxers, calypso singers assumed *noms de guerre* – the champions of the 1920s, for instance, were Attila the Hun (Raymond Quevedo) and Roaring Lion (Rafael de Leon).

Calypso quickly acquired a reputation for excellence beyond Trinidad. By the 1930s it was being broadcast throughout the British empire by the BBC, and its stars had been invited to New York to sing alongside Fred Astaire. Its fame gave Trinidad a presence in the wider world. For the first time in its history, the colony had a distinctive voice. The transformation of calypso, from a diversion for agricultural labourers on a small Caribbean island to an internationally acclaimed style of entertainment, coincided with changes to Carnival itself, whose celebrations, after an unruly adolescence, had matured into something a little less furious. The degenerate processions of semi-naked drunks waving chamberpots full of urine and engaging in bottle fights had given way to teams of themed masqueraders who paraded in an orderly manner through the streets of Port of Spain, the capital of Trinidad. Attila the Hun summarised the transformation in the lyrics to his classic of calypso, 'History of Carnival '(1935):

> *Carnival of long ago you used to see*
> *Half-naked women for the* Pisse-en-lit
> Shak shak *and* vera *in their hand*
> *Twisting their body as they lead the band*
> *You weren't safe in your own home*
> *Through accident bottle and stone*
> *But today you can hear calypso*
> *On the American radio.*

In addition to developing a new class of music for their festival, Trinidadians also invented the only genuinely new musical instrument of the twentieth century – the steel drum – to help them celebrate. The instrument was created by cutting the bottom section off an oil drum, beating the base until it was concave, and tuning this surface with a blow-torch and a hammer. Oil drums were in plentiful supply for Trinidad had become a producer, and its economy had changed from being based on agriculture to supporting primary industries. Once again, a development in the nation was reflected by an innovation in the national festival.

The original steel drums were worn around the neck on a cord and played with a pair of rubber-tipped drumsticks. They had a range of one octave or less and produced a bright, yet arresting sound. The impact of the new instrument was limited at first, for it had been invented just prior to World War II, for three of whose years the celebration of Carnival was suspended. However, steel drums appeared en masse on VE Day in 1945 and their music electrified the Trinidadians. Development work, meanwhile, proceeded on the instrument – by using larger sections of oil drum, pan makers found they could produce pans with different octaves, and before long a steel band had almost the same range as a symphony orchestra, and as many musicians. Steel bands quickly took over from the Bamboo Tamboos, the bamboo-playing rhythm sections that had emerged when the British banned drums, as the principal marching force at Carnival. Not only was their sound startling, but also the appearance of their musicians:

> *They were soaked with sweat. It was the second day of carnival and they had probably been beating almost non stop for 36 hours. In bands like that to keep going was an honourable thing; a bandsman would open his pants and urinate as he marched rather than drop out. Yet they stood straight as the royal palm, beating the scarlet worded pans that hung heavily on their bellies. They groaned with pleasure. It was a wild, sweaty, dirty, straggling band altogether, jumping and spinning like drugged unruly ecstatics. The noise was terrific, hammering, unsponsored, cruel as a violin shrilling in a silver desert.*

Rivalries sprang up between the bands, most of whose members came from Trinidad's slums, and they held spectacular streetfights with one another throughout the Carnivals of the late 1940s and early 1950s. Band members considered themselves the spiritual heirs of the people who had enlivened the festival with 'bottle and stone' during the previous century. They made a strong impression on the Coronation Carnival of 1952, a special celebration held in June of that year to mark the ascent to the throne of Queen Elizabeth II, during which there were eight major steel band battles which left hundreds injured and one man dead. Their sound, however, was tantalising, and by the mid-1950s steel band music was being broadcasted by the BBC alongside Gilbert and Sullivan operas. Notorious at home, but famous abroad, the steel bands followed the same route of development as calypso singers, in that they acquired a sense of their own worth. Men who had been invited all over the globe to perform before heads of state no longer felt compelled to brawl in the streets. The element of competition between the bands was preserved, however, although bands now limited their challenges to a trial of musical prowess during Carnival. This new maturity was also reflected in a change in the status of Trinidad itself, which obtained independence from Great Britain in 1962. There were no longer any colonial authorities to protest against, and the new country had to stand on its own in the world.

The various influences that have shaped Trinidadian society since independence have also had their impact on its Carnival. Prior to the 1960s, the majority of celebrants were men, a statistic reflected in the intensely competitive rituals that grew up around the festival. However, from the 1970s onwards, the women of Trinidad took to its streets in increasing numbers, and their presence affected the tone of the celebrations, making them less confrontational, and more overtly sexual. It appears that Carnival served the same role in the emancipation of women as it did in that of slaves, offering a platform on which the pleasures of liberty could be expressed. Finally, the East Indian population of Trinidad, the descendants of agricultural workers imported from the Sub-continent after the termination of slavery, who hitherto had remained on the periphery of the festival, began to contribute to the celebrations. While these had their own traditions of drumming and stick-fighting, it was not until the late 1970s – when a movement to make Trinidad a republic had come to the fore, and marches were held under the banners of 'Indians and Africans Unite' – that they made their presence felt at Carnival, enriching its festivities with Indian rhythms, dances, costumes and chants, and contributing to a derivative of calypso named soca.

As a result of the accretion of all these influences, both recent and more distant in time, Trinidad Carnival has evolved into its present form – an exuberant, competitive, creative festival that reflects the character of a nation. The orphan child of French *émigrés* has grown into a sophisticated adult, and is itself a parent, for Carnivals based on the Trinidadian model have been founded and flourish in Toronto, London and New York. Indeed the London offshoot, the Notting Hill Carnival, is the largest street party in Europe.

*

Trinidad Carnival is a movable feast. Its dates are determined in accordance with those of Easter, and fall within a month-long period comprising the last three weeks of February and the first week of March. Officially it consists of just two days – Shrove Tuesday and the preceding Monday. However, work on the songs, steel band arrangements and costumes that will be premièred at Carnival begins months before the festival commences, and Carnival-goers start their training for the official period of hedonism several weeks in advance. There is a semi-formal sequence of preliminary events to help them with their regime. These consist of the knockout rounds of calypso contests, called 'tents' after the marquees in which they used to be held, and 'fêtes' – all-night parties where the dance music composed for that year's festival is trialled. The tents open for business from the new year onwards. They offer up to twenty different calypso singers every night, each of whom performs two songs. Singers who do not please the audience are received in silence and with stony faces. In the past, inadequate calypsonians were removed from the stage by the neck with a shepherd's crook. The singers who charm the audience, however, are greeted with rapturous applause, are called back for encore after encore, and hear their lyrics being sung in the streets the next day.

While the calypsonians are engaged in their preliminary competitions, the steel bands are rehearsing for five hours a day, seven days a week. Each band works under the guidance of an arranger on a single tune, with which they hope to captivate the masses during the festival. Steel bands participate in regional contests several weeks in advance of Carnival, followed by semi-finals ten days before, and the ten finalists that these produce, plus last year's champion, dispute the Carnival crown at a contest named Panorama, which, although it falls outside the official boundaries of the festival, is viewed as its opening event.

Panorama is held in Queens Park Savannah, a public gardens in the centre of Port of Spain. The Savannah is graced with the grandstand of a now defunct racecourse, opposite which a temporary stand is erected, and a long thin stage resembling a runway inserted between the two. From midday onwards on the Saturday prior to Carnival proper, a succession of steel bands are wheeled on to the stage. Each takes twenty minutes or so to set up, for a band can consist of a hundred musicians, who are disposed in an intricate arrangement in order to project the required sound. Once all its performers are in place, each band then performs a single tune, for which they are allotted a maximum of ten minutes. During this short period, the band is joined by a host of its supporters: the men bare chested, the girls in the tightest and briefest of shorts, who dance furiously around the stage, attempting to whip the audience into a similarly frenzied state. The music builds towards a crescendo, and while the crowds are partisan and reserve their applause for local bands, if a rival is exceptionally moving they will surrender to the music and the entire crowd will break out dancing. The bands are capable of producing a formidable range and volume of sound, and when the arrangement is sweet the melody blends effortlessly with the rhythm, compelling people to their feet.

As a consequence of the prolonged breaks between tunes, the overall pace at Panorama is gentle. It is a long, hot day under the tropical sun, and the attention of the crowd is fixed on itself as much as the music. The audience of 25,000 or so arm themselves with picnics and entertain each other with rum and pleasantries. Trinidadians are not shy of making themselves heard and will shout out witticisms, which will provoke other quips, so that the scene is not unlike a debating chamber, with comments, ditties and insults flowing back and forth between sections of the crowd. Interestingly, the habit of critical observation in plain prose or extempore verse seems to have been long established as a Trinidadian past-time at public gatherings. In 1863, the author Charles Kingsley observed locals at a race meeting on the Savannah improvising songs that poked fun at passers-by, and while he was shocked at their presumption, he was delighted by their inventiveness.

Panorama also incorporates the Trinidadian limbo-dancing championships, a discipline that deserves to be in the Olympics, as a counterbalance to the high jump, on account of the exceptional co-ordination, flexibility and nerve that it demands. Instead of being tested on how far they can leave the ground, limbo-dancers are invited to see how low they can go. They are required to pass under a pair of bars, without touching the bars, or allowing any portion of their bodies other than their feet to touch the floor. The bars are lowered in successive rounds of the contest, until they are eight inches or so off the ground. They are wrapped in burning rags that have been soaked in petrol, whose flames add risk and colour to the proceedings.[1]

Panorama and its associated entertainments are followed the next day by *Dimanche Gras*, literally Fat Sunday, on which the calypso championships are celebrated, together with the selection of the most outrageous Carnival costumes for that year, of which more later. Both events take place in the Savannah on the same awkward stage as Panorama, although the mood in the audience on Sunday changes from the casual to the fervent, from partisan support for a local steel band to the jubilant reception of what have become the favourite songs in Trinidad. The calypso championships, for the title of Carnival Monarch, are interpreted by Trinidadians as a kind of state of the nation address, and the themes chosen by the finalists are accepted as being a faithful record of the scandals and intrigues that have interested Trinidad over the preceding year.

Carnival proper begins immediately after midnight on Dimanche Gras. The timing is a relic of colonial rule and dates to 1841, when a ban was issued prohibiting all forms of entertainment bar churchgoing on Sundays, in a vain attempt to

---

1 Curiously, limbo-dancing originated as a mourning rite: the relatives of a dead person were required to pass under a board from the coffin at the funeral, this action representing the journey that the soul of the deceased was required to undertake from the physical world to the afterlife.

limit Carnival creep. The festival possesses a ceremonial starting cannon that is fired in Port of Spain at about 2 a.m. on Monday morning, but revellers do not wait for its signal before seeking release. From midnight onwards the streets of the city fill with people covered from head to toe in mud. They gather for a ceremony known as J'Ouvert, from the French for 'day opens', and their aim is to rid themselves of the world beyond Carnival and engage the festival without reserve. J'Ouvert originated amongst emancipated slaves, as a ritual to exorcise the evil memories of subservience and to revel in the earth in whose ownership they had, at last, been granted a share. It shows a contempt for clothing – a preference for the sensation of dirt under the fingernails and a mud-caked skin. And not just any common or garden mud: the nastier the better, for unlike purity, filth can always be improved upon – with the sump oil from a worn-out engine, with housepaint or horse manure.

J'Ouvert is a deliberate fracture between the order that reigns outside of Carnival and the freedom of expression that characterises the festival. In contrast to the organised ceremonies that are to follow, J'Ouvert is spontaneous: Trinidad Carnival begins in anarchy. Trucks loaded with generators, amplifiers and walls of speakers steal their way into Port of Spain and pump music through its streets. People congregate to dance, and to apply mud and other filth to one another and to strangers, whether willing or not. Mud dries on to their skins in patches, resembling crocodile scales. Their hair is matted and clotted with dirt, and their clothing is sodden and sticks to their flesh. The application of filth to the bodies of friends and strangers is accounted one of the special pleasures of Trinidad Carnival: 'The mud, cold against warm skin in the early morning, causes pores to raise as it makes contact. Then, tingling as it begins to dry . . . The coverage must be complete. Then you return the favour. Bathing every limb in mud. All in the darkness . . . Now it's time to get the rhythm that will keep you going from 2 a.m. till sunrise.' The rhythm that the celebrants of J'Ouvert are seeking is deep and strong, and their dancing openly sexual. It is a celebration of physical contact, of flesh on flesh. Couples dance thigh to thigh, running their hands over limbs, legs and breasts. People writhe together in groups, slipping their bodies over one another, while they are refreshed with buckets of iced water from the rum stalls, and with mud by passers-by.

TRINIDAD EXPRESS NEWSPAPERS

J'Ouvert is haunted by the ghosts of Carnivals past. It parades all the demons that the Trinidadians encountered and slew on their journey to independence. Some of J'Ouvert's celebrants wear costumes over their mud, and their disguises are those that were the favourites of the French planters of the late eighteenth century – devils, revolutionaries, clowns and transvestites. Those in old-world disguises are accompanied by similarly antique and enigmatic figures from Carnival's adolescence, including Bats,

Bedwetters and Midnight Robbers. These last are individuals dressed in showy capes with a robber box under one arm who accost passers-by and threaten them with violence on a titanic scale, unless they are rewarded with some token gift. Midnight Robbers were a feature of nineteenth-century Carnival, when they would wander the villages and towns of Trinidad, terrorising children for their pocket money and challenging each other to verbal duels as to which of them was the most malevolent. A good Midnight Robber required a talent for hyperbole and the ability to project a sinister demeanour, and the craft has undergone a revival as these social skills have come back into fashion.

J'Ouvert celebrates confrontation, as well as contact. It presents opportunities to smear mud upon, to dance with and to menace perfect strangers. This last activity is the province of the Jab-Jab Men, a class of celebrants who adorn themselves with horns, dildos, mud and a pointed tail, perform obscene dances, lap up puddles on all fours, threaten passers by with pitchforks and lick them with their tongues. In keeping with the spirit of competition that pervades Carnival, there are prizes for J'Ouvert King and Queen. Competitors aim to look as ugly as possible, and their costumes appear the product of a careless and hasty psychopath. Some carry placards with messages scrawled on them in felt pen, others decorate themselves with the contents of dustbins. It is all very punk.

The logic behind J'Ouvert is compelling: since Carnival represents a different social equilibrium in which the boundaries of acceptable behaviour are expanded, the sooner these new limits are tested the better. Interestingly, J'Ouvert has been replicated abroad, thus demonstrating that it is not only the hygienic elements of Trinidad Carnival such as steel-band medleys that touch a universal chord.[2] By daylight on Monday morning J'Ouvert is winding down. Its celebrants return home to

---

2 J'Ouvert's greatest overseas triumph has been in New York, where it now forms an essential part of the Brooklyn carnival held each Labor Day weekend.

wash away the sweat and dirt they have accumulated, for Dirty Mas, as J'Ouvert is also known, is succeeded by Pretty Mas, where instead of being dulled by mud, and ruled by disorder, the Trinidadians dress like angels, dust their bodies with glitter, compose themselves into uniformed bands, and parade through the streets of Port of Spain.

Pretty Mas, the principal ceremony of Carnival, is a formal event, consisting of a procession of *Mas* bands – large organised groups of people in themed costumes – around a designated circuit. Each band can consist of up to 8,000 people, divided into sections, every section wearing a different type of costume, which together form a common theme for the band, such as 'Viking gods and goddesses'. Pretty Mas is competitive, and prizes are awarded to the most imaginatively turned-out band. The range of Mas band themes underwent a creative expansion through the twentieth century that is typical of Carnival – from the limited assortment of French stereotypes, through biblical and colonial motifs to pure fantasia. The evolution is reminiscent of that of Trinidad itself over the same period. A sense of this progress can be gained by a glance at the themes chosen by the winning bands during the past forty-eight years: in 1955, the champion theme was Imperial Rome; in 1960 (when the independence movement had come to the fore), Ye Saga of Merrie England; in 1963 (first Carnival after independence), Gulliver's Travels; in 1978 (republicanism), Know Yuh Country; in 1988, Out of This World; and in 2001, the Unexplained Sea. The themes chosen in any one year, like those of the calypso songs, are believed to reflect the state of the nation in Trinidad, and although playing Mas is reckoned to be undiluted pleasure, the costumes of the masqueraders also serve for social comment.

Participation is encouraged in Carnival to a far greater extent than at any other event of a similar scale, and anyone can join a Mas band. They begin to recruit six months in advance of the festival. Mas camps are set up in shops which display the costumes that each section of the band will wear, and one simply chooses from the selection, pays the required price, is measured up, and the outfit will be ready for collection a week before the festival begins. While some costumes may be reserved for people with special skills such as stilt-walking, it is otherwise an entirely democratic process. Masqueraders supplement their costumes with rum flasks, body glitter and dancing shoes.

While the Mas bands have increased in size, and in the complexity of their presentation over the years, the costumes of their members have tended towards the revealing. Many consist of little more than G-strings and bikini tops, albeit hung with tassels and adorned with feathers, beads and sequins, while the theme of the band is left to head-dresses, props and ornaments. This trend has been attributed to the present dominance, in the sense of abundance, of women in the Mas bands, who outnumber men five-to-one, and who prefer to wear less, both in order to show off their charms, and to increase the freedom of their dancing. Whether the theme of a band is carried by costume or props, they are spectacular ensembles, which are intended not only to be admired by the crowds, but also to be brought to life by their wearers. According to Peter Minshall, a leading designer for Pretty Mas, 'Mas is dancing sculpture. Mas is human energy in performance on a huge scale.' The costumes for the bands are prepared by an army of seamstresses, some part time, others employees of large companies – for the ingenuity in design and dexterity in execution of Carnival outfits in Trinidad has gained the nation an international reputation for the manufacture of fancy dress. The talents of Peter Minshall, for example, were called upon to mastermind the opening ceremonies of both the Barcelona and Atlanta Olympic Games.

Playing Mas embodies the laudable philosophy that (pace voyeurs) it is more fun to join in than to look on. Each Mas band is in itself a mobile party. The bands are accompanied by music in the form of truck-mounted sound-systems, and they proceed along the Carnival route to a rhythm known as 'chipping', which is a shuffle in time to the music that combines self-expression with forward motion, and conserves energy for 'breaking away', which is said to occur when the music seizes an entire band, who dance with a passion and intensity that invites exhaustion. While they are breaking away, Mas players 'wine and jam'. These are not a drink and a condiment, for Carnival has spawned its own vocabulary, but rather are ways of dancing during the festival. Wining, which involves moving the hips round and round in time to the music in imitation of coitus, is a perfect demonstration of George Bernard Shaw's maxim that dancing is 'a perpendicular expression of a horizontal desire'. Wining can be done solo, or with one or several companions of either sex. It is a contact sport. Jamming, in contrast, is obeying instructions embedded in the music, such as 'Put your hands in the air!'

JALISCO TOURIST BOARD

After chipping, wining, breaking away and jamming, the next most important form of behaviour on display along the Carnival route is flirting. This activity, in Trinidad, is not a discreet example of the genre. Instead of relying on amorous sighs, sidelong glances, and coded hand signals, Mas players telegraph their desires and mime their intentions. The air is awash with pheromones, the music is overwhelming, and freedom of expression rules. Even if aspiring lovers do not succeed in communicating their proposals to the paragon that they desire to possess, their gestures will have been noticed by a hundred other pairs of eyes, some of which may be receptive.

The Mas parade course leads via a series of street parties, and even its quietest legs pass through crowds of people cheering and dancing, who infiltrate the bands for a wine or two. Refreshments are available en route – there are bars and food and drink stalls at strategic points along the track, in the style of water stations along the path of a marathon. From the air, the Mas parade resembles a giant rainbow snake squeezing its coils through a convulsive crowd. Mas bands parade on Monday afternoon and evening, and all day Tuesday until midnight, the official end of Carnival. Tuesday is the day when the bands are judged, the costumes come out in all their glory, and the Mas players dance as if the world were about to end.

Adjudication takes place in the Savannah, whose stage marks the finishing post of the Mas parade route. Bands are judged as to their appearance, the creativity of their chosen theme and the spiritedness of their display. They are divided in three categories by size – small (up to 200 members), medium (up to 1,500 members) and large. A large band can take more than an hour to cross the stage, for the parade is televised and all its members will try to linger under the cameras, hoping to prolong their stay in the limelight by indulging in newsworthy exhibitionism. The Mas bands are led across the Savannah stage by their Kings and Queens. These are individuals dressed in costumes up to 30 feet tall and as many wide in each direction, which would look impressive on the face of a pyramid or atop a colossus, let alone adorning a single man or woman. They radiate outwards and upwards from their wearers and explode into colours. Indeed, so overwhelming are these creations that it is often hard to spot the person at their centre. Despite their great size and complicated construction the costumes are designed to move in time to the music, and to bring to life the subject of their theme. It is permissible to support outlying parts of these *folies de grandeur* on wheels, but they must be capable of being carried by their wearers.

The Kings and Queens of the Mas bands compete for separate festival titles. Although there are cash prizes, these barely cover the cost of the costumes, and people do not aspire to be King or Queen of Trinidad Carnival for love of money. Their mission is rather to explore the bounds of human dress and to win glory for a year. Many design and build their costumes themselves. Indeed, Trinidad has long been an eager if unlikely market for aerospace technology as would-be Kings and Queens search for ever lighter, stronger materials from which to construct their alter egos. A biologist would file their efforts under display behaviour along with the peacock's tail – as an example of runaway sexual selection. The costumes certainly function as a fitness indicator, for they can weigh several hundred pounds, and are sensational demonstrations of creativity. That of Geraldo Viera Jnr, 2001 Carnival King, for example, whose theme was 'Winds, an Element of Change', was of a similar size to a double-decker bus seen side on. It consisted of a row of four Mayan masks, each man-sized, sporting illuminated moving dreadlocks in red, purple and yellow, linked horizontally by 10-foot membranes shaped like bat wings that had been embellished with sequinned flames; the ribs of the wings sprouting totemic antennae ornamented with horned drums; the rear of the wings fanning out into a plumed tail 12 feet high and as many deep; and at the centre of the costume, Geraldo Viera Jnr, from whose shoulders rose a pillar three times his height mounting another giant mask topped with a head-dress radiating spears of colour. This spectacular work of art moved in time with its wearer as he danced to the music, spouted fireworks from the mouth of its upper mask, and finally incorporated a synchronised light show.

Once the bands and their respective monarchs have crossed the

TRINIDAD EXPRESS NEWSPAPERS

Savannah stage they are joined by friends, family and admirers, and the tempo of the celebrations changes. The Mas players set up for a last lap of the course, the pace of the music slows, costumes are discarded piece by piece, and as midnight on Shrove Tuesday approaches, Carnival closes with scenes that would not have disgraced a Roman Saturnalia. Those who have not danced, drank and flirted themselves to a standstill seek out partners for a Carnival fling, to be consummated in the open air. Indeed, the festival does not so much fade as fall apart. People collapse into each other's arms or stagger home, tailed by crowds of children eager to collect unwanted costumes and their props.

There is a final Carnival championship to be adjudicated, that is decided more or less at the stroke of midnight on Shrove Tuesday. This is the Road March title, which is awarded to the composer of the most popular song of Carnival. It is settled by taking note of which songs the Carnival bands are playing as they pass certain check-points along the parade route. In some years one tune can captivate festival-goers to the oblivion of all else: 'Man, de song so sweet dat the whole ah Trinidad shoulda get diabetes, whole day nutten else dey playing, de song so sound dat if yuh resting up during the first chorus and verse by the second yuh so fired up wid energy that yuh bound tuh move.' Although such peerless tunes are rare, when they occur they are believed to encapsulate the spirit of Trinidad over the preceding twelve months, and instead of remembering a year as a number, Trinidadians recall it by the name of the winning Road March song.

Until quite recently, it was considered taboo to mention Carnival after it had ended, and children would throw stones at anyone who transgressed. The festival stopped as abruptly as if it had run into a brick wall, the radio stations which had played nothing but calypso dropped it absolutely, and Trinidad enjoyed a Lent of almost monastic calm. Its population claimed to suffer from a syndrome known as 'burn-out', whose symptoms included an aversion to bright lights, alcohol and sudden movements. Notwithstanding burn-out, the festival has begun to extend itself into Ash Wednesday beach parties, and the blackout on Carnival music post-Carnival is no longer observed. Interestingly, the trend for Carnival to last beyond its traditional terminus has led to a certain unease amongst Trinidadian commentators, who consider it a threat to the integrity of the festival. While anyone complaining that Carnival has become too lubricious is dismissed as crying wolf, there is a school of thought that holds that the true spirit of the festival depends upon it being limited by time, so that Trinidad can focus its inventive powers on a few days each year, after which the slate is wiped clean and creative efforts can begin afresh for the next event.

However, the time limitations do not apply to Carnival's offspring. Just as the festival helped slaves to express their freedom, so their descendants have returned the compliment, and liberated Carnival from its old-world ties to Lent and its roots in the calendar. Copies of the Trinidad event flourish in Sydney, New York, Amsterdam, Toronto and London, and these celebrate the festival at very different times of the year, with no reference to its original purpose as the last fling before a fast. Carnival is no longer bound to the end of winter in Europe because a West Indian island nation has set it free.

It is not uncommon to find festivals flourishing in cultures other than those that nursed them. Just as Trinidad adopted a foreign ceremony, transformed it and then exported it worldwide, so many other types of ritual have been transplanted to foreign lands. Festivals have been carried abroad by migrants, have been introduced to pagans by missionaries, and have been imposed by conquerors on the conquered. However, the styles of celebration that have met with the best reception in new territories are those, like that of Trinidad, which provide some simple form of entertainment, with a universal appeal, that inspires in their participants a sense of playing truant from the rest of the year.

Perhaps the most successful example of a festival that has been adopted far and wide is an event staged every Shrovetide in a pretty English country town. Shrovetide is the English name for the carnival period, and while the English do not have a carnival tradition per se, they nonetheless possess a parallel custom of making a ritual farewell to meat for Lent, saying their adieus with pancake races, and brutal physical contests involving balls. On the same days each year that Mas players wine, jam and break away in Trinidad, the inhabitants of the English town celebrate a similarly energetic festival, which likewise revolves around a series of contests, albeit in the physical, rather than the creative sphere.

KEITH LOMAS

IV

~

A FRIENDLY
KIND OF FIGHT

Imagine the following: you have stepped into a bar in a foreign country, where a television set is showing a football match. The volume has been turned up loud and the monologue of a commentator fills the room, its tones urgent, the emotion intelligible, if not the language, rising over a babble of whistles, cries and groans. A number of young men are visible on the television screen, some dressed in red, others in yellow, milling around on an area of grass, passing a ball between them. Then one of the reds sprints wide, the voice of the commentator becomes animated, the camera zooms in on the player so that he fills the screen as he receives the ball on his chest, drops it to his feet, eludes two men in yellow with a spectacular display of dexterity, then swivels, glances up and lashes the ball away. The commentator is howling 'GOAL! GOAL!', as the camera shows the ball fly through the air, just beyond the reach of a despairing individual dressed in green and wearing gloves, and stretch the back of a rectangle of netting. Within a very few seconds, perhaps a hundred million men and women around the world, many wearing an identical red shirt to the footballer who has scored, right down to the name and number on their backs, will leap into the air, as if jolted simultaneously by an electrical charge, and shout out together in exultation. Such an amazing co-ordination of emotion is something leaders of religious or political organisations could only dream of inspiring, yet it happens nearly every week, at any time of day or night, and all because of twenty-two men chasing a small leather ball.

The television audience of a football match are, after a fashion, participating in a festival. They respond emotionally to every instant of play – they bite their lips in anxiety, hold their breath in trepidation, and cheer aloud with pleasure. The match transports them to a different world, where time is transformed into an eternal present, complete with replays, and the actions that the viewers follow with such rapt attention have special meanings and consequences which are only relevant to the ceremony in progress. This ninety-minute ritual is so compelling that football has become the most popular form of spectacle entertainment on the planet. Its 2002 World Cup drew a television audience of over 38 billion, which is the equivalent of every living human watching at least six of the competition's 111 matches. Such statistics, which demonstrate that soccer has more followers than all the religions in the world combined, suggest that the game touches a universal chord, that to be human is to admire football.

The global popularity of football is sometimes accounted as a triumph of both the British public school system and the Victorian ethos of fair play. The former codified an ancient style of ball game played throughout Great Britain, the latter gave the refined product the moral force to conquer the world. Together, they converted football into a portable ritual that, like the Christian mass, could be celebrated almost anywhere, needing only willing souls and a few props for its performance. However, there are fundamental philosophical differences between the rites of mass and football, for the charm of the game derives not from a creed, nor the elegance of its rituals, but from its appeal to the urge to compete, to divide the common herd into winners and losers.

The competitive instinct that is responsible for the global appeal of football can be seen at its most naked at an annual festival celebrated in the English town of Ashbourne. Ashbourne Royal Shrovetide Football, played between teams of several thousand, on a pitch 3 miles long, divided by a river, whose boundaries include both town and countryside, is a direct ancestor of the modern games of soccer, rugby, American Football and Australian Rules, yet it is restrained by few of the regulations that characterise its offspring. While murder, manslaughter and transporting the football by vehicle are strictly forbidden, the teams are otherwise free to use whatever strategy they think best to wrestle the ball towards their opponents' goal. In addition to being short on rules, Ashbourne Royal Shrovetide Football lacks the strict boundaries between spectator and participant that limit the contemporary game. Members of either sex are free to join a match at will and to retire from competition at any time.

The festival takes place amidst beautiful rural scenery and derives additional charm from its unpredictability. It lasts for two days, during which at least two games will be played. For much of each game the football itself is obscured beneath a seething mass of players, known as the Hug, which proceeds very slowly along narrow streets, over field and stream, trampling flat whatever it crosses and steaming all the while. Ashbourne Royal Shrovetide Football is an unruly kind of dance, an exuberant celebration of the joys of competing with thousands of similar-minded people, that further allows its participants to turn a familiar landscape into a wonderland. For the duration of the festival the centre of a respectable county town, usually a place of labour and commerce, becomes the stage for a series of violent struggles, and civic order makes way for festive chaos. The resulting spectacle has been described as resembling a 'cross between Rugby, Football, and a civil war'.

Although, prima facie, Shrovetide Football may appear an unlikely candidate for the paternity of the most popular form of entertainment on the planet – it does not have the music, the dancing, the decorations, or conspicuous consumption of other ceremonies that have been imitated far and wide – a glance at its history, and that of football per se, will reveal how the Ashbourne game has survived unchanged for centuries, and why its spirit has inspired so many people in a multitude of cultures.

The leisure activity of manoeuvring spherical objects with our hands and feet seems to have developed in parallel in a number of ancient civilisations, including those of China, Meso-America and Greece. In China, football can be traced as far back as the Han dynasty, when soldiers played a game that involved kicking leather balls stuffed with feathers into square nets. This activity was celebrated in a Taoist eulogy:

A round ball and a square goal
Suggest the shape of the Yin and the Yang.
The ball is like the full moon,
And the two teams stand opposed . . .
And let there be no partiality.
Determination and coolness are essential
And there must not be the slightest irritation for failure.
Such is the game. Let its principles apply to life.

Li Yu, AD 50–130

Ball games enjoyed an entirely separate genesis in the Americas. The favourite pastime of the Mayans was an elaborate contest staged in giant stone stadia, involving a solid rubber ball, and teams of men dressed in padded belts whose decoration depicted the sacred toad, gatekeeper to the underworld. In addition to serving as a popular entertainment, the game had profound religious significance. The losing team were sacrificed to the gods, their hearts were cut out, their bodies were decapitated and their heads added to the racks of losers' skulls that adorned the ball court.

In Europe, the Greeks were playing with balls some centuries before the birth of Christ, and credit their invention to Aganella, 'a fair maid of Corcya' who presented the 'first ball that ever was made to Nausicaa, the daughter of King Alcinous, and taught her how to use it'. Interestingly, the Greeks regarded football as a game for girls, believing it insufficiently rugged to allow men to vent their natural aggression. Hellenic sexism vanished when the Romans took to playing ball games, one of which, Harpastum, meaning 'abduction', a favourite of the Roman legionaries, was remarkably similar to modern rugby. It was played on a rectangular pitch, marked out with lines, and the objective of each team was to carry or kick the ball over the goal line of their opponents. Harpastum was a respectable pastime, and not only for soldiers. The learned Athaneseus recorded his approval: 'Harpastum . . . is the game I like most of all. Great are the exertion and fatigue attendant upon contests of ball-playing, and violent twisting and turning of the neck.'

It is likely that the Romans brought Harpastum to Britain, where it survived them and gradually degenerated into the style of game that is still played at Ashbourne today. There is, however, a second school of thought that holds that football is native to Great Britain, and commenced life as a Celtic fertility rite, in which a ball representing the sun was rolled across fields prior to their being planted. A third theory as to the origin of the game agrees that the sport is indigenous, but claims that it originated in Walton-on-Thames where it arose spontaneously to commemorate a victory over Viking marauders, the head of whose leader was kicked around the battleground after his troops had been put to flight.

Whatever its origins, football makes regular appearances in British records from the twelfth century onwards, usually in the context of legal documents that paint it as a violent pastime. Indeed, early match reports are often little more than casualty registers listing fatalities, broken limbs, stab wounds and incidental damage to property. The game is recorded as having been played the length and breadth of the British Isles, from Kirkwall, in the Orkney Islands, to St Columb in Cornwall, and had an unsavoury reputation in every place. Football was perceived as a sport of the mob: it was not so much a game as a pretext for the bestial fits of the animal masses. It suffered centuries of persecution under various kings, commencing with Edward II (1307–27) at whose command football was banned in the streets of London: 'For as much as there is a great noise in the City caused by hustling over large balls, from which many evils may arise, which God forbid, we command and forbid on behalf of the King, on pain of imprisonment, such game to be used in the City future.' Laws against football were also passed by King Henry IV, Henry VIII, and Queen Elizabeth I, who decreed that anyone caught playing the game was not merely a criminal but a sinner. Footballers were punished with a week in prison, and after paying their debt to society were compelled to do penance to satisfy their crime against the Church. Regal repugnance for the game was shared in Scotland, where King James I (1406–37) issued the absolute prohibition 'that na shall man play at the Futeball'. The usual reasons given for persecuting football were twofold, namely that it was violent and that it was useless, for it distracted men from or incapacitated them for worthwhile occupations such as archery practice and work.

Football attracted the particular ire of the Church, as the mob tended to play on holy days and Sundays. That the days set aside for rest and worship should be profaned by so turbulent a spectacle inflamed the pious, for 'any exercise which withdraweth us from godliness, either upon the Sabbath or any other day, is wicked and to be forbidden . . . for as concerning football playing, I protest unto you that it may be rather called a friendly kind of fight than a play or recreation, a bloody and murthering practise than a fellowly sport or pastime . . .'. Even Shakespeare frowned on football, recording his distaste in *King Lear*, where the loyal Earl of Kent insults the treacherous Oswald by calling him a 'base football player' (Act I, Scene 4).

Oppression and criticism notwithstanding, football was too important to the people to be eradicated. Englishmen were willing to risk prison and damnation in order to play. Why? The game of the Middle Ages was notable, if anything, for its brutality, and favoured strength and savagery over ball control. Even the scant rules prohibiting murder and manslaughter that are observed in Ashbourne today do not seem to have existed 500 years ago, when murderers were strung up and disembowelled without a second thought, so that over-vigorous play carried the risk not only of death but of a death sentence. So why did people risk their freedom, their souls and their bodies for the chance of pursuing a ball?

It seems that there were a variety of reasons, some ritual, others practical. Football matches were usually part of other celebrations – centrepieces to traditional holidays, which the people felt to be theirs by inalienable right, and to be beyond the interference of princes and priests. Games of football also served as initiation ceremonies for apprentices, and as such were not merely contests but rites of passage. As for the practical reasons for playing football, some games were contested in order to assert public rights of way, which had to be kept open through use, and can be seen as a sort of ceremonial mass excursion, while others were used to rally a crowd in protest, in order to combat attempts to circumscribe the freedom of the people. For example, a football match was held in Ely in 1683 whose true purpose was not sport, but rather to destroy the dykes that had been erected to drain the fens, and which would have deprived local rush-cutters of their livelihood. Similar examples of direct action occurred throughout the country: in 1740, 'a match of futtball was Cried at Kettering of five hundred men of a side, but the design was to pull down Lady Betey Jesmaine's Mills'.

Persecution of football and other traditional pastimes was redoubled in the nineteenth century, and a host of new legislation was enacted with the twin purposes of establishing public order and instilling piety and sobriety into the common people, in the latter case by limiting their temptations to be otherwise. The phrase on the lips of every social reformer was 'rational recreation'. It was acknowledged that the people must have their pleasures, but also that these pleasures should be decent and above all explicable in accordance with the strict moral code that prevailed in the age of steam. Sports involving cruelty to animals were the first to be curtailed, and such popular entertainments as bull-baiting, bear-baiting, cock-fighting, dog-fighting, badger-drawing and chicken-stoning (the list is long and sanguinary) were outlawed one by one. The next to come under attack were sports involving humans. Prize-fighting was banned outright and various pieces of legislation, including the Highways Act of 1835, which threatened fines or imprisonment to any person who obstructed public roads by playing at 'Football or any other Game on any Part of the said Highways' were introduced with the intention of suppressing the traditional matches. The game at Ashbourne fell foul of the

Highways Act in 1860, when one of its players was convicted of obstructing a cart. At his trial, it was noted that the teams 'prepared mostly as if for a deadly struggle' for the encounter, dressing in padded clothing and hobnailed boots. The conviction was appealed, but the appeal failed, and a mock obituary for Ashbourne football was circulated in a satirical broadsheet:

> It becomes our painful duty to record the death of the Right Honourable Game Football, which melancholy event took place in the Court of Queen's Bench on Wednesday Nov. 14, 1860 ... For some months the patriotic Old Man had been suffering from injuries sustained in his native town, so far back as Shrovetide last year; he was at once removed (by appeal) to London, where he lingered in suspense till the law of death put its icy hand upon him, and claimed as another trophy to magisterial interference one who had long lived in the hearts of the people. His untimely end has cast a gloom over the place, where the amusement he afforded the inhabitants will not soon be forgotten.

In the event, the obituary proved to be premature. A year later football was revived in Ashbourne and by 1880 was enjoying such robust good health that police had to be called in from as far away as Derby to quell the traditional riots that accompanied the game.

Whereas Ashbourne survived the nineteenth century, many similar games that were contested throughout the British Isles did not. The annual football match at Inveresk in Scotland, for instance, played between teams of married and unmarried women was a typical victim of the rational recreation movement. It was considered improper that maids and matrons should scratch each other's eyes and breasts in order to gain the possession of a ball, and such was the power of moral opprobrium that the traditional spectacle was extinguished. One by one such time honoured amusements fell foul of legislation, of the dislocation engendered by the industrial revolution, and ultimately were superseded by a new generation of ball games. These last were the result of a sea change in attitudes towards sport in the middle and upper classes of Great Britain. Games, football especially, had been discovered to be a good way of keeping public schoolboys under control, who otherwise expressed their urge to compete by staging riots. Various forms of football were included in the curricula of, among others, Eton, Winchester, Rugby and Harrow. At each of these schools rules were invented to make the game a controlled explosion of adolescent passion that took place within a defined area of terrain, between clearly delineated teams of players. The result was rational tribalism – schoolboys pledged their faith to their house team, and focused their energy on its contests with other similar social units. In Winchester, for example, the spectacular annual pupil revolts which, until 1818, had had to be put down by the army with fixed bayonets, vanished upon the introduction of a violent, if codified form of football.

Old boys carried their affection for the tribal rituals of their youth into their adult lives. In order that the alumni of different schools might compete against one another, they decided to draw up a set of universal rules. Those for football were settled by a group of ex-public schoolboys over the course of a meeting in a London pub in 1863. However, their formula did not allow for 'hacking' – kicking other players in the shins whether they had the ball or not – and a second set of rules was drawn up by pro-hackers which were later to become the basis for the modern game of rugby.[1] As soon as football's rituals had been codified

---

1 A member of the hacking lobby issued a sombre, if prophetic warning to the nascent Football Association of the likely consequences of prohibiting the time-honoured custom: 'you will do away with the courage and pluck of the game, and I will . . . bring over a lot of Frenchmen who would beat you with a week's practice'.

their performance spread rapidly across Great Britain and throughout the world. By 1900 the game was being played or watched by millions of people every weekend, and had been taken up as far away as Argentina and New Zealand.

The success of the new generation of ball games resulted in a change of attitude towards the older forms of contest. Instead of being rejected as mob brutality, they gradually were acknowledged to be a part of the national heritage. In the case of Ashbourne, the journey towards respectability commenced in the last decade of the nineteenth century. Prestigious visitors, including peers of the realm, were engaged to start the annual matches. Local grandees recorded taking their daughters to watch them. Shrovetide Football also acquired an association with patriotism. Its players took up singing 'Rule Britannia' and 'God Save the King' before the start of a game, and when they volunteered to serve in World War I, they carried a football with them to the trenches as a reminder of the values they were fighting to preserve. This was used in the first ever away fixture of the Ashbourne game, played on Shrove Tuesday, 1916 in the French village of Sous St Ledger. After the war, the reputation of Ashbourne football continued to ascend until it reached the summit of respectability. Its progress was rewarded with the ultimate mark of recognition in 1928, when the Prince of Wales performed its opening ceremony, and confirmed its title as Ashbourne Royal Shrovetide Football.

Despite the elevation in its status, the character of the game has remained unaltered up to the present day. A few changes have been made to its limited rules, and one new one – that the ball may not be transported by motor vehicle during play – has been added. The players too have remained true to the time-honoured principles of the contest. While they no longer lose their trousers or their hats during a match, for braces and headwear have gone out of fashion – and the whiff of aftershave has appeared on their bodies alongside those of beer, whisky, silage, coal tar and sheep dip – they are still evidently the descendants of the dangerous-looking mobs that so terrified middle England for nearly a millennium.

Ashbourne Royal Shrovetide Football takes place amid some of the prettiest countryside in England. The town of Ashbourne is situated at the southern end of the Derbyshire Peak District, which, to judge by the abundance of palaeolithic remains in the vicinity, has been a desirable landscape for humanity, and related hominoids, for at least fifteen hundred thousand years. The festival lasts for two days – Shrove Tuesday and Ash Wednesday, which usually fall in February, when winter still clings to the land, and the sun rolls along the horizon at eye level, delivering more brilliance than warmth. Signs of regeneration are apparent in the landscape – daffodils and snowdrops have emerged, their coloured petals rendered all the more striking against the sombre background of bare trees and muddy brown fields whose puddles reflect a leaden sky.

Ashbourne rises from the surrounding countryside like a high-masted boat on a turbulent sea. The 215-foot steeple of St Oswald's, its thirteenth-century church, tapers to a needle that scratches against the bellies of the clouds. The town itself is a large settlement that manages to be both stately and pretty. It is famed for its gingerbread and arrangements of flowers as well as for its football. Indeed, tradition is a fickle mistress, for whereas she gives some communities elegant festivals, appropriate to their attractive surroundings, where the sexes decorate each other with garlands, and mingle and dance amidst sumptuous decoration, the tumultuous nature of the annual celebrations of Ashbourne requires it to be protected rather than adorned. Preparations for the Shrovetide Football only begin on the day that the festival commences, and the town is made ready for the revelry with barricades. Shop fronts are boarded up with timber balks and chipboard, for only essential institutions such as pubs and casualty wards will stay open during the event. On rare occasions gestures have been made in the direction of ornamentation – in

2003, for instance, special strings of Union Jack bunting were hung between the buildings on Church Street, the main thoroughfare of Ashbourne, in order to commemorate a second visit by a Prince of Wales – but otherwise Ashbourne strips rather than dresses for action.

The residents of the town are divided into two for the purposes of the festival. Those Ashburnians who were born on the north side of the River Henmore, which runs through the middle of the town, are known as the 'Up'ards' and those born on the south side as the 'Down'ards', and it is these factions that comprise the teams who will dispute the Shrovetide Football matches. While there are inevitable rivalries between the groups, for most of the year they mingle easily and intermarry freely – indeed, they are only strongly tribal for the duration of the games.

The players are animated by the same spirit of minimalism in preparation that guides the municipal authorities of Ashbourne. Shrovetide Football is a festival that requires little personal

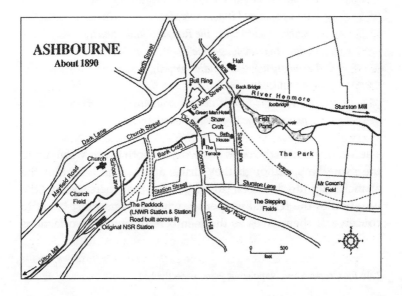

commitment prior to the event itself. Players do not spend months working on a costume for the match. They value durability and protection above elegance in their clothing, and dress, like their ancestors, 'as if for a deadly struggle', augmenting the traditional hobnailed, steel toecapped boots with wetsuits for water play. Nor do they follow any formal training regime before competing, although rugby, butchery, agricultural labouring and wrestling are all accepted to be useful forms of preparation. Outsiders are permitted to join either team – at their own risk.

Preliminaries to the festival consist in the main of drinking ale. The Up'ards and the Down'ards assemble on the morning of Shrove Tuesday in Ashbourne's public houses, and once they have shipped enough pre-match nourishment, they prepare their lungs for the athletics ahead by singing patriotic favourites and the Shrovetide Football Song:

> *There's a game that bears a well-known name,*
> *Though foes do it deride,*
> *For years and years it has been played,*
> *And why should it now subside?*
> *It's helped us conquer the Russians and French,[2]*
> *In days that are long gone by,*
> *For many a gallant soldier played,*
> *Who under the sod doth lie;*
> *'Tis a good old game, deny it who can,*
> *Is football played by Englishmen!*

The atmosphere in the pubs is rowdy, for both teams warm up in the same bars, although they drink apart. It is here that the artificial divide between townspeople that persists for the duration of the festival is opened, when players must begin to conceive of themselves as the members of one of two factions

---

2 In the Crimean and Napoleonic wars respectively.

about to wage war. This task is complicated by the absence of team strips. Neither side carries any identification – not armbands, nor headscarves, nor even any particular colour. The competitors can work up neither pride nor rancour with reference to a uniform, they cannot be Pavlovian about red, for instance, and so must dig up their aggression from within.

The kick-off for the festival, known as 'turning up' the ball, takes place from a brick-built plinth beside Ashbourne's municipal car-park, when a local dignitary or national celebrity launches it into an expectant crowd. The first game begins each day at 2 p.m. and potentially lasts until 10 p.m. Every game is decided by a single goal. The goals are situated three miles apart – one at Sturston Mill, to the east of Ashbourne, and the other at Clifton Mill to the west of the town. Each consists of a stone pillar on the banks of the River Henmore. A goal is scored, and the match won, by tapping the ball three times against a circular millstone embedded in each pillar. If a goal is scored before 5 p.m., a new ball is 'turned up' and a new game started. If the goal is scored after 5 p.m. then there is no more play for that day. No more than three games have ever been played in a single day, and no more than four have been completed over the two days of the festival.

The balls are handmade from shoe-leather and are filled with chips of cork. They are larger and very much heavier than a soccer ball – indeed, they are very hard to kick at all. The exterior of each is painted with the Union Jack and embellished with the details of the match in which it is to serve. If a goal is scored with the ball, it is given to the scorer. If none occurs in the match, it is given to the person who turned it up. The balls are beautifully assembled, and however much damage they may suffer during a match, are repainted after they have dried out and are kept and prized as heirlooms.

The opening ceremony of Ashbourne Royal Shrovetide Football is wonderfully uncomplicated. The individual honoured with turning up the ball is carried shoulder high from his place at a pre-match luncheon table to the plinth in the Shawcroft car-park, escorted by a crowd of players. The pubs empty and the teams assemble round the plinth, where they sing 'Auld Lang Syne' and 'God Save the Queen', and the mayor of Ashbourne issues them with the traditional request that they respect private property and do not destroy buildings, businesses or gardens. The view at the start of the game for the person charged with turning up the ball is breathtaking: a crowd of thousands, a forest of arms, a multitude of open mouths singing and issuing battle cries, and a sea of eyes, many glazed over with testosterone, all intent on a painted leather sphere.

DAVE BURGESS/DAILY TELEGRAPH

As soon as the ball is launched into the crowd it disappears from sight. A knot of several hundred people forms around its vanishing point. This is the Hug, a kind of giant, steaming rugby scrum, inside which the ball will pass much of each match. The Hug is not the place for those who pride themselves on being pale and interesting. Bodies compact towards its centre, like car bumpers crumpling at the point of impact. Broken ribs, dislocated shoulders and severe bruising are common injuries inside the Hug; asphyxiation, exhaustion and the smell of a hundred men sweating out beer are no more than incidental hazards. Visitors tempted to join the mêlée are advised to heed the frank warning once passed on by a local to an outsider on the verge of diving in: 'If you go in there you will be knocked down, trampled on and crushed.'

The Hug proceeds through the streets of Ashbourne in the general direction of one or other of the goals. Its pace is slow, but its progress is inexorable. It moves like lava – an amorphous mass that swells over walls, through gardens, engulfing vehicles (the game now has right of way over all forms of traffic), and submerging whatever lies in its path. While effort on the individual level is by and large wasted, for each person in its midst must dedicate as much effort to protecting themselves as to assisting in the forward motion of the ball, the cumulative destructive force of the Hug is considerable. It can overturn cars, collapse stone walls and cave in shop fronts. Players on both sides observe an unwritten code that it should be steered clear of any very dangerous obstacles, such as plate-glass windows, and ensure that it is kept out of the town's churches, its cemetery and its memorial gardens. Despite such precautions, the Hug behaves as if it was an independent being, picking its own route through Ashbourne according to its whims. There is an instance, for example, of it passing in its entirety through a fish and chip shop, entering by the front door and leaving via the rear, leaving a trail of customers, waiting staff, pickled eggs and battered cod in its wake.

The topography of the pitch provides each of the teams with its particular strategy during a game. Clifton Mill, the goal of the Down'ards, is located downstream of Ashbourne so that the Down'ards have the advantage of the current, and aim to Hug the ball into the Henmore river, and use the force of the water to aid them to their objective. The Up'ards, in contrast, whose goal is upstream of the town, are on the defensive during 'water play', and their strategy is to keep it to a minimum, by directing the Hug away from the river. The general tactics of both teams are to use the Hug to establish position, then to throw or kick the ball clear to runners who are posted around its flanks, or lurking in strategic places, who may then break away towards their goal. The goals and their approaches are defended by guards, of shorter wind but greater bulk than the runners, and each team also has specialised water players, renowned for their indifference to cold, and the low value that they place upon their front teeth. Indeed, the position any player assumes is by and large determined by their physique, and fear level.

Cold water is a speciality of the festival, and once play has made a round or so of Ashbourne, it gravitates towards the river. When Shrovetide falls in early February the Henmore is sometimes frozen, though not thickly enough to support the Hug. Conversely, if the weather has been gentle, the river can be swollen with meltwater, and although it is seldom more than neck deep its waters are sufficiently frigid. In centuries past, players who spent too long in the river suffered from and sometimes died of hypothermia. In modern times, they have taken to wearing wetsuits in order to conserve their stamina while the Hug is in the Henmore.

The absence of team colours and numbers make it hard for the outsider to admire the complex deployment of players through the streets of Ashbourne, its river, and the countryside beyond. A Frenchman watching a similar match in the nineteenth century, and unable to detect the elegant disposition of its teams, remarked 'If this is what they call football, what do

they call fighting?' Although the Ashbourne game may appear gloriously artless on first acquaintance, its players claim that its tactics are as intricate as those employed at the highest level of chess. This complexity stems in part from the nature of the pitch. The level of the river, the presence or absence of ice on the town pond, the quantities of slurry in a particular field must all be taken into account, in addition to any changes in the terrain that have occurred over the preceding year. Indeed, failure to notice change can lead to disasters. In the 1971 game, for example, the first after the Henmore had been re-routed through a culvert, the Up'ards instinctively made for the old river bed, now covered over, thus missing a break-away and losing the match.

Like Trinidad Carnival, Shrovetide Football has developed a vocabulary of its own. The ball is called the 'Leather', and floundering after the Leather in the river, or through a muddy field is known as 'sprottling'. While the players are sprottling, their wives and mothers encourage them with cries of 'Rollick it!', and if the women feel that the Leather is not being rollicked hard enough, they are not above risking their beauty and joining in. Women have even scored goals in Shrovetide Football, the first of the fair to achieve this distinction being Mrs Doris Mugglestone in 1943. Her strike for equality was recorded by the local press: 'a new factor arose when Mrs Mugglestone jumped in and proceeded to tear the Hug apart. It survived the shock and when Down'ards threw in all their weight near the top of the Fishpond meadow it was about forty strong with a high proportion of women . . . A combined effort by the female forces sent the Hug staggering across to the opposite bank. This vigorous Amazon stuff was something new to the "water rats", but they bore it with fortitude.' The comely maids of Ashbourne, latter-day Nausicaas, continue to contribute to play, although none has got her name on the scoresheet since Miss Nora Wibberley in 1957.

It is impossible to predict the course of a game of Shrovetide Football. Each match is something of a magical mystery tour of Ashbourne and its environs, which serve as a giant playground for the duration of the festival. As a general rule, once a Hug has been formed, the town explored, and the players have refreshed themselves in the river, the game tends towards open country. It assumes a slightly brisker pace once play is clear of Ashbourne. There are fewer obstacles, and if the Hug is still intact it is easier for the mass of players to manoeuvre around or through a bog than along a narrow alley. The Hug presents an inspiring spectacle in the fields at sunset, when the shadows of its constituent players are drawn out long, and the red and orange rays of the dying sun lance through the steaming knot of bodies. Play continues well after night has come: if the ball is still in the streets of Ashbourne, under the sodium glow of their lamps; if in the naked countryside, illuminated by torches and the faint radiance of the new moon.

Once darkness has fallen the tactic of hiding the ball comes into its own. It is permissible to conceal, or bury the Leather, so long as it is kept intact. Although a Hug can continue for a long time without a ball at its centre, its absence usually is swiftly detected and the festival becomes an elaborate game of hide and seek until it is found. Players have hidden balls in railway tunnels, beneath their grandmothers sitting at their knitting, in the mud at the bottom of the fish pond, and in the middle of the coal-stack in the station yard. Hiding the Leather has lost something of its tactical value since the redrafting of a 'no ball' rule in 1991 that requires the game to be restarted with a fresh ball if the original has not been seen for over an hour. Hitherto, if a player succeeded in hiding a ball it was accepted wisdom that he or she would retire to a public house and meditate on the science of strategy while the town was being searched. Balls sometimes passed six of the eight hours allotted to a game under a couch or locked in a garden shed.

Whether the Leather has been smuggled, wrestled or run out of Ashbourne, by the time it reaches a goal its design has usually been battered off its surface and its shape is no longer any more than an approximation of the spherical. Play sometimes pauses when the ball is in the vicinity of a goal, while the players who are around it draw straws to see who will be given the honour of scoring. Etiquette demands that if, say, there are five players about the ball, four Up'ards and one Down'ard, and the Down'ard wins the right to score, his opponents are honour bound to accompany him to the other end of the pitch and help him goal against themselves. The end of a hard-fought game is a peculiar time to introduce the luck of the draw. A player who has exhausted his reserves of strength in running, fighting, sprottling and rollicking can be deprived of the glory of scoring and the prize of getting to keep the ball on the turn of a coin. In chess terms it is the equivalent of putting an opponent in check then offering them the opportunity to decide the result of the game with a round of Pooh-sticks. While the introduction of uncertainty at the eleventh hour serves to reduce the chance of individual glory, and to reinforce the ethic of teamwork up until the final instant of play, it is unlikely that the custom was

introduced for the purposes of improving the morals of the
players. The scoring etiquette rather seems intended to ensure
that, over the course of several festivals, players who make
regular contributions are at one time or another rewarded.

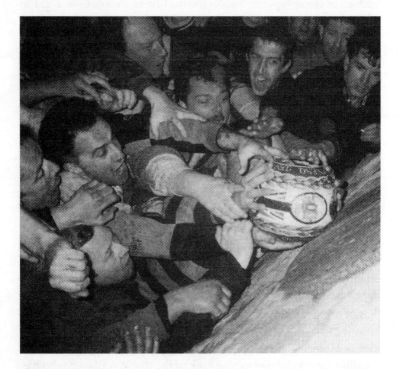

The Shrovetide game does have its local heroes, although these
men do not receive a fraction of the flattery and rewards of their
contemporaries in professional football. The fame of their
exploits, however, can be expected to continue for a far longer
time. For example, the deeds of Joe 'Ninety' Burton, who was at
his peak as a player in the first decade of the twentieth century,
are still spoken of with awe. A contemporary described him as
playing 'a wonderfully hard and vigorous game and his red head
was always noticeable in the thick of the fray. He was not over

scrupulous in his methods – he would admit it – and was a decidedly "high kicker", sometimes indeed, when the ball was not there!' Moreover, exponents of the Shrovetide game can achieve immortality not only for their athleticism but also for their villainy. In the infamous Shrove Tuesday contest of 1972, for instance, a key Down'ards player named Doug Sowter amazed his own team, and delighted the opposition by smuggling the ball out of the Hug and goaling for the Up'ards. His treachery has yet to be forgotten or forgiven.

The goals, Clifton Mill and Sturston Mill, as their names suggest, were once water mills astride the River Henmore, and a score was made by touching the ball against their mill wheels. Both were demolished in the twentieth century, and to mark their former locations, stone plinths have been erected on the river bank, each with an immitation millstone embedded in the face that overlooks the water. A player goals by standing in the river and tapping the ball three times against the millstone. The scene around the goal at the moment of a score is inspiring. Each plinth resembles a monolith – a standing stone raised into position for the purposes of worship – and the crowd cluster in the river around its base with arms raised as if in adoration, while steam drifts upwards from their bodies like clouds of incense. Resistance is maintained to the last inch, and the lucky individual who has drawn the right to goal may find the last few yards of water blocked by ranks of defenders four deep. The usual tactic employed by attackers at this stage is the phalanx – a cluster of heavyweight players who use their fists to batter through an opening for the individual with the ball.

Goalscorers at Ashbourne describe the event as being charged with emotion, and seem to compete in hyperbole to express their elation. Kirk Maskell, who goaled in 2002, announced that the feeling had been 'better than winning the National Lottery' and Pete Millward, who scored the subsequent year, not to be outdone, claimed the experience to be a greater wonder than witnessing the birth of another human being: 'I have got seven children and I have been present at every birth, but I have just goaled a ball and there is no feeling like it.'

It is a long walk back to the start for both teams, whether elated by victory, or defeated and exhausted. The festival continues after play has ended for the day in Ashbourne's public houses, where Up'ards and Down'ards mingle freely once again – the surge of enmity that polarised them throughout the match has been dissipated, the testosterone generated has been washed away by the icy waters of the Henmore. Pubs and breweries have long and honourable connections with Shrovetide Football, and local brewers produce speciality ales such as 'Tearbrain' and 'Old Shrovetider' to assist the players in replenishing lost body fluids. While they rehydrate, the competitors warm down with patriotic airs, and a few choruses of the Ashbourne Football Song. Devotion to an ideal England runs deep and strong through the players. It is as if they regard themselves as the keepers of a sacred flame, as the guardians of one of the mysteries of what it is to be English:

> For loyal the game shall ever be,
> No matter when or where
> And to treat that game as ought but the free,
> Is more than the boldest dare;
> Through the ups and downs of its chequered life
> May the ball still ever roll,
> Until by fair and gallant strife,
> We've reached the treasured goal,
> It's a good old game, deny it who can,
> That tries the pluck of an Englishman!

The pleasures of effort enjoyed by the Shrovetide Footballers are such that any incidental pain that they might suffer is ignored. The game may be uncomfortable at times, but players do not participate with the express purpose of hurting themselves. In contrast, pain, particularly the self-inflicted variety, is considered grounds for celebration in a number of cultures. Examples of festive pain range from the ritual tortures and mutilations that enliven initiation rites in tribal societies to the self-denial imposed by Islam on its followers during Ramadan. The celebration of suffering is justified on various grounds. In some cultures pain is inflicted in order to inure their members to hardships, whereas in others it is endured as an exercise in piety, or as a form of atonement for misdeeds. This last class of self-chastisement is common in Christian societies, where it travels under the name of penance.

Penance need not be brutal. Indeed, the Catholic Church has vigorously opposed some of the more exuberant kinds of self-immolation that have sprung up amongst the faithful over the centuries, burning the leaders of medieval flagellant sects at the stake for heresy, and more recently, requiring the Filipinos, who have themselves nailed to crosses over Easter, to desist from making a spectacle out of their faith. More gentle forms of penance are, however, encouraged, in particular over Lent – the forty-day period after Shrovetide – and meditation on suffering is advocated during the Easter celebrations that follow.

An elegant city in the south of Spain has made an art form out of these milder types of penance, where they have been seized upon as an opportunity to celebrate the bittersweet aspects of life. Mourning dress never goes out of fashion within its precincts, and its citizens are masters at weeping sensual tears. These prodigies of melancholy put all their arts to the test during a week-long festival that involves feats of penitential endurance, while simultaneously transforming self-chastisement into an exquisite type of hedonism.

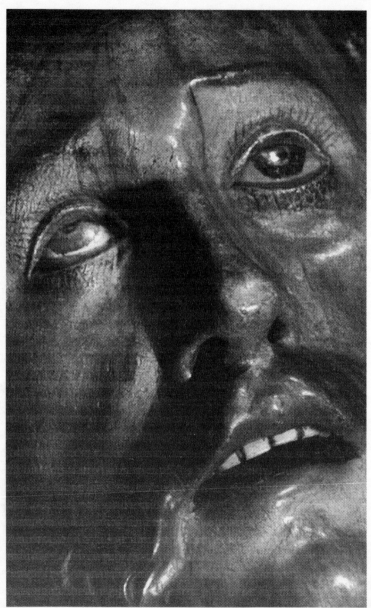

R.OLID

V

THE AGONY AND
THE ECSTASY

They that sow in tears shall reap in joy

PSALMS, CXXVI, 6

When Hippocrates, father of western medicine, went to visit his
friend Democritus the philosopher on the Greek island of Aldera
in the fifth century BC, he found him in his garden 'busy in cutting
up several beasts, to find out the cause of . . . melancholy'.
Democritus had taken to dissection in the conviction that misery
was the result of an anatomical malfunction, that somewhere
within the body of every living creature was an organ responsible
for happiness, which once identified would enable him to cure
sad people of their woe. That he was unsuccessful in his quest is
evident in the fact that people are still prone to dejection nearly
two and a half millennia later – not even Prozac can end

melancholy. This innate capacity for sorrow that so fascinated the Greek philosopher is recognised and encouraged every Easter week in Seville, the capital of Andalusia, during the festival of *Semana Santa*. For eight consecutive days and nights the melancholy can dress in mourning and weep and grieve to their heart's content, while their senses are charmed with doleful music, the scents of candles, incense and orange blossoms, and a spectacle of penance unrivalled since the fourteenth century when the cult of the flagellants was at its prime.

Semana Santa is first and foremost a Christian festival, whose purpose is to commemorate the suffering that Jesus Christ underwent on the cross, in order to win a life in heaven for His followers. While this may seem an unpromising cause for hedonism, it has become so refined in Seville as to present the opportunity to indulge in the most exquisite nuances of sorrow. It may be miserable, but it is also magnificent. The festival consists of a series of processions in which floats mounting tableaux of Christ in His agonies, or images of His mother the Virgin Mary, are carried through Seville upon the shoulders of the faithful, preceded by brass bands, surrounded by flowers and candles and followed by costumed penitents. Together, these constitute a Passion Play, which uses the streets and squares of the city as its stage, and which dramatises the last week that Christ spent as a man in a suitably splendid and sorrowful manner.

The unabashed weeping, the solemn penance and the open grief that characterise Seville during Semana Santa are at odds with its usual reputation. The city is home to many of the traditions and figures that the world considers to be quintessentially Spanish – flamenco music, Byron's Don Juan, Carmen, marmalade oranges, the Inquisition, guitar playing, the fervent worship of Christian images, and also to many of Spain's greatest painters and writers. Its citizens are perceived of as romantic, carefree and sensuous, the last sort of people one would expect to dress up in mourning and press handkerchiefs to their eyes. This apparent contradiction is explained by the history of the city: for over 2,000 years, Seville has alternated between glory and ruin, and as a consequence two contrary influences have shaped the character of its people: the first the accumulated hedonism of a wealthy and cultured succession of civilisations; the second, the inevitable melancholy that followed the overthrow of each of these through wars, plagues and persecutions.

The city made its historical debut as a Carthaginian settlement, and interestingly archaeological remains indicate that the Carthaginians offered special veneration to images of young, fertile women, thus prefiguring the reverence held today for the carved Madonnas that are carried in the processions of Semana Santa. The Carthaginians were driven out by the Romans in 206 BC, who christened the town Hispalis, and established a colony for veterans of the Punic wars close by. This settlement was the birthplace of Trajan and Hadrian, two of Rome's greatest emperors, who lavished splendid monuments on it, thus giving it its first taste of glory. Shortly afterwards, in a swing from magnificence to devastation that is typical of the history of Seville, it was sacked by marauding Mauretanians.

Christianity arrived in Seville during the twilight years of the Roman empire, when the city too was in decline. The new religion was greeted with persecution, and in AD 287 Seville was blessed with its first two martyrs, Saints Justa and Rufina, a pair of virgins who took offence at a lewd pagan idol which they smashed, and who were imprisoned, tortured and executed for their pains – Saint Justa perishing on the rack, Saint Rufina by strangulation. Despite so inauspicious a debut, Christianity flourished in Seville, and once a method of calculating when Easter fell had been established in AD 325, its adherents celebrated Holy Week, the oldest and most important of Christian festivals, with fasting and prayer vigils.

In the Holy Land, meanwhile, Easter celebrations were taking on a shape that anticipates the Semana Santa celebrations of

Seville by 1,000 years. Pilgrims from Spain and the rest of Europe made the arduous journey east in order to visit the places where Christ had lived, preached and perished. Thousands gathered in Jerusalem every Easter to re-enact their Saviour's final days as a man. Crowds retraced His journey from the Mount of Olives to Jerusalem, assembled in the garden of Gethsemane on the anniversary of His betrayal, and held a vigil before the great relic of the True Cross that culminated on the night of Good Friday with a service commemorating the passion of Christ. This last event according to Aetheria, a fourth-century pilgrim, was a sombre occasion, at which 'the sobs and lamentations of the people exceeded all description'.

While pilgrims were developing the celebration of sorrow in the Holy Land, Seville was overrun and settled by the Visigoths, a race of barbarians that had emerged suddenly, in historical terms, from the forests of Germany and snatched Spain from Rome. The Visigoths were Christians, albeit heretics of the Arian persuasion who denied the divinity of Christ, and while Seville was in their hands Easter celebrations languished. The single bright note of their rule was provided by St Isidoro, a Christian polymath who compiled an encyclopedia and a thesaurus, wrote commentaries on Holy Week and preserved the work of many classical writers for posterity.[1] However, the Visigoths were too fond of fleeting pleasures to form a lasting administration and were ousted from Seville in AD 712 by Muslim Arabs crossing from north Africa, who ruled the city for the next 500 years.

Inspired by rosewater, sherbet and hashish, they celebrated Isbilaya (Seville), jewel of the thrice-blessed kingdom of Al-Andaluz, in their poetry, in their histories and by adorning it with gardens, orange groves and palaces. Isbilaya was one of the

1 In addition to canonisation, St Isidoro has been nominated for other posthumous honours, including selection as the patron saint of the internet. His saint's day falls on 4 April.

largest and most magnificent cities in Europe. But melancholy was never far away – the city was too beautiful to be left unmolested and became a prize disputed by the members of a united faith. Al-Mutamid, its poet king, was deceived into surrendering his rule in 1085 to the Almoravids, an austere sect of desert Muslims. These latter had little time for narcotics, gardens and poetry. Their monument to the city is the Giralda, a stately tower that stands in the centre of Seville, the fenestration and ornament of whose lower storeys depict the face of a woman in tears, symbolic of the fate that was in store for its builders.

The Christian reconquest of Spain commenced in the same year that the Giralda was constructed, and Seville was returned to the Catholic fold by King Ferdinando II on 3 November 1248. During the centuries for which the city had been in Islamic hands, Christianity in the wider world had developed doctrines, and an accompanying iconography that focused on the suffering Christ had undergone in order to ensure the redemption of the faithful. Instead of representing the Saviour as a lamb or a fish, crucifixes had come into fashion, and Christians sought to probe the mysteries of their faith through self-immolation and penitence. These aspects of their worship were boosted by the appearance of the Black Death a century after the reconquest of Seville, which killed a third of the population of Europe, and animated the remainder to chastise their flesh in order to appease God's wrath. Encouraged by St Vincent of Ferrer (1350–1419), sects of flagellants arose who would lash themselves with whips and iron rods as demonstrations of faith, and this mode of worship spread through Spain down to Seville. Their bouts of castigation were accompanied by sweet, rhythmic music, whose sound was said to be capable of 'moving hearts of stone and bringing tears to the eyes of the most stolid'.

Christianity had also acquired gentler forms of devotion during the centuries that Seville had been governed by the infidel, including Passion Plays, which were theatrical performances that re-enacted scenes from the life of Christ, in order that the illiterate masses might better understand the mysteries revealed in the New Testament. These became favourites of the people of Seville and were staged in its new cathedral, on which work had commenced in 1401. It was built on a grand scale – the ecclesiastics who planned it boasted that it would be 'so large that those who see it shall think that we are mad', and from the mid-fifteenth century onwards, entries appear in the accounts of this behemoth relating to the purchase of decorations and props to be used in the annual Easter dramatics.

The late-medieval period witnessed the appearance of the

Hermandades, or brotherhoods of penitents, who currently parade during Semana Santa. These organisations trace their roots to the reconquest, when the guilds of the city established associations to rescue wounded soldiers and to give the dead a Christian burial. For the first century or so of their existence, the Hermandades were charitable bodies devoted to tending the sick. However, both their number and their functions increased dramatically upon the advent of the Spanish Inquisition in 1487, which was headquartered in Seville. This infamous branch of the Spanish civil service was responsible for the country's morals, which it defended with a truly bureaucratic zeal, making popular festivals of its successes against pagans and schismatics in the form of spectacular *autos-da-fé* – acts of faith, during which penitents dressed in striped pyjamas were received back into the Church and the condemned, distinguished by their dunce's caps were burned to death at the stake. The Inquisition introduced a note of misery in an age when Seville was otherwise on the ascendant. Jews and other non-Christians were forced to convert or emigrate. Many members of these groups joined or established Hermandades in order to demonstrate their credentials as good Christian citizens, and the Hermandades drew up elaborate rulebooks, which were as much statements of faith as the statutes of associations, and which were submitted to the ecclesiastical authorities for approval.

By the turn of the sixteenth century all the elements of the current Semana Santa celebrations were in place. Self-mortification and penance were accepted forms of devotion; Passion Plays depicting scenes from the life and death of Christ were popular entertainments; and a large number of Hermandades keen to demonstrate their piety had come into being. All that was missing was the inspiration to combine them into a single event. The inspiration arrived in 1521 when Don Fabrique Enriquez Ribera, the First Marquis of Tarifa, returned from a pilgrimage to the Holy Land and sought permission from the Church to institute a Via Dolorosa in Seville. His intention was to establish a route of the same distance that Christ had had to carry the cross on his way to execution, along which Don Fabrique could walk as an act of penance. Walking the real Via Dolorosa in the Holy Land had been revived as a must-do activity for pilgrims, and it had been fitted out with stations to identify the points where Christ had slipped, or been lashed by Roman soldiers. Several European cities had already set up their own Via Dolorosas, so that people unable to travel might demonstrate their faith, and the Marquis of Tarifa wished to add Seville to the list. Permission was granted and he set a course of 977 metres, the same distance that Jesus had had to cover, from his own house in the centre of Seville to a cross set under a dome outside the city walls named Cruz del Campo.

The concept proved popular amongst the Hermandades, who began to promenade along the Via Dolorosa, in particular at Easter, their members either laden with crosses, or armed with whips to use upon themselves and one another. As had been the case with the followers of St Vincent, they covered their faces while indulging in self-mortification, and further adopted the pointed headgear of the victims of the Inquisition as an icon of repentance. These parades became so numerous that in 1607 Cardinal Nino de Guevara, Grand Inquisitor, formulated a set of rules in order to control them. His regulations specified routes along which each of the Hermandades were required to proceed, and also set down the order in which they were to march.

At the same time as these important developments in the history of the festival were occurring, Seville was enjoying a purple patch and had become, once again, one of the richest cities in Europe. Its fortunes had soared with the discovery of the Americas, for it had been granted a monopoly over all of Spain's trade with its New World possessions. The women of Seville wore mantillas of Chinese silk, embroidered in Mexico; its men smoked Havana cigars, paid for with Peruvian silver. The city was the epicentre of the golden age of Spanish writing in the sixteenth and seventeenth centuries. Cervantes began *Don Quixote* in its prison,

Lope de Vega and Góngora graced its streets. Painters, including Velásquez and Murillo, produced some of their greatest works in Seville, many of which still adorn its churches and palaces. Some of this wealth and creative energy was applied to the production of elaborate props for the Hermandades, whose processions had grown into popular spectacles, displacing the Passion Plays in the affections of the people. Their members no longer carried only crosses and flails, but also elaborate tableaux, named *pasos*, which displayed Christ crucified, and sometimes entire scenes from His last days as a man.

Not only did the Hermandades introduce images of the Saviour to their parades, but also copies of the Virgin Mary, for as they had grown in importance, from being simple charitable bodies to organisations with real power, both within the city and the Catholic Church, they had assumed the role of dogmatists on a number of key articles of faith. Amongst these was the doctrine of the Immaculate Conception, which many of the brotherhoods incorporated within their regulations – those of the Hermandad de Silencio, for example, required and still require all of its members to 'believe, proclaim and defend, to the point of bloodshed . . . that the Most Saintly Mary, Mother of God and our Mistress, was conceived without original sin'. As a consequence, and in order to give a form to the purity that they had pledged themselves to defend, Madonnas were commissioned and carried through the streets of Seville, whose citizens demonstrated their appreciation for these icons through gifts of precious stones and priceless robes.

In a typical reversal of fortune, while Seville was awash with wealth, its population was halved in 1649 by a plague epidemic, and the contrast offered by sudden and ugly death in splendid surroundings was once again displayed to its citizens. The city had scarcely recovered when it lost its monopoly over the South American trade to Cadiz in 1717, and it began a century of decline into genteel poverty. However, while its fortunes ebbed, its Semana Santa celebrations went from strength to strength. The

Hermandades and Seville continued to play a key part in the
politics of the Catholic Church, in particular those relating to the
Counter-Reformation, an attack that had been launched against
Protestants in the sixteenth century, and then revived to oppose
the age of enlightenment. Its objective was a glorious rebuttal of
reason, its grounds for war the premise that human faith was
more important than human rights. The processions at Easter
became ever more elaborate, and the images that were paraded
increasingly baroque. It is during this period that Semana Santa
settled into its present form, drawing on nearly two millennia of
experience of splendour and suffering to produce the spectacle of
today, notable for its elegant manipulation of the emotions of all
those who gather to witness Christ dying in the streets of Seville.

The contemporary celebrations of Semana Santa are renowned for
their emotional power, which derives not only from the solemnity
of their subject matter, but also from their appeal to the senses,
each one of which is deliberately stimulated during the course of
the festival. The sense of smell is tantalised by the aromas of roses,
orange blossom, incense and candles; that of hearing by the
barefoot tread of penitents, the sound of men and women
weeping, the tragic and strident notes of an improvised lament,
and the noise of nearly a hundred brass bands; touch is satisfied
via the lips when they kiss the images of Christ and His
sorrowing mother, the entire passion of the instant and the festival
concentrated upon and released through that contact; taste is
sharpened through fasting, and vision is overwhelmed by the
spectacle of entire crowds lost in emotion.

These sensual stimulants are present on a colossal scale, and the
magnitude of the festival is also an important aspect of its power.
All of Seville is in some way involved in Semana Santa. It is a
demonstration of identity as much as piety. The series of
processions from every corner of the town to the cathedral at its
centre, which together make up the rituals of the festival, unite
Seville piece by piece – the footsteps of the penitent members of

the Hermandades are the stitches that incorporate the residents of each suburb within a greater entity, that make them part of an ancient and intricate composition.

Although not all the eight days for which the festival lasts are official holidays in Seville, its businesses are run on skeleton staffs, according to rotas that allow every worker time off to follow their local icon to the cathedral. A total of fifty-seven Hermandades parade during Semana Santa, and display 112 images between them. Some set out at dawn for the cathedral from their respective chapels scattered throughout Seville, whilst others do not venture forth until the sun has set. All the parades are arranged in accordance with a strict timetable, to avoid a gridlock of penitents developing around their destination.

The form of each of these processions is more or less identical, and consists of the transportation of images of Jesus, the Virgin Mary, and a supporting cast of Apostles, Roman soldiers, New Testament personalities such as King Herod, and various farmyard animals to the centre of the city and back again. The images are life-sized and carved from wood. They are painted to make them appear as life-like as possible, indeed, realism is the dominant aesthetic factor in their execution. They are either carried singly or arranged to form tableaux.

The images are conveyed on pasos, wooden altars which are intricately carved, lavishly decorated with silver, gold and tapestries, and carefully ornamented with banks of flowers and candelabra. Pasos are large, heavy assemblies, weighing several tons, and are carried on the shoulders of between twenty and forty penitents, known collectively as *costaleros*. Their sides are boxed in, or covered with brocade down to ground level, so that all that is visible of the porters is their feet. It is hard physical work to carry a paso – a row of poles concealed beneath the frame rests on the shoulders of the porters, who are arranged in lines like galley slaves. Costaleros were once recruited from the docks and paid by the day, but nowadays almost all are volunteers from the Hermandades – indeed, many pay for the privilege of carrying a paso. The costaleros are concealed in order that they do not distract attention from the power of the images on the pasos that they bear, and therefore they cannot see where they are going and are directed by a *capataz*, an external pilot, who guides them with verbal instructions and a gold knocker attached to the front of the paso. His instructions are brief, and often lyrical. When the costaleros are called upon to take up their load, for instance, the capataz raps sharply on the paso and calls out '*Al Cielo con Él!*' – 'Towards Heaven with Him!'

The pasos form only part of each procession. Between them, the Hermandades field approximately 60,000 costumed participants during the course of Semana Santa. Each paso is accompanied by between 500 and 3,000 members of the Hermandad, and usually by one or two brass bands, although some, such as *El Silencio*, march in absolute silence. Usually, each Hermandad arranges itself as follows: at its head is the *Cruz de Guia* – the guiding cross – carried by a costumed and hooded Hermano. The cross is succeeded by *nazarenos*, ranks of Hermanos dressed in gowns, their heads and faces concealed by pointed hoods which resemble inverted ice-cream cones, a fashion introduced in the days of the Inquisition and imitated since in America by the Klu-Klux-Klan. The nazarenos carry crosses, banners and candles. They are arranged according to seniority, so that the youngest members of the Hermandad march at the front of the company, and the most senior including the *Gran Hermano* – the Big Brother – precede the paso of Christ. The figures of Jesus on the pasos are life-sized, and aim to show His person, His expression, and His wounds so that they appear both real and painful. They are vivid *aides-mémoire* of the suffering Christ underwent for the redemption of His followers, and they are very effective. Behind the paso, if the Hermandad is not sworn to silence, is a brass band, and following that a group of marching sinners in uniform, called *penitentes*, who are dressed in cloaks and hoods like the nazarenos, but in their case the hoods are thrown back to reveal their faces. The penitentes are authentic penitents. They proceed barefoot and carry one, or sometimes a pair or more of heavy wooden crosses. Some wear manacles around their ankles, although the more sanguinary displays of self-mortification that were popular in the Middle Ages were banned in the nineteenth century, thus severing the festival from any overt links with the pleasures of sado-masochism. Interestingly, many Sevillanos mourned the passing of flagellation, which they considered to be good for the health, and which had been a favourite of the spectators at Semana Santa.

Next in the marching order comes a paso bearing an image of the Virgin Mary. This section is headed by more nazarenos, followed by the paso itself, and perhaps another band. The Madonnas are decked out with trailing veils embroidered in gold, while they themselves wear extravagant jewellery and garlands of pearls. It has become a tradition that the flowers on their pasos are arranged and the Virgins dressed by Seville's homosexual community. Every procession attracts a tail of aficionados, known as the *bullo*, who are the particular followers of each Madonna, and who believe that their favourite image has aesthetic merits infinitely superior to any other on display during Semana Santa. Sevillanos take their allegiances to their Madonnas very seriously, and marriages between members of different sects have been known to be prohibited on the grounds of a clash of virgins.

These, then, are the mechanical elements with which the festival will evoke a tempest of melancholy – tens of thousands of penitents dressed in sinister costumes, that conceal the identity of their wearers, thus focusing attention on the images of beautiful women in tears, or a man on the way to his execution; other visual prompts depicting the symbolism of suffering such as crucifixes, lilies and candles; music that is simultaneously solemn and strident, and all of these supported by the beauty of Seville itself, which is dressed by nature with the delicate blossoms and the vibrant colours of spring.

An entire week would be too long to spend in festive dejection, and emotions during Semana Santa build in accordance with the timetable provided by the historical Easter week. The festival commences on a light-hearted note on Palm Sunday with a paso that depicts the arrival of Jesus in Jerusalem mounted on a donkey. *El Burrito* (the Little Donkey), as this float is known, is a favourite with children, and their loyalty is cemented by the handfuls of boiled sweets handed out by the nazarenos who accompany it. From this optimistic starting point, the pasos show the successive degradations that Christ suffered, and lead towards the awful inevitability of the forthcoming crucifixion. There is a paso mounting the Last Supper; another paraded the following day depicting the Betrayal; a third, which is carried through Seville the day after, that shows Herod passing the sentence of death, and so on.

An example of one of the busier of these compositions is carried by the Hermandad of the Mystery of the Exaltation. In addition to Christ Himself, it contains eight other figures and a horse, all life-size, and depicts Jesus, nailed to the cross, being raised into a vertical position. He is overlooked by the two thieves who were executed alongside Him, a brace of Roman centurions, and the horse. The tableau is alive with effort, and has been laid out in accordance with Renaissance laws of perspective and composition. In each front corner, labourers strain on diagonal ropes to heave the cross upright. The horse rears. The waiting thieves, like Christ, wear only loincloths, and are positioned so as to focus attention upon the agonised figure of the Saviour. Their hands are bound at the wrists behind their backs, and their poses are models of dejection.

R.OLID

It is a mistake to conceive of such pasos as decorative idolatry. They must be understood in their role as the descendants of the Passion Plays, and their images as no more nor less than wooden actors. Their contribution to the festival is to enhance the sense of spectacle, and they are appreciated and applauded by the crowd. Their magnificent decoration, whether seen in blazing sunlight or by the flicker of candles and lanterns, is powerful enough to provoke a sense of awe, especially if encountered in a narrow street, where a paso can appear like a stranded galleon, and the spectators in the houses alongside can reach out and touch its images. Their exuberance, however, does not detract from the solemn nature of their subject matter, and they play an essential role in establishing the grave tone that pervades the festival.

Passions mount as Semana Santa progresses, according to the course of events of the first Holy Week, towards a climax that occurs in the *Madrugada* – the pre-dawn hours of Good Friday, the hours Christ spent dying on the cross, which culminated in the delivery of His body into His mother's arms. It is during this period that some of the most famous and emotionally powerful pasos appear in the streets, and from the point of view of a hedonist, that the festival achieves its full potential as a majestic expression of misery. As many as a million people gather along the routes that the pasos will take towards the cathedral, many of whom have come ready to be moved to tears at the sight of their Saviour or His grief-stricken mother.

Six Hermandades parade during the Madrugada, and three of the images that they transport are considered to be the most emotive of the entire festival. These are the Christ of the Great Power, *La Esperanza de Triana* and Our Lady of Hope of Macarena. The two versions of the Madonna provoke not only a tempest of melancholy, but also a storm of rivalry as to which of the pair is the more beautiful and therefore the more inspiring. The effect that the appearance of these images has on the waiting spectators is enhanced by night, for all three venture forth in darkness, and the candles and lanterns of the pasos, and the full Easter moon floating over Seville, surround them with radiant auras.

The Christ of the Great Power is the first to appear. He is known as the Lord of Seville and is carried by members of the wealthiest and most influential of all the Hermandades which, to give it its full name, is the Pontifica y Real Hermandad y Cofradia de Nazarenos de Nuestro Padre Jesus del Gran Poder y Maria Santisima del Mayor Dolor y Traspaso, usually abbreviated to *El Gran Poder* – the Great Power. Spectators will have passed hours, if not the entire day waiting alongside his route, handkerchiefs at the ready, for his arrival. Most will learn of his approach from the music of his band, for the Hermandad of the Great Power fields nearly 3,000 brothers in its parade, and the ensemble takes an hour to pass any particular point on its route.

Upon first acquaintance the music at Semana Santa sounds strident and disconcerting – a confusion of wailing brass, and drums beating a slow tempo best suited to a funeral march, which provoke sensations of alarm and sorrow – a listener can feel the hairs rising on the nape of their neck. Interestingly, it has been used to great effect as background music to the shootouts in spaghetti westerns. An indication of its sound can be gauged by the titles of some favourite pieces: 'Amargua' (Bitterness), 'Sangre' (Blood), 'Misercordia en tus palabras' (Pity in your Words). However, once the listener has become accustomed to its raw tones, both its passion and its melody emerge. It is music not just to cry but to sob to. It is both tragic and triumphant. Every drumbeat has a finality to it, as if the procession was marching to an execution, and at any instant the drums might cease and the crucifixion commence. It also has something of the gypsy lament, of the *Canto Jonde*, of the primeval wail. Its volume is beautifully modulated, from the quiet, yet plaintive notes of a single cornet, backed by drumbeats like the tramp of muffled footsteps, to a blazing crescendo and a rhythm that would drive an army forwards.

The paso on which El Senor del Gran Poder is mounted, while

simpler in design than the composite tableaux of some Hermandades, is nonetheless breathtakingly opulent. Christ stands life-sized and upright in its centre, dressed in a purple robe, bearing His cross upon one shoulder. His head is tilted and He looks forward and downwards, with an expression that is profoundly introspective. Carved by Juan de Mesa in 1620, the image is acknowledged to be a masterpiece. El Gran Poder walks on a bed of red carnations, and is illuminated by baroque lanterns, chased from solid gold, one on each corner of the paso. The decoration of his paso is exuberant baroque, an intricate, yet harmonious arrangement of cherubs, angels, foliage, mostly gilded, interspersed with enamelled plaques depicting scenes from the crucifixion. The costaleros who carry the paso have been trained to impart a sway into their step as they proceed, in order to suggest motion to the image they carry, so that it seems as if Christ Himself is walking to his crucifixion.

The sense of solemnity is further enhanced by the flicker of candlelight playing on the grave expression and weary posture of the image, by the clouds of incense that hang in the still night air, by the sobs of women who watch singly, their shoulders shaking, or who clutch one another to share and to ease their grief. The costumes of the nazarenos that accompany El Gran Poder cast phantasmic shadows. Their pointed hoods have only slits for eyes so that they appear faceless, and their slow, measured tread makes them genuinely sinister. From time to time their eyeballs blaze red with reflected light from beneath their hoods. The image they surround is projected in shadows many times life-size on to the walls of buildings, trembling in the candlelight, so that Christ appears to shake under the weight of the cross He is carrying towards Golgotha.

True connoisseurs of melancholy hold that the emotive force of El Gran Poder viewed under the Easter moon is only equalled, and perhaps surpassed by, depending on their personal allegiances, the paso of either the Virgin of Hope of Macarena or La Esperanza de Triana. While the images of Christ that are paraded during Semana Santa are complete statues, often naked bar a crown of thorns and a loincloth, the images of the virgins, beneath their voluminous gowns, are no more than a bust in the sculptural sense, that is attached to a cylindrical torso along with a pair of articulated arms. This is a stroke of presentational genius, for it means that all that is visible of each virgin are her face and hands, thus focusing attention on her expression and her gesture. In effect, every white carnation, lily and candle flame, every ounce of worked silver and every square inch of costly brocade on the pasos, exist only in order to direct the eye towards not just a face but an emotion.

Every Madonna is depicted in one of two conditions, either *dolorosa* (pained) or *armargua* (bitter). At the risk of being partisan, I shall describe only La Triana, who is dolorosa. She is dressed in a snowstorm of lace, whose embroidery is as intricate as ice crystals. She is crowned in gold and has more jewels than a duchess. Her emeralds alone are priceless. Indeed, the expensive style in which such images are maintained is a plain, if effective measure of the esteem that they command. She is presented in a tunnel of white flowers and candles, and the profuse decorations of her paso are composed to focus the attention of the spectator upon her expression of sorrow.

Close up, she is as realistic as a waxwork. La Triana is a young woman of no more than twenty-one. She has an oval face with symmetrical features. Her dark eyes are almond shaped, her eyebrows pencil thin. She has real eyelashes, and wears mascara. Crystal tears adhere to her cheeks. She has a rosebud mouth, whose lips are swollen with blood. Between them the tip of her tongue is just visible – a little slice of erotic pink. Her expression is simultaneously sorrowful and carnal, and her mystery derives from the direction of her gaze, for her eyes possess an elusive quality, like the Mona Lisa Smile, and are fixed upon a calamity that we cannot see. She is at her most enchanting at dusk, when the candlelight from her paso begins to sparkle in her emeralds and her tears.

R.OLID

La Triana's route through Seville leads her from her home in the Capilla de los Marineros (Chapel of the Sailors), across the River Guadalquivir, through a number of narrow streets and on to the cathedral. Her progress is uneven. Parts of her course are so packed with spectators that even the funereal pace of her paso has to be slowed. At every step she is saluted with shouts of *'Que guapa!'* – 'What a beauty!', and sobs. She makes a number of official stops to honour the chapels of other Hermandades and, until it was demolished, she used to pause in front of the prison in Triana, which was usually filled with her admirers, to allow them to sing out:

Abrir las puertas carceleros
y asomarse a esas ventanas
que está aquí la Soberana
Madre del Dios de los Cielos
y Esperanza de Triana!

Open the shutters, warder
and put your head out the window
for here is the Sovereign Mother of the God of Heaven
Our Lady of Hope of Triana!

La Triana also makes unscheduled pauses, to allow her costaleros to rest, or to receive the salute of a *saeta* – an improvised song of praise, a spontaneous ejaculation of faith from a spectator who has been overcome with emotion. Saetas are also planned, for they are a form of art and famous flamenco and opera singers will position themselves at strategic points along the route – on a balcony above a small square, for example, that is certain to be crowded with grieving spectators. If they are moving, listeners will stifle their whimpering and hear the singers out in silence. It is spontaneous theatre, with a tragic theme, a public catharsis in which the saetas express in song the anguish depicted on the face of La Triana.

Semana Santa is a demanding festival to attend, for it is impossible to remain impassive, an aloof observer of pageantry. Tears are contagious and as the festival proceeds through the Madrugada, and entire crowds become convulsed with sorrow, even the sunniest of optimists will be tempted to join in. The target of both spectators and participants alike is a state known as *el sobrecogimiento*, which has been translated as meaning 'complete debauchery and ultimately sacredness of all the senses all at once'. It is a mixture of awe and self-indulgence, and simultaneously a form of release, that purges those who experience it. Even in an age when people are accustomed to seeing the exotic and fantastic in two dimensions via screens, and thus are less susceptible to spectacle than their ancestors, Semana Santa overwhelms. It was formulated in an era where sin and sorrow were considered fundamental to the human condition, and thus is better able to relieve the afflicted than the transient consolations offered by a visit to the shops, to the cinema, or any other contemporary form of recreation. The festival achieves this influence over spectator and participant alike by making suffering beautiful. In the words of the Sevillano author Manuel Machado, 'if you have seen Semana Santa you can say, without the slightest risk of exaggeration or hyperbole, that you have seen the most beautiful of your dreams converted into the most beautiful of realities – a thousand times more beautiful than your own dream'.

The celebrations continue for two further days after the Madrugada, during which the mood of the festival alters. Saturday is calm, like the still air that precedes a change in wind, and Easter Sunday is exultant – every trace of sorrow has vanished and there is a sense of relief of an ordeal endured and overcome. The festival of Easter is not merely to mourn the execution of Christ, but also to celebrate His Resurrection, although in order to indulge in melancholy, the people of Seville tend to close their minds to the triumphant message of the festival until the day on which it occurs. Semana Santa is a celebration of new beginnings as much as of repentance. Women buy new clothes and new shoes to follow the processions, and these latter have sometimes been blamed for all the weeping. The bars do a brisk, if respectful trade, for there are those who have been overcome with the sobrecogimiento, and who wish to *beber sus lagrimas* – literally, drink their tears. *Capellitas* ('little chapel-goers'), a local type of fanatic, make tours of all the chapels where the images are housed, in order to collect a souvenir ribbon from each. Finally, Seville's bullfighting season starts on Easter Sunday, and two weeks later the city explodes with exuberance at its *Feria de Abril*. Just as Semana Santa is the perfect demonstration of the solemn side of the Sevillano character, the Feria shows it at its most joyful and vivacious.

The images paraded in such opulence at Semana Santa in order to provoke the emotions of the faithful, and to focus their thoughts upon certain incidents in the life of their Saviour, are acknowledged to be no more than exquisitely carved pieces of wood – visual prompts that trigger a certain state of mind. Although they are treated with enormous respect, the homage paid to them falls far short of outright worship. Furthermore, no extraordinary spiritual benefits are promised to those who attend the festival. Observing the rites of sorrow does not guarantee an eternal reward.

In contrast, a festival held in an ancient, indeed legendary city on the east coast of India offers its participants the spectacle of wooden carvings that are not merely representations of gods, but the real thing, and one of whom is not just any god, but the Lord of the Universe himself. In addition, those who journey to the festival are guaranteed that their present lives will be their last, an enticing prospect to the average Hindu, whose beliefs are centred around the doctrine of reincarnation, and whose spiritual goal is to escape the treadmill of rebirth. Even hedonism can become a burden – a body can only take so much living – and even the most pious find it hard to avoid committing actions that might compromise their next existence. As a consequence, a festival that promises to free its participants from having to repeat themselves in other lives is a compelling, not to say righteous attraction, as are the incidental physical pleasures that it offers to believers.

VI

CHARIOTS OF
THE GODS

The world will end, perhaps not for the first time, in the present Age of Kali, the Hindu goddess of night and blood sacrifice, the erotic mistress of destruction. The end will begin in AD 431496 when our overcrowded planet has been stripped of all vegetation and anything still living will be dying of hunger, whereupon firestorms will descend and scorch away the rivers and oceans so that the earth becomes as 'naked as a turtle's back'. Rain will follow and flood the empty land, marking the beginning of a new cycle of ages. Vishnu, the first creator, will reappear, asleep upon the surface of the ocean, his dreams pregnant with the secrets of new life. After Vishnu has dreamed for more than a million years, a lotus will blossom from his navel, and creation reoccur. Men will walk the earth once again and when they die their souls will return to the treadmill of reincarnation. Thus runs the Hindu account of the cycle of existence, whose low point is no less dreadful for being distant, and which offers a sobering prospect for those who are fated to return to earth and see it all come to pass.

Happily, there is a way to escape the rigmarole of reincarnation and thus avoid being present at the predicted apocalypse, when the tears, urine, blood, lymph and every other form of fluid in our nearly liquid bodies will be sucked clear and vaporised while firestorms atomise cities and the rocks on which they are built. The solution takes the form of a pilgrimage to Puri, a town on the east coast of India, and participation in *Rath Yatra*, its principal annual festival.

Puri is one of India's four *Chaar Dhaams* – places where the great god Vishnu still spends time on earth. At Puri, the god has taken up residence, along with his brother and sister, in several hand-carved logs of wood. These roughly shaped if striking creations are believed to be real gods, and the wooden avatar of Vishnu is venerated as Jagannath, the Lord of the Universe. Jagannath is housed in an immense stone temple where he has a retinue of 6,000 priests and 14,000 servants. Every day, he is washed, dressed, entertained and fed, then chaperoned through a crowded social calendar, the highlight of which is the festival of Rath Yatra – when he and his siblings take to chariots for their annual excursion to a nearby pavilion. Their chariots are dragged through Puri by thousands of eager pilgrims, and their progress is wildly applauded by a million or more spectators, who surge around the moving vehicles in order to catch a glimpse of the face of Lord Jagannath. Their number, and the strength of their devotion stem from a promise contained in the sacred texts of the Hindus that guarantees *Moksha*, or liberation from the cycle of reincarnation, to anyone who sees Lord Jagannath during Rath Yatra, thereby excusing them from attendance at the terminal firestorms of the Age of Kali.

The resulting spectacle has amazed and sometimes horrified foreign visitors for nearly 700 years. Friar Oderic, the first European to witness the giant chariots being towed through the tumult of pilgrims observed: 'many ... who have come to this feast cast themselves under the chariot, so that its wheels may go over them, saying that they desire to die for their God. And the car passes over them, and crushes them, and cuts them in sunder, and so they perish on the spot.' Subsequent travellers were equally fascinated by the fanaticism of the pilgrims: 'They voluntarily offer up their wretched lives,' wrote Sebastian Manriquez, a seventeenth-century adventurer, 'throwing themselves down in the centre of the road along which the procession passes with its chariots full of idols. These pass over their unhappy bodies, leaving them crushed and mutilated. Such men are looked on as martyrs.' Puri developed a gruesome reputation in the West, and a corruption of the name of its resident god gave a new word to the English language – 'juggernaut', signifying a 'large, overpowering force or object . . . [an] institution or notion to which persons blindly sacrifice themselves or others'.

The spontaneous, if flamboyant, suicides during the festival of Rath Yatra that had caught the eyes of Friar Oderic and Manriquez continued to puzzle successive generations of foreign observers, who likewise failed to see the advantage that being crushed to death offered to its participants. The attraction that they could not appreciate was the prospect of instant Moksha, a temptation some few pilgrims each year could not resist, for according to their creed, there was no better time at or place in which to die than during Rath Yatra in Puri.

However, few latter-day pilgrims to the event attend with the specific motive of seizing the posthumous incentives on offer on the spot. Puri is not only famed as the abode of Lord Jagannath, and for a blood-soaked annual spectacle, but also as an attractive seaside town where all faiths can meet in equal worship to meditate upon the sublime. Moreover, the rigours of the Indian caste system are suspended for the duration of Rath Yatra, thus enabling Hindu pilgrims to enjoy a social freedom, including the liberty to walk among, and even to eat alongside their betters, that they might otherwise only dream of. Finally, *Tirtha*, the Sanskrit word for pilgrimage, has the further meaning of 'an action in itself virtuous' so that 'truth, forgiveness, control of senses, kindness to

all living beings and simplicity are also Tirthas', and a visit to Puri
enables every pilgrim to exercise these commendable qualities.

The story of how Vishnu, in the form of Lord Jagannath came
to take up residence in Puri, and to issue the promise of Moksha
to all who paid a visit to him is set out in the pages of the *Skanska
Purana*, a Hindu account of India's sacred places, whose contents
are accepted as holy writ. Briefly, a long time ago, a penitent king
named Indradyumna wished to do merit in this world and
consulted the gods via his dreams as to the best method. He was
advised to proceed to Puri where a temple dedicated to Vishnu
lay buried under sand dunes along the sea shore.[1] He was to find
and rebuild the temple, whereupon Vishnu would return in
person and make the place his home. Indradyumna located the
buried temple, constructed the new edifice, and waited for the
god of his dreams to appear, whiling away time in the interim by
sacrificing horses. Vishnu duly arrived in the form of a log of
driftwood (in fact the unburned portion of the body of his
Krishna avatar)[2] which was chiselled into an appropriate shape
by the hands of Vishwakama, cabinet-maker to the gods, and
installed in the temple. His mission accomplished, King
Indradyumna inaugurated Rath Yatra, during which Vishnu-
Krishna-Jagannath was paraded through the streets of Puri in a
chariot, for the benefit of all those pilgrims who yearned to gaze
upon the face of the almighty, and the festival has been celebrated
ever since.

---

1   Interestingly, the legend is reflected by the true fate of the magnificent Sun
    Temple at Konarak, only 20 kilometres north of Puri, which is covered from
    pediment to Sikhara with erotic carvings, and which lay hidden beneath sand
    dunes for a period of nearly 300 years.
2   In addition to animating tree trunks, Vishnu also visits earth from time to time
    via a series of avatars, or incarnations. To date these have included Matsya the
    fish, Vamana the dwarf, Narasimha the man-lion, and Krishna, a beautiful
    youth identified by his blue skin, who performed a number of legendary deeds
    in the service of mankind and its sacred cows, and who once made love to
    thirty-three cow girls thirty-three times every night for thirty-three consecutive
    nights.

The historical evidence as to the origins of Puri, its resident gods, and the festival of Rath Yatra is less clear cut. The first record of a spiritual influence at work in the area is on a polished stone column, erected by Asoka, the greatest ruler in the history of India, in the third century BC, whose inscription notes that its patron, sickened by warfare and slaughter, had elected to convert to Buddhism. The region was considered sacred to Buddhists for the next 500 years, and was reputed to have been the resting place of the left front tooth of Gautama Buddha himself, which had been salvaged from his funeral pyre. The Buddhists of this period celebrated chariot festivals, of a similar style to those performed in Puri today, which may have been the precursors of Rath Yatra. Over the following centuries, Hinduism gradually displaced Buddhism, and Lord Jagannath made his historical debut in Puri in the ninth century AD. Thereafter, records of the presence of the god, and references to his festival flow thick and fast. By the time that Friar Oderic chanced upon it in 1321 it was already centuries old, and the motives for attending well established.

From that period onwards the reputation of Puri begins to shine bright in secular as well as religious sources. Jagannath and his sacred abode were celebrated in poetry and song, and the spiritual advantages of a visit were widely disseminated. The *Panchasakha* poets of the fifteenth century, whose work was dedicated to the glorification of the Lord of the Universe, introduced a note of hedonism to his worship. Indian Baudelaires, they embraced the sordid in their lives, and feigned to disdain it in their writing. They appear to have reasoned that since oblivion was at hand, when the worthless world of the flesh could be bid adieu for ever, it mattered little how the intervening days were spent. Sentiments such as

> *O Forgetful mind, why do you forget?*
> *Don't you remember that the vulture of Time is flying about?*

are typical of Panchasakha thought, and some of their best work was produced in bars and brothels.

Their contempt for the material world had a prophetic streak –
Puri was conquered by Muslims in 1592, and while its new rulers
permitted the continuation of Rath Yatra, they made life miserable
for its celebrants. Although the spiritual reputation of Puri had
created a deep first impression on the advancing Islamic hordes,
not often noted for their tolerance of idols, and had moved their
general to proclaim 'This country is no fit subject for conquest, or
for schemes of human ambition . . . it belongs to the Gods, and
from end to end is one region of pilgrimage,' internecine strife
persisted for the century and a half of Muslim government during
which period the Jagannath temple was sacked a number of
times, and its resident gods were removed to safe hiding places
on several occasions.

Nonetheless, the fame of Jagannath continued to spread –
western adventurers who passed through Puri carried home more
tales of fanaticism during Rath Yatra; and within India, spiritual
leaders including Guru Nanak of the Sikhs visited the town and
paid testament to its unique aura. Ashrams were built around its
temple, and pilgrims began to travel to Puri from ever further afield.
Jagannath even made some converts from Islam, including the poet
Sal Beg, the son of Puri's Muslim ruler, who prayed to the Lord of
the Universe for help as he lay on a battlefield covered in wounds,
and upon his recovery dedicated his life to praising his saviour.

Stability returned in 1803 when the British assumed control of
what is now the Indian province of Orissa. Puri was taken under
their direct administration, and an investigation was made of the
affairs of its palatial temple and the gods within. The colossal
scale of the establishment prompted the British to attempt to
impose a management committee, a step that was vigorously
opposed in India and Britain, both Hindus and Christians
complaining of sacrilege. Opposition was particularly strong in
Great Britain, where returned missionaries whipped up a storm
over the scandalous implications of a British government running
a pagan institution. They were assisted in their case by regular
and lurid accounts of pilgrims to the Jagannath temple hurling

themselves under the chariots of its idols, a spectacle which moved British writers to join the Panchasakha poets and celebrate the Lord of the Universe in verse:

> *A thousand pilgrims strain*
> *Arm, shoulder, breast and thigh, with might and main,*
> *To drag that sacred wain,*
> *And scarce can draw along the enormous load.*
> *Prone fall the frantic votaries on the road,*
> *And calling on the God*
> *Their self devoted bodies there they lay*
> *To pave his chariot way.*
> *On Jaga-Naut they call,*
> *The ponderous car rolls on and crushes all,*
> *Through flesh and bones it ploughs its dreadful path.*

Not only did the gods that they found in their temporal charge appeal to the sense of the macabre of the British, but they also awakened their intellectual curiosity, not least of all with their unusual morphology. Instead of being many limbed, like most Hindu representations of deities, the divine residents of Puri consisted of little more than the tree trunks from which they had been hewed, painted in bright colours, and decorated with cartoon character faces. In further contrast to the delicate craftsmanship that the British expected of Indian carving, Lord Jagannath and his siblings were clumsily executed – giant squat effigies with stumps for arms, manic smiles and eyes the size of dinner plates.

The British were likewise amazed by the sheer complexity of the rituals surrounding the gods, which were more intricate than those that governed the court life of a feudal ruler. The gods were attended by a host of priests, servants and *Devadasis*, or brides, who together numbered in their tens of thousands, each one of whom dedicated their working lives to the service of Lord Jagannath. British scholars developed a number of theories of their own to explain the curious form of the deities, and the

fanatical adulation they received, thus adding to the body of myth surrounding their presence in Puri. These theories included the suggestions: (a) that the gods were Buddhist in origin – personifications of the symbolic triad of Buddha, Dharma and Sangha, which had survived from the centuries when the region was a place of Buddhist pilgrimage; (b) that the deities were the rainmaking gods of the local tribes, who had been converted to Hinduism; and (c) that they were the survivors of a secular ceremony once observed in the region, during which the king who had ruled for the past twelve years was sacrificed and a new one crowned. This ceremony bore many stylistic similarities to Rath Yatra. The king embarked for death in a chariot drawn by his subjects, and killed himself by cutting off his lips, nose and eyelids, and then attempting his arms, at which point he usually expired. The featureless visage of Jagannath, it was reasoned, might be in imitation of a damaged human king, and the elaborate care paid to the inanimate substitute a reflection of the attention once given to a flesh-and-blood ruler.

The enigma of Lord Jagannath, and the mysteries surrounding his temporal abode in Puri have continued to grow since the end of British rule in 1947. The release promised by a sight of his features during Rath Yatra, together with the disdain for worldly matters that this justified, found a new audience in the 1960s. The International Society for Krishna Consciousness, known colloquially as the Hare Krishna movement, was founded in 1966 to spread the god's promise and to praise his virtues in the industrialised world, and its votaries still enliven many European and North American cities with their dancing and chanting in celebration of the Lord of the Universe. In the following decade, George Harrison of the Beatles composed a popular song ('My Sweet Lord') that honoured the Krishna aspect of Jagannath, which has resulted in fresh generations of people singing his praises, unconscious of the true object of their devotion.

The contemporary festival of Rath Yatra begins on the second day of the first bright week of the month of *Asadha*, which can fall at any time between mid-June and mid-July, for the Hindu calendar is lunar, divided into twelve months, each comprised of a bright fortnight when the moon is waxing, and two dark weeks when it wanes, and it does not match up with the Gregorian calendar from year to year. The festival lasts nine days, commencing with the outward journey in chariots of Lord Jagannath and his entourage from his temple to a pavilion some 3 kilometres distant, followed by a ritual sojourn lasting a week, and terminating with a return ride to the starting point.

Although Rath Yatra may be viewed as a single event, it is also part of a continuous round of festivals. Since the gods that it parades are deemed to be alive, they require constant attention – it is not simply a matter of taking them down from an altar once a year, dressing them up and then showing them in public. They must be cared for, entertained and worshipped for every hour of every day of the year, and they are the objects of elaborate daily ceremonies that last from dawn until the time when they are put to bed. They are awakened each morning, fanned and 'washed' by placing a mirror in front of them and pouring water over their reflections. They are then fed, dressed and led through a busy whirl of appointments. Lord Jagannath maintains a full social calendar, containing twelve major festivals in addition to Rath Yatra. He has an extensive wardrobe of uniforms to fulfil his various official duties. In the month of *Magha* on the night of the full moon, for instance, Lord Jagannath appears as Gaja Udharana Vesa – the 'appearance He had while killing a crocodile in order to save an elephant' – and during Rath Yatra itself he undergoes several changes of dress.

The cycle of rituals leading up to Rath Yatra commences in May with *Snana Yatra*, a bathing festival during which Jagannath and his brother, Balarama, are dressed as black and white elephants respectively, and washed with pitchers of water carried from a sacred well within the precincts of his temple. Snana Yatra is followed immediately by *Anavasara*, a fifteen-day period during which the deities are said to be ill, and are sequestered and kept on invalids' diets. During Anavasara, the decoration of the Gods is touched up to ready them for their chariot ride. Whenever two months of Asadha occur in a single year, which event happens at intervals of between twelve and nineteen years, Jagannath and his siblings are remade from scratch. A dedicated caste of temple servants are sent into the jungle in search of a Neem tree, which will be used to make new bodies. The proper tree distinguishes itself by twelve signs. These include limitations on the number and shape of branches that it bears, and the presence of a cobra's nest among its roots. Once it has been identified, felled and trimmed, its leaves and branches are respectfully buried. New gods are carved from its trunk under Brahminical supervision, and when they are ready, the divine essence[3] concealed in a hollowed out section of

---

3 A secret substance or item that has never been seen by human eyes. Legend holds that it is the fabled *Nilmadhava* or blue mountain of the Puranas, which may be a giant sapphire.

Lord Jagannath's old body is transferred by a blindfolded priest to the new. The used bodies are then cremated and their ashes buried.

Throughout the month that the deities are being washed and spruced up for their annual outing, pilgrims gather in Puri in readiness for Rath Yatra. In centuries past many arrived via the arduous process of prostration, a form of locomotion resembling that of a caterpillar, in which the pilgrims lay face down on the ground, rose so that their feet stood where their face rested, lay down again and so on, sometimes for journeys of many hundreds of miles. Nowadays, most reach the town by a dedicated train service, the Jagannath Express, which arrives each dawn from Calcutta. Puri is also known as *Shankha Kshetra* – the City of the Conch – and its topography is represented in antique maps as having the form of a conch shell, with its skirt submerged under the sea, and the Jagannath temple at its centre. This mythical shape cannot be discerned by the naked eye, although, according to Hindu philosophy, all that is visible is in fact illusion – *Maya* – and the enchanting, if scruffy, seaside town on view obscures a deeper presence – *Purosottama-Kshetra*, the Abode of the Gods.

Once pilgrims have found their bearings and performed ritual ablutions they make haste to the Jagannath temple at the metaphysical centre of Puri, which is set within a vast and imposing enclosure, resembling a walled city. The temple occupies a particularly auspicious spot, and the mere sight of it, according to Hindu theology, is 'sufficient to procure inestimable blessings. Even to be beaten with sticks by the priests who serve [there] is reckoned of peculiar merit.' Its holy of holies, where Jagannath resides, is a towering *Sikhara* built of ribbed and fluted sandstone which resembles a giant cactus, which once served as a navigation mark for European explorers and traders voyaging over the Bay of Bengal. The walls of the temple enclosure are crenellated, with breaks in the battlements for chutes down which food and other refuse is thrown to the sacred cows, of which Puri contains a vast number, scavenging below.

On the day that Rath Yatra commences, the gods are woken up inside the temple at 5.30 a.m., washed, fed, and dressed for their journey. Their holiday portmanteaux are made ready, containing all the clothing they will need for their sojourn away from home. While these preliminaries are in progress, crowds begin to gather outside the main gate of the temple, and on the Grand Road – the thoroughfare along which Lord Jagannath and his siblings will travel in their vehicles to their destination, the Gundicha pavilion. The Grand Road is built as wide as a motorway in order to accommodate the chariots of the gods and a million pilgrims. Its borders are fringed with the corporate hospitality tents of local businesses, each erected on a raised platform to provide a grandstand view of the action. Behind these, every rooftop is packed with spectators, and the dazzling hues of the women's saris flutter like psychedelic bunting along the parapets. In between the hospitality stands, a smattering of stalls offers food, fruit juices, devotional items and souvenirs to clumps of pilgrims, who coalesce as the Grand Road fills up. Families with excited children jostle against saddhus – itinerant, ascetic holy men with faraway eyes and ashes smeared on their foreheads – against beggars exhibiting their deformities, and against the odd 'sky-clad' Jain, stark naked except for a face mask to prevent the accidental murder of flies.

Crowds are densest around the main gate of the temple, where three giant chariots are waiting in a line, each one as tall as a four-storey building. These consist of ornate, multi-layered platforms, constructed entirely from wood, and crowned with helmet-shaped domes wrapped in cloth of various hues. Each of the principal gods rides alone, and is identified by the colours on their chariot – red and yellow for Lord Jagannath, red and blue for his brother, Balarama, and red and black for Subhadra, their sister. These vehicles, the original juggernauts, are built from scratch every year by a dedicated caste of carpenters to a formula that specifies and names every component. To the eye, they are simultaneously intricate and rustic. While the carvings that decorate their pillared platforms are elegantly executed, their wheels, each taller than a man, are imperfect hand-formed circles. All three chariots are adorned with wooden horses, spirit guardians and a divine charioteer, sculpted from the waist up only and plugged, like a toy, into the platform of the vehicle. Lord Jagannath's driver is called Daruka, his horses (all named, like Santa's reindeer) are Shankha, Balahaka, Shveta and Haridashva, and his vehicle itself is Nandigosh.

The process of manoeuvring the gods from the sanctum sanctorum of the temple to their chariots is prolonged, on account of the bulk of the deities, in particular that of the Lord of the

Universe. Jagannath is about 8 feet tall, 6 feet in diameter and weighs several tons. He requires sixty temple servitors equipped with ropes to transfer him to his juggernaut. His progress through the temple can be followed by observing the movement of the crowds on its rooftops, and there is a tremendous cheer when he appears at its gate. Jagannath sallies forth surrounded by a knot of servants, led by a priest carrying a heart-shaped emblem mounted on a pole. He is advanced to a rhythm called *pahandi*, which is considered to add dignity to his motion. His body rocks and bobs as he proceeds, his head-dress, arranged like a peacock's tail, fans out with each step. He is attended to all the while by servitors waving yak-tail fly whisks. As the living god commences to travel up the ramp of split coconut trunks that leads into his vehicle and his inertia begins to tell, head ropes are attached to assist him into position. Once he is in place beneath the centre of his chariot's dome, various other images and idols, and his luggage, are brought up to join him. The Raja of Puri puts in an appearance in his role as foremost temple servant and sweeps the area around Jagannath with a golden broom. The platform fills with semi-naked priests, various castes of servants, and musicians equipped with cymbals and drums who clash and hammer out a rhythm. More and more people force their way onboard, until the superstructure of the chariot is obscured by writhing flesh. Fully loaded, Nandigosh weighs close to a hundred tons.

From an elevated perspective, the scene on the Grand Road – now flooded from border to border with pilgrims, amongst whom the three chariots standing in line-abreast rise up like rock outcrops from a turbulent ocean – is bewitching. The mind is fascinated by the notion that a path for such large vehicles could be cleared through such a press of people. The starting time for the chariots is fixed for 4 p.m. Shortly before the off, those aboard do their best to provoke the surrounding crowds into a frenzy of adulation. A priest stands on the yoke behind the black wooden horses which are to 'draw' Nandigosh – depicted rearing on their

hind legs and pawing the air – and whirls a whip above their heads, urging these carvings on. Meanwhile, the passengers of the chariot rock back and forth, simulating motion, drums boom, gongs bang and the crowd around yell encouragement, as if they were cheering on the favourite at a racecourse. Many pilgrims are moved to song. An eternal favourite is the 'Jagannathastakam':

> O Lord of the Gods! Take away from me all attachment
> To the bonds of this world which is so impermanent.
> Its useless pleasures are all evanescent!
> O Lord of the Ydava clan!
> Dissolve all my sins through your compassion!
> O Lord and Master of the lowly and the fallen!
> Bestow on me the benediction
> That I may find, beyond this mortal existence, a secure seat
> Close to my true haven, next to your lotus feet!
> O lord Jagannatha, Lord of the Universe!
> O my Master! Grant my eyes a glimpse
> Of your beauteous countenance!

Nandigosh is hauled by a pair of coir ropes, each 250 feet long and about 5 inches in diameter. Rough to the touch, they shed an orange-brown dust that stains the hands of the people who pull on them. The tractive force is made up principally of volunteers, for towing Nandigosh is accounted a form of devotion. In order to start the chariot going, the tow ropes must run in straight, parallel lines, so that the 4,000-odd people attached to them are in its path. When the strain is taken up the ropes stretch, Nandigosh quivers, then shoots forward like a champagne cork. Many pilgrims choose this moment to prostrate themselves before Lord Jagannath. First they break a coconut on the asphalt – the shell smacks down and splits with a crack, spilling milk – and then they lie on their faces in front of the advancing vehicle. Police with rattan canes and megaphones do their best to ensure a clear run – handicapped people are helped aside, and the crowds

pressing forwards for a glimpse of their god are forced apart.
There is, however, no way of controlling the vortex of people in
front of Nadigosh, where those sincere in wishing for a perfect
death have the perfect opportunity.

The actual death tolls for Rath Yatra make disappointing
reading when set against its sanguinary reputation. Although
there seem to have been vintage years – 1796, for instance, when
'no fewer than 28 Hindus were crushed to death' – a glance at
British records from the nineteenth century reveals a surprisingly
slight body count. 'That excess of fanaticism which formerly
prompted the pilgrims to court death by throwing themselves in
crowds under the wheels of the car of Jagannath,' wrote A.
Stirling, the collector of Orissa, in 1818, 'has happily long since
ceased to actuate the worshippers of the present day. During the
four years that I have witnessed the ceremony, three cases only of
this revolting species of immolation have occurred.'

So why hang back when heaven waits? In the words of a
Panchasakha poet,

> Why do you, O mad mind,
> Sit in a shipwrecked boat?

It seems that either the early European visitors to Rath Yatra
exaggerated the carnage, or that there has been a decline in the
level of zeal since their visits. The latter explanation for a present-
day reluctance amongst the pilgrims to seize their chance is
contradicted by a steady increase in their number, suggesting the
'many' suicides reported by Friar Oderic to be wide of the mark.
Besides, the festival is so impressive a spectacle that it seems
positively intended to dissuade its celebrants from ending their
lives while it is in progress. There is an atmosphere of happiness
and expectation in the crowds at Puri, such as might be
encountered amongst visitors to an amusement park, flushed
with adrenaline as a result, or in anticipation of subjecting
themselves to a surfeit of G-forces. Emotions are intense around

the chariots when they are rolling, but the progress of these is erratic. They move to secret gastric rhythms, in spurts and contractions, and the pauses in between allow tensions in the crowd to diminish. Participants never quite reach the pitch of temporary collective insanity – of divine madness – that can only be released through self-sacrifice. There are, however, many lesser offerings that the pilgrims can make. Mutilations which are not life-threatening are common during Rath Yatra and are generally well received by the crowd as demonstrations of intent. Even if few have faith enough to seek Moksha on the spot, anyone making a go of it is appreciated, and the spectators 'applaud them heartily and regard them as the very acme of devotion'. Recent examples of piety include devotees cutting out their tongues to offer up to Jagannath, and ritual throat slashings, said to produce 'spectacular, although non-fatal results'.

Pilgrims may further be tempted to put off oblivion in order to enjoy the traditional freedom of association between the sexes at Indian chariot festivals, when, according to Abbé Dubois, an eighteenth-century observer, 'Decency and modesty are at a discount.' The Frenchman noted, with disapproval, that pilgrims took advantage of the crowds and confusion to enjoy sex with strangers, and that it was a common practice for clandestine lovers, 'who at other times are subject to vexatious suspicion, to choose the day of the procession for their rendezvous in order to gratify their desires without restraint'.

Nandigosh usually takes several hours to cover the course from the temple to Gundicha Mandira, the pavilion inside a walled garden where the gods are to pass the next seven days. However, there have been years when the chariot has proven impossible to drag, no matter how hard the pilgrims strain. Such stoppages, which can last for days, are attributed to divine intervention. An oft-quoted occasion on which Nandigosh refused to stir occurred in the fifteenth century, when Balarama Das, the first of the Panchasakha poets, attempted to climb aboard directly after leaving a brothel. He was ejected at once, for being unclean, whereupon the chariot froze, indicating Lord Jagannath's displeasure. Motion was only possible once the decadent poet had been allowed back on. A similar delay was recorded in 1814: 'The sight here beggars all description,' wrote a British observer. 'Though Juggernaut made some progress on the [opening day of the festival], and has travelled daily ever since, he has not yet reached the place of his destination.' The year in which our correspondent was writing was, incidentally, a good year for demonstrations of faith on the part of the pilgrims: 'one lady devoted herself under the wheels, and a shocking sight it was. Another also intended to devote herself, missed the wheels with her body, and had her arm broken. Three people lost their lives in the crowd.'

Whether Nandigosh has succeeded in conveying Lord Jagannath to his destination or not, the crowds thin towards sunset, and people gravitate towards Puri's beach, where other entertainments associated with the festival are in progress. The devout pause at Swargadwara, a burning ghat located on the waterfront in between hotels, whose name translates as 'the Gate of Heaven'. A steady breath of wind from the sea blows clean salt air through its enclosure, stretching women's saris like flags, shaking the palm trees, while overhead crows set their wings and bank on its gusts. Here, pilgrims may reflect on what might have been, for not only is Puri the perfect place to die, it is also an auspicious spot in which to be burned. Indeed, elderly pilgrims sometimes journey to Puri with the express purpose of ending their days there, 'lulled to their last sleep by the roar of the eternal ocean'. There are firewood vendors amongst the souvenir stalls on the road leading to Swargadwara, equipped with stacks of cut wood and man-sized brass scales, who sell the relatives of anyone lucky enough to die in Puri the precise weight of fuel required to reduce their loved one to ashes. Cremations are carried out in the open air. Each corpse is bound into a shroud and placed on an oblong pyre of wood that takes fire easily and burns fiercely, for as Sebald observed, 'It is not difficult to burn a human body – the king of Castile burned large numbers of Saracens with next to no fuel.' Attendants armed with poles pop the skulls of the departed and push any errant matter back into the pyre. Once it has burned through the debris of bones and ashes is collected and scattered in the sea. This is the fate of the despised flesh of anyone who has achieved Moksha during Rath Yatra.

At sunset, just after the last funeral pyres at Swargadwara have expired, a beach fair commences. Tourists and pilgrims mingle on the sands, new India rubbing shoulders with the old. Under hurricane lamps and strings of fairy lights powered by car batteries, food and souvenir stalls, both sacred and secular, set out their goods. There are camel and pony rides, and even saddhus are not above climbing astride an animal and racing along the sands, feet bouncing in the stirrups, hair flying with the wind of passage, their faces set by years of austerities, of tramping dusty roads from temple to temple, breaking open and grinning like children's at the thrill of speed.

Amongst the numerous explanations advanced for Rath Yatra has been the claim that it functions as a rainmaking festival, and the annual refurbishment of its gods is taken to be symbolic of the regeneration occasioned by the onset of the summer monsoon, with which the festival coincides. Whether through divine intervention or meteorological probability, the cloud banks that develop in the Gulf of Bengal during each day roll in over Puri on the evening breeze and when night arrives rain descends in large warm drops that burst like grapes against the rooftops, terminating the beach fair and sending pilgrims hurrying for shelter. Only the town's resident population of sacred cattle are unperturbed by the nightly downpours, and pick over sugar cane pressings and coconut husks discarded by juice vendors along the Grand Road.

In past years, pilgrims in search of nocturnal entertainment of an improving nature during Rath Yatra could escape the rain by securing the company of a Devadasi, or 'bride' of Lord Jagannath. These were real young women, in the service of the temple, who did not restrict their favours to immortals. At its peak, Puri had over 10,000 women who had dedicated their lives to ministering to the phantom lusts of idols and the physical needs of men of spirit. Upon retirement, they were branded on their breasts and, more importantly, allowed to inherit property – a material advantage in a society which expected widows to share no more than their husbands' funeral pyres. Although the Devadasis have all but vanished, some of their traditions remain alive. Their less suggestive dances are still performed during the festival by amateur groups, composed of the daughters of decent families, although these shows do not encourage the audience participation that was a hallmark of the Devadasis' golden age.

Jagannath and his entourage pass seven days at the Gundicha pavilion, during which they hold open house to the faithful, and are subjected to minor, if intricate, rituals and various changes of clothing. On the third day after their arrival, a minor drama is staged outside Gundicha, which draws the crowds back to the Grand Road. This ceremony, a part of Rath Yatra called *Hera Panchami*, choreographs what is known in police vernacular as a 'domestic incident'. Lakshmi, the wife of Jagannath, who is left to look after his temple while he is absent, is deemed to suffer an attack of jealousy. She is carried, in the form of a small metal icon, to Gundicha where she breaks, via a human proxy, a piece off Nandigosh in a fit of pique, before returning home surrounded by approving women.

When their time is up the gods take to their chariots once again for the ride back to the Jagannath temple. They travel the same route as the outward journey in reverse, attracting the same eager crowds of worshippers, to whom they present a last chance to embrace Moksha before the festival closes. The pace, however, is easier on the return leg. Most pilgrims will have seen the face of their idol already and so enjoy a better control over their piety. The gods stop halfway down the course at Mausi Ma, the temple of their aunt, who presents the Lord of the Universe with a slice of his favourite cheesecake. When Jagannath reaches his own abode, a final piece of theatre is acted out for the benefit of the pilgrims, quite possibly intended to convince any remaining Doubting Thomases that the gods who live in Puri are real. This last ritual, called *Duara Pita*, consists of a ceremonial disagreement between Jagannath and his wife, who refuses to let him enter his temple. He is carried to gate after gate, each of which is slammed in his face, until at last Lakshmi relents, and he is granted permission to come home. The part of the Lord of the Universe is spoken by temple priests, and that of Lakshmi by Devadasis, who improvise on behalf of the goddess, for the entertainment of the pilgrims. The ceremony has an especial resonance with its audience, as it demonstrates that the gods share another quality with the living – the tendency to argue with one another. To be alive is to have and to show emotions, to be petty as well as magnificent.

Many pilgrims stay on in Puri after the conclusion of Rath Yatra, in order to attend other festivals in the packed calendar of Lord Jagannath, and to enjoy the spiritual atmosphere that pervades the town. Those, however, who are forced to desert the lotus feet of the Lord of the Universe for the world of Maya will expect, in addition to the posthumous advantages gained from attending Rath Yatra, immediate and tangible benefits to result from their visits. These are said to include 'sublime visions, strengthened transcendental consciousness . . . improved digestion and the elimination of waste products'. Some pilgrims even declare that they have been charged by the religious power of Puri to such a degree that anyone they touch upon their return to their homes will receive an electric shock. The continuing belief in the efficacy of a Tirtha to Lord Jagannath's abode is summed up by a Hindu proverb: 'What is important is not the object worshipped but rather the depth and sincerity of the worship,' the purity of whose sentiment suggests that pilgrims will continue to attend Rath Yatra, and possibly to mutilate themselves with traditional abandon, until 431496 AD when the firestorms arrive to mark the termination of the Age of Kali and the beginning of the end.

As the monsoon rolls over the east coast of India and pilgrims disperse from Puri to their villages and towns across the Sub-continent, Europe settles into the dry summer months that form its principal season for celebrations. Shortly after Rath Yatra ends, a festival is held in northern Spain, close to the foothills of the Pyrenees, which also offers its participants the opportunity to step into the path of danger. However, whereas pilgrims to Puri confront the chariots of their gods with the settled and presumably joyful expectation of death, the aim of celebrants at the Spanish event is to survive their encounter with danger, and to test their bravery rather than their faith. Indeed, with the exception of the chance of being killed by moving objects, the Spanish and the Indian fixtures could not be more different. In Puri, for example, the sale of alcohol is banned for the duration of Rath Yatra, and pilgrims must rely on bhang *(cannabis, sold legally in government-run shops) for stimulation, whereas drinking to excess is a feature of the Spanish event.*

Perhaps the key to the difference between the two places and their festivals is to be found in their respective treatment of livestock. Cattle are sacred in Puri, and according to the Hindu creed, 'He who kills the cow of a Brahmin will go after death to hell, where he will forever be the prey of serpents, and tormented by hunger and thirst . . . after thousands of years of horrible sufferings he will return to the world to animate the body of a cow and he will remain in this state as many years as the cow has hairs on its body . . . at length he will be born a Pariah, and will be afflicted with leprosy for a period of ten thousand years.' In Spain, in contrast, these creatures are killed with considerable ritual in front of paying audiences, as part of the ceremonies of the festival.

PAUL NEWTON

VII

THE PLEASURES
OF THE CHASE

Danger is a stimulant in common use, enjoyed for the pleasurable adrenaline rush that it induces. A multitude of ways have been perfected for facing danger, that range from wrestling grizzly bears to watching horror movies, all of which have the same goal: to tease the body into releasing its most exciting hormone and so provoke that 'rarissima avis' – a natural high. Happy the hedonist who is easily frightened, for they will be bathed in adrenaline if surprised by a mouse. The brave, however, need to work a little harder to stimulate their adrenal glands. A hundred and fifty thousand or so of this latter class gather on 6 July each year in the city of Pamplona in the north of Spain, in order to excite themselves at its annual festival, which offers its participants the opportunity to live very dangerously indeed. The *Fiesta de San Fermin*, officially a celebration of the life and works of the patron saint of wineskins, is best known for its *Encierro de los Toros*, or running of the bulls. This dawn ritual is performed every day of the week-long event, and offers adrenaline-lovers the chance of being chased through narrow, twisting streets by 600-kilogramme fighting bulls, which have been bred to kill on sight. For those of fainter hearts, who prefer to take their danger by proxy, there are bullfights every evening; and for both the bold and the timid there are fireworks by night, and a non-stop round of drinking, singing and dancing through the streets of an attractive and ancient stone-built city.

The fighting bulls are not the only form of peril on offer at the festival, for its celebrations are relentless, and frightening examples of the dangers of excess are visible from the instant that it opens until the moment when it shudders to a halt. Indeed, San Fermín is best avoided by those who are fastidious in their attire, who disapprove of animals being killed for entertainment, or who are possessed of an over-acute sense of smell. Danger is a great provoker of sweat and urine, as is wine, which is laid on for free in horse troughs during the festival. When copious quantities of these man-made liquids have been spilled on to the streets and evaporate, and their vapours mingle in the hot summer air, a distinctive odour results that is reckoned to be a feature of Pamplona *en fête*. However, for those sound of liver and limb, who are partial to crowds of dancing inebriates, and to risking their lives by running in front of savage beasts, San Fermín offers a foretaste of heaven.

The principal stimulation on offer at the festival – being chased by a wild bull – has a surprisingly broad appeal. Despite the energetic mass extinctions performed by generations past, and the consequent rarity of dangerous animals today, they nonetheless continue to fascinate humanity. For example, people who have never seen one in the flesh are frightened of tigers, or are terrified of sharks even if they have yet to swim in salt water. Indeed, savage and powerful beasts trigger such universal associations that they are used to sell products as diverse (taking tigers for an example) as breakfast cereals, petrol and tiger-striped lingerie. Bulls, likewise, are considered to be evocative, and their generic qualities of bravery, power and fertility have been harnessed to promote aftershave, Spanish brandy and condoms.

The qualities attributed to bulls are borne out in the flesh, and are supplemented by ferocity, for while there are many contenders in the animal kingdom for the title of Most Dangerous, the strain of fighting bull[1] that supplies the animal contingent during the festival of San Fermin has a genuine claim, and it does not need to be cornered, trodden upon or hungry to demonstrate its fatal potential. It is quick, nimble, and uses its hundreds of kilos of sinew to punch holes with its horns through skin, through muscle and through bone. Once a bull has stabbed a horn into a victim, it tosses them through the air, then follows through with another charge. The *morilla*, the hump of muscle in its neck, is strong enough to throw a horse and armoured rider over its back. The double action of stabbing and tossing creates multiple internal injuries as the horn jags around inside the body of whatever creature the bull happens to have impaled. If alone, a bull will attack a man on sight, and will not cease attacking until it has killed or died in the attempt. Its ferocity and the efficacy of its natural armament have been tested against lions, panthers and tigers, in every case with only one result: victory to the bull. In the last match between a bull and a Bengal tiger, held in 1904 in a steel cage in the Plaza de Toros of St Sebastian, the bull dispatched the tiger, smashed the cage, charged the crowd, and was only stopped by a volley of rifle fire from the police.

The danger and excitement involved in taking on one of these creatures was one of the earliest matters that humanity thought fit to record for posterity, probably as a celebration of their hunting skills. In the Pindar cave in Spain there is an 8,000-year-old depiction of a confrontation between a wild bull and two men. The bull has been pierced by a spear, and both the men lie wounded on the ground beside it, one of whom is in a state of sexual arousal, presumably as a result of the encounter. Indeed, evidence of prehistoric bull cults, dedicated to the veneration and the slaughter of wild bulls has been uncovered in places as diverse as

---

1 The taurine participants at San Fermin are from a different strain to the common or garden bull, and one which has not yet been domesticated. Its females have yet to be milked, or its males yoked to a plough.

Crete and Siberia, suggesting that wherever mankind encountered them, their pursuit was accorded a special significance.

When other types of cattle were tamed at the dawn of history, and used to provide milk and labour instead of meat and danger, men continued to seek out the wild variety to enjoy the singular pleasures that it offered face to face. Bull killing was considered a gentleman's sport in Imperial Rome, where it took the form of a ritual contest, a single combat between the bull and a mounted knight, armed with a lance. The Romans introduced the sport to Spain, and it is possible that it was practised in the settlement they established in 73 BC at Pamplona, named in honour of the great general Pompey. Pamplona flourished for three centuries under Roman rule, and suffered for seven more under their successors, the Visigoths and the Moors. Its strategic location on the Ebro river, and its proximity to the pass of Roncesvalles leading into France, resulted in the sack of the city on several occasions, and its total destruction in 924 at the hands of the Moorish Prince Abd al-Rahman III. The habit of taking on wild bulls seems to have been lost throughout the Visigoth and Moorish periods.

After the Christian reconquest of northern Spain, Pamplona was repopulated, and the sport of killing bulls was revived. Spanish records from the twelfth century attest to its practice as a trial, in the style of the Romans, of a knight's courage. The revival was not limited to Spain's equestrian orders – Italian nobles also resumed the challenge of facing a bull in single combat. The bulls even made a comeback in the Colosseum of Rome itself. In 1332, a bull-killing contest was staged in the hub of empire of the ancients in accordance with the rules of chivalry: young gallants wishing to demonstrate their valour and to obtain the favours of young women of equal birth made their appearance on the sands of the famous amphitheatre, each adorned with an emblem or motto that declared their amorous intentions, or frustrations, and their indifference to danger. 'If I am drowned in blood, what a pleasant death!' read one such, which proved prophetic, for 'The combats of the amphitheatre were dangerous and bloody. Every champion successively encountered a wild bull; and the victory may be ascribed to the quadrupeds, since no more than eleven were left on the field, with the loss of nine wounded and eighteen killed on the side of their adversaries.'

The inherent risks of bullfighting ensured its continuing popularity as a chivalric pastime, and it also developed as a sport for peasants, especially during festivals. In 1385 it was recorded for the first time in Pamplona, and subsequent references provide a picture of the popular style of spectacle that was evolving: a square was barricaded off, and bulls with flaming torches attached to their horns were used in gymnastic displays, then slaughtered with spears. References to bull-killing by both paupers and princes appear with increasing frequency over the next century and a half, by which time these spectacles had become sufficiently widespread to come to the attention of the Vatican. In 1567, Pope Pius V issued an edict which threatened excommunication to any prince who permitted bullfighting in his country and which denied a Christian burial to anyone killed by a bull. The intention of this Papal Bull was not so much to suppress cruelty to animals, but rather to prevent the death of so many Catholics.

The Pope's command was not respected in Spain, for shortly afterwards King Philip II (1556–98) founded the Real Maestranza de Caballeria in the hill town of Ronda for the purpose of providing martial training to his knights, which included killing bulls. In the rest of Catholic Europe, however, taurine entertainments were extinguished. Belated Spanish support for Pope Pius arrived nearly two centuries later in the form of King Philip V, who considered that bullfighting made his country appear uncivilised and archaic. Religious and regal disapproval, however, were not enough to suffocate the sport. While the king could dissuade gentlemen from fighting bulls, the commoners were harder to restrain, and the animals continued to be hacked to death by crowds of excited peasants at provincial fiestas.

After the withdrawal of mounted nobles from the sport, a

revolution occurred in the manner in which bulls were killed. In 1724, Francisco Romero, the first great *matador* to fight bulls on foot, established a method by which he could kill them without the need for a horse or spear. The spectacle of a single man armed with a sword and a cape taking on the ancients' symbol of virility, and using his skill and bravery to overcome a creature many times superior in strength, proved wildly popular, and resulted in the birth of the modern *corrida*, or bullfight. Pedro Romero, son of Francisco, refined the ceremony his father had invented and killed 5,600 bulls over a career lasting thirty years. The demand for bulls for such spectacles grew to the extent that they had to be farmed in order to ensure a reliable supply. By the nineteenth century dedicated Plazas de Toros, or bullrings, had been built all over Spain, including in Pamplona, to accommodate the new style of bullfighting, and legislation had been introduced to regulate the spectacle.[2]

In the days before motorised transport bulls were herded long distances from the ranches on which they had been reared to the places where they were to be fought. In several towns, a custom arose of running alongside or behind the bulls as they were driven up to their corrals. The Pamplonan innovation of running in front of them, a very much more risky exercise, seems to have occurred at about the time of the construction of its first bullring in 1843. This exercise quickly became a popular feature of the town's annual festival, and by the time that Ernest Hemingway brought it to the attention of the world in his novel *Fiesta* (1927), the taurine entertainments on offer in Pamplona had become the pre-eminent attraction of the festival of San Fermín, even taking precedence over the ceremonial procession of an effigy of the eponymous saint. Despite thirteen recorded deaths in the intervening years, and more than 200 non-fatal gorings, the *encierro*, as the event is

2 Interestingly, at the same time that Spain was legislating in favour of bullfighting, the courts of Great Britain were busy suppressing it. Until the first quarter of the nineteenth century, many British towns had bullrings where bulls were baited before being slaughtered for food; many also held bull-runs, during which crowds of apprentices chased the animals through the streets.

known has gone from strength to strength. It is perhaps the most dangerous in existence to be organised by a municipal authority. Indeed, the entire festival has an air of peril to it, an edginess which is heightened by the prodigious amounts of alcohol consumed and the frequent and sudden use of fireworks.

The Fiesta de San Fermin begins each year at 12 noon on 6 July with a short ceremony in the Plaza de Ayuntamiento, Pamplona's central square. Participants in the festival, known as *Pamplonicas* or *Sanfermines*, begin to gather in the square an hour or so before the start, and by the time the festival is due to commence, they are packed together shoulder to shoulder to form a solid body of people. The Sanfermines, both male and female, all wear the same costume, consisting of white clothing, a red sash and a red neckerchief. This uncomplicated dress code licenses its wearers for hedonism, providing them with both a communal identity, and an individual passport to pleasure. By the simple expedient of tying two pieces of scarlet cloth around their bodies they declare themselves ready to party. It is unusual to find such egalitarianism in festival dress, which generally is employed to make its wearers stand out, rather than reduce them to being members of the ranks of a uniform army. It is, nonetheless, an effective way of making everyone equal for the duration of the festival, converting lawyers and labourers alike into a distinct class of celebrants.

The Sanfermines await the *chupinazo*, a single rocket fired to declare the fiesta open, with surprising decorum. Although many will have taken their breakfast from a bottle, etiquette demands that they curb their excitement until the starting rocket. At midday precisely its trail curls up into the sunshine, against which its flash is just visible, and when its bang reaches the square below an instant later it is answered with cheers, and a volley of champagne corks from the waiting crowd. The wine is discharged over everyone within range, and these return fire with raw eggs and bags of flour. Within a few minutes most people in the square are covered with a mixture resembling uncooked batter. No one rushes home to change, as the initial barrage is only a foretaste of the relentless bombardment on its way. Pamplona has been described as 'an ordeal by noise and wine', and it is inevitable that the Sanfermines will receive more drink and food on their white clothing during the course of the festival. Indeed, the depth of an individual's commitment to the event can be gauged by the stains they have accumulated, and those with too few are helped on with wine, mercurochrome and pig's blood by sympathetic strangers.

The festival revolves around two daily events – the morning encierro, at which its participants have the opportunity to face its most famous hazard, and the afternoon corrida, where they may watch matadors take far greater risks and so enjoy their danger secondhand. The hours in between are whiled away with what is best described as a general round of excess, which may be viewed in the light of a handicapping system that renders some Sanfermines, whether through inebriation or exhaustion, entirely unfit for participation in the next encierro, while persuading others that being chased by bulls for fun for free is a pleasurable and worthwhile exercise.

Inspiration in liquid form is vital to the festival and in order to facilitate drinking on the move, many Sanfermines equip themselves with *botas*, leather wineskins fitted with a nozzle and a carrying strap, ranging in size and materials from the scrotum of a bull to the entire hide of a goat. Examples of the latter are often constructed so that their shapes retain those of their original owners, with the vestiges of a leg on each corner. Botas are utilised by holding them at arm's length then squeezing them gently so that they jet out a fine stream of wine which is caught in the mouth. They are a remarkably clean delivery system, so long as both the hand that squeezes and the head that receives are steady. Once the festival is more than a few hours old, however, the unmarked portion of celebrants' clothing is usually criss-crossed with slashes of red from missed mouthfuls.

The music for the continuous round of dancing that characterises the event is provided by the brass *charanga* bands of the *penas*, which are social clubs dedicated to entertaining their members and the masses during San Fermín. In addition to a band, each pena has a clubhouse in the centre of Pamplona, whose bars are kept open every hour of every day through the course of the festival, and which are open to all comers. The penas take the business of maintaining the momentum of the festival very seriously, often providing relays of bandsmen to take over the instruments when one group has played itself to exhaustion. These altruistic individuals also act as vigilantes, waking anyone trying to snatch some sleep with a trumpet blast to the ear. The charanga bands wander through the streets of Pamplona like nomads, each followed by a flock of dancers. From time to time the bands will halt, then their attendant crowd will sink into a crouch in time to the music, and spring back to their feet with a cheer. This manoeuvre is repeated for hours at a stretch, and has the effect of thoroughly confusing its participants, so that they lose track of both time and place.

The peculiar state of mind generated by the relentless celebrations during San Fermín, and the resulting sense of disorientation were captured by Hemingway in *Fiesta: The Sun Also Rises*:

> the fiesta had really started. It kept up day and night for seven days. The dancing kept up, the drinking kept up, the noise went on. The things that happened could only have happened during a fiesta. Everything became quite unreal finally and it seemed as though nothing could have any consequences. It seemed out of place to think of consequences during the fiesta. All during the fiesta you had the feeling, even when it was quiet, that you had to shout any remark to make it heard. It was the same feeling about any action. It was a fiesta and it went on for seven days.

The first encierro of the festival takes place on the morning of 7 July. Preparations commence around 6 a.m. The streets along which the bulls will run are cleared and sprayed and heavy wooden barricades are erected to close off the route and so prevent the bulls

rampaging through town. Six bulls are run in each encierro. These
are kept in a corral overnight where they may be admired by any
Sanfermines wishing to scare themselves before the event
commences. The appearance of the *toros bravos* is striking, even
when viewed strolling round a pen, for they are very much more
muscular and alert than domesticated cattle. The morilla, the
tossing muscle between their shoulder-blades is particularly
eyecatching, as are their horns, which in contrast to the decorative
appendages carried by tame breeds are fighting weapons, as
evidently deadly as the teeth in the jaws of a shark. The majority of
the bulls have black hides, against which their red eyes stand out
like glowing coals, and their white horns like polished ivory.

The bulls are kept calm in their pen, and will be accompanied
throughout the run, by an equal number of steers. The steers are
larger and clumsier that the bulls, with dappled hides and large,
nervous eyes. They are a vital control system, for when fighting
bulls run in company they are in thrall to their herding instinct,
and hence are relatively manageable. However, should one
become separated from the group, it turns psychopath in an
instant and will attack any living thing that it sees.

The route travelled by the bulls from their corral to the Plaza de
Toros is 900 metres long, partially uphill, and twists through
cobbled streets. Its starting line is beside the corrals, and its finish
is in the bullring. The course is divided into discrete sections, each
with its own name, like the bends and straights of a Grand Prix
track, and each is graded according to the likelihood of being
gored. The first section, *Santo Domingo*, which runs uphill from
the corral along a street of the same name, is accounted very
dangerous. The bulls are full of energy after twenty-four hours of
confinement, and the street is lined with houses leaving few
opportunities to escape. The route then enters a square, from
which it exits via a narrow street named *Mercaderes*. This section
is considered one of the safest, as the street has barricades along
one side over which the panicking may clamber. The route next
takes a sharp right-handed turn into *Calle Estafeta*, and this is the

most perilous part of the encierro. The bulls skid around the corner and sweep along the left-hand side of the course. Although they have slowed, they are still travelling fast enough to cover 100 metres in less than six seconds, so they cannot be outrun, and there is nowhere to hide. Sometimes they lose their footing on the corner which increases the risk of a bull becoming detached from the herd. Pamplonans advise that visitors who do not know their *izquierda* from *derecha* should not attempt this section. Estafeta leads into a short stretch named *Telefonica*, where the principal risks come from collision with other spectators, or the late arrival of a bull that has broken free from the pack. Telefonica terminates in a narrow underpass leading into the bullring, and when the bulls are through the tunnel, have crossed the ring, and are safely penned, a rocket is fired to announce the end of the spectacle. The entire encierro is usually over in three minutes, but appears to last for far longer. It is one of those events like the launch of a spacecraft where time is measured out in seconds and the passage of each is marked by some momentous event.

Crowds gather by the corrals at the start of the route well before the bulls are due to be released. Many carry rolled-up copies of that morning's newspaper which they wave in the air while singing a devotional song to a little statue of St Fermin in a niche beside the start:

> *We ask San Fermín,*
> *As our Patron,*
> *To guide us in the Bull Run,*
> *And to give us his Benediction.*

The statue is draped with the ubiquitous scarlet neckerchief, and is attributed with miraculous powers, including the ability to turn aside a bull that appears certain to gore one of the saint's admirers.

About five minutes before the encierro commences, police move the crowd of several thousand forward along the route, and remove those who are too drunk to walk. In the past, those Sanfermines who clearly were unfit to run were clubbed on the head and thrown off the course to prevent them suffering greater injuries. The atmosphere is jovial, people slap each other on the back and spray wine from their botas into their own and others' mouths. There is also a tension that underlies the bravado – the smell of sweat can be discerned amidst the fumes of alcohol and urine that rise from the freshly swept and watered streets. At 8 a.m. a rocket goes up – the bulls are loose – but instead of pandemonium, time stands still – nothing happens – then there is a murmur, a clatter of hooves, people struck with last-minute doubts slip out through the barricades, although any that show signs of panic are jeered by the crowd on the balconies overhead. All of a sudden, every runner sets off at once, bumping into those in front. It is at this point that fear starts to take hold. The crowd bunches up, people collide and trip, the fallen grab at legs to try and haul themselves up, the shrieks of spectators further back down the run get closer, the urge to sprint is overwhelming, but impossible to realise, and the run takes on all the aspects of a bad dream, when the dreamer is powerless to escape an imminent danger, his legs and arms flailing as he tries to swim through a sea of white and red clad bodies.

JIM HOLLANDER

PAUL NEWTON

The greatest danger of the encierro is a *toro suelto*, a bull that has broken away from the herd and run berserk. Most of the fatalities recorded at the festival have been caused by toros sueltos. Amazingly, aficionados of the encierro, those locals who run every year, pray for the chance to take on a lone bull with nothing more than their copy of that morning's newspaper. They hang back in doorways as the crowd sweeps past, ready to leap out and accost the bulls. Their aim is to provoke and evade a charge, and the successful completion of this manoeuvre is said to result in the release of a positive torrent of adrenaline.

The encierro terminates inside Pamplona's bullring, which is filled to the brim with spectators who enjoy a dramatic view of the arrival of first people then animals, which mixes comic instants with occasional tragedies. Shortly after the rocket has gone up to announce that the bulls are free, runners begin to emerge from the entry tunnel. Some of these early arrivals are crazed with fear, even though the watching crowd know that they could not have seen a bull. They are regaled with sarcastic applause as they claw their way to safety over the barriers around the edge of the ring. The true progress of the encierro is indicated by a chorus of cheers and screams approaching the bullring along the streets outside. All of a sudden, the mouth of its tunnel starts to vomit clumps of people on to its sands, tangles of red and white figures who disengage and either dash for its perimeter, or stand their ground, hoping to wring out a last dribble of adrenaline when the bulls arrive. The climax of the event is usually over in a flash – the bulls and their steer chaperones burst into the sunlit ring, whirl around its perimeter like the eddies of dried leaves that the wind makes in autumn, then are sucked out the far door into their pens, leaving the odd body in their wake. When they are gone the breathless runners stretch up their arms and spin round on their heels, entranced by the view from the middle of the ring – a vast, white host of spectators, laughing, chanting and dancing, splashed with the scarlet of their scarves and sashes.

The encierro is followed by other taurine entertainments in the bullring. Shortly after the bulls have been penned, *becerros*, immature bulls with padded leather balls sewn on to the tips of their horns are released on to its sands. The Sanfermines form human pyramids in front of the gate through which the becerros appear, and account themselves fortunate if selected for the first charge. These less dangerous encounters may be viewed in the light of a warm-down for the brave, for facing peril is a wonderful exercise in perspective, and the becerros seem absurdly dainty after the toros bravos that preceded them. They provide the opportunity for amateur bullfighters to practise their cape-work, and to experience first-hand the sensation of being thrown through the air. The becerros are recaptured after breaking a few bones, the bullring empties and the Sanfermines hasten away to resume their traditional rhythm of drinking and dancing.

*

The corrida, the second daily ritual that punctuates the festival commences every evening at 6.30 p.m. Whereas the encierro is a practical test of the nerves of the Sanfermines, the bullfight itself is rather an examination of their ability to witness danger and bloodshed. The bullfight is first and foremost a spectacle of death. Every bull that comes flashing into the ring will leave it as a corpse.[3] If it surrenders its life with valour, fighting until the sword of the matador touches its heart, it will receive a posthumous ovation. If it hesitates, however, its body will be jeered as it is dragged away by mules. The corrida is a trial of human courage, as much as an opportunity to admire the same quality in another creature. The matadors who have been engaged to kill the bulls are expected to stand their ground in front of the same animals that their audience have run away from that morning. They too will be criticised or applauded, according to the way they conduct themselves in the ring.

Corridas involve the death of six bulls, which are killed by three matadors in turn, in descending order of seniority. Thus the longest qualified matador will slay the first bull, his immediate junior the second, and the least qualified the third. The process is then repeated in the same order. If a matador is killed by a bull or gored so that he is unable to continue, the most senior matador must kill his bulls for him. If two matadors retire injured the remaining one must kill all the bulls, or he will be sent to prison for a week. Each matador is assisted by a group of assistants known as *peones*, two mounted and two or three on foot, who serve to assist him in preparing the bull for the climax of each fight, when he will face it alone on the yellow sands.

The form of an individual bullfight has been described by Kenneth Tynan, the eminent English theatre critic, as a tragedy in three acts, each of which is intended to manipulate the emotions of the spectators in different ways, and to enable these to build

---

3 *Pace* very rare exceptions, when an extraordinarily courageous bull is granted its life at the end of a fight.

towards a peak that coincides with the death of the bull. Briefly, and in general terms, these three acts, known as *tercios*, are as follows:

First Tercio

This part of the fight is intended to display the strength and aggression of the bull, and to test its courage. It commences with a brief pageant, in which the matadors and their peones march across the arena in the style of Roman gladiators to salute the governing officials of the corrida. Each matador is dressed in a ceremonial costume known as a *traje de luz*, or 'suit of lights'. These are extremely tight-fitting, particularly around the crotch, are embroidered in gold, silver and brightly coloured thread, and glitter in the sunshine. After the procession, the ring is cleared, and the first bull enters to the sound of trumpets. The matador advances to meet it, carrying a large lilac and mustard coloured cape, whereupon the bull charges. They perform a series of passes together, in which the bull demonstrates its savagery and the matador his grace. Meanwhile, two *picadors*, mounted peones armed with lances, enter the arena and take up their stations at opposite points on its perimeter. The matador lures the bull towards one or other of them, and when it is in position, feet on or over a concentric circle painted on the sand of the arena, he retires. The picadors wear steel-leaf armour on the side that they present to the bull, and their horses are protected with padding that resembles mattresses. The horses are also blindfolded and their ears have been stuffed with straw so that they cannot see or hear the bull.[4] The picador clangs his armoured leg against his iron stirrup and levels his lance at the bull. If it is brave it will charge without hesitation. It dashes in and hits the horse with a *whump!*, like a boxer punching a heavy bag. At the same instant, the picador thrusts his lance into its hump. The lance is fitted with

---

4 Until the 1930s, when effective armour was developed, most horses used in corridas were killed by the bull on the first or second charge. Nowadays, veteran mounts are employed that are seldom injured.

a crossbar, to stop its point penetrating more than two inches. The purpose of this action is to weaken the tossing muscle, so that the bull will carry its head lower, and thus enable the matador to reach over its horns when the time comes to kill. It is at this point that first-time visitors to the corrida, and any others who may have forgotten, are reminded that the purpose of the spectacle is to slay an animal. It is rare to see creatures being injured deliberately, and the blood welling up from the hole stabbed into the bull by the picador's lance has a sobering effect upon any who have been intoxicated by the initial charges and swirling capes. The first tercio is the least popular part of the fight, often provoking spectators into a fury on behalf of the wounded bull.

Second Tercio
This act is a decorative interlude, which aims to relieve some of the emotion provoked in the previous tercio. It is a graceful spectacle involving the placement of pairs of *banderillas*, wooden sticks wrapped in ribbons with steel harpoon points, in the hump of the bull. Its notional purpose is to correct any tendency the bull may have to favour its left or right horn. The matador, or one of his peones, approaches the bull with a banderilla in each hand, provokes a charge, then runs in a semi-circle past the bull and stabs the banderillas into its hump while evading its horns. The second tercio is the only overtly gymnastic part of a bullfight, and should be the only time that both man and bull are running. Matadors, in general, eschew running – it is not considered to be a useful skill for taking on a fighting bull. Similarly, many do not follow an exercise regime in between corridas. El Gallo, a famous matador of the 1920s, when asked what he did for exercise, replied that he smoked Havana cigars. 'What do I want with exercise, Hombre?' he continued, 'What do I want with strength? The bull takes plenty of exercise, the bull has plenty of strength!' Between two and four pairs of banderillas are placed in the bull within a space of five minutes. Each pair presents the crowd with a minor and independent drama, that brings man and bull

together for an instant of danger. If the man succeeds, the memory of his co-ordination and agility remains frozen in the minds of the spectators. If, however, he is caught by the bull, he is tumbled over in an instant to screams of fear from the crowd. It is a matter of professional pride not to show pain when gored. El Litri, one of the stars of the ring of the 1950s, summed up the necessary stoicism simply and evocatively: 'when I feel the horn go in, I just switch off, like an electric light'.

JIM HOLLANDER

Third Tercio

The final part of the corrida is the soul of the spectacle, with only the bull and the matador in the ring, the one to die, the other to kill. The

JIM HOLLANDER

matador changes his cape for a smaller, scarlet *muleta* and a sword.
He makes a formal dedication of the life of the bull to a member of
the crowd, or to the entire crowd, and walks out to meet it alone on
the sand. His aim is to lead the bull through a series of passes under
the muleta, during which he will demonstrate his bravery and
elegance, and then to kill with a single thrust of his sword. Matadors
are judged by three qualities – their ability to *parar*, *templar* and
mandar. The first quality measures the capacity of the matador to
stand his ground in the face of a charging bull, the second his co-
ordination and timing in front of the bull, and the third his ability
to dominate his adversary. In addition to, and over and above these
three, the matador must be brave: 'Without valour, bullfighting is
like the sky without the sun: it is still the sky, but without radiance
and beauty. The [aspiring matador] must demonstrate three things:

valour, valour, and valour. Art can be learned, but valour is innate, like seductiveness in the eyes of beautiful women.'

The series of passes the matador performs in the last tercio is known as a *faena*. The length of an individual faena is up to the matador, although all are limited to a maximum of fifteen minutes. If the matador perceives that the bull is strong and brave, he will perform as many interlinked passes as possible, aiming to draw the bull ever closer to his body, until the blood running down its flanks is smeared over and dulls the brilliance of his suit of lights. It is like watching an act of hypnosis, during which the man controls every movement of the animal with a piece of coloured cloth. If, however, the bull charges awkwardly and hunts the matador instead of his cape, the latter will call for his killing sword and aim to end the fight.

When the matador prepares to kill the crowd falls utterly silent. He stands side on, two or three yards away from the bull, furls his muleta in his left hand, and extends it towards his adversary, its bottom edge close to the ground. He needs to be sure the attention of the bull is attracted by the cape and not fixed on him. He points his left toe towards the bull, slides his right foot backwards, raises the sword to shoulder height so that its hilt is a few inches in front of his eyes and sights along the blade. His body arches, as if he was drawing a bow, the sword an arrow ready for flight: he pushes his cape along the ground towards the bull, then launches himself through the air. The bull follows the cape and the sword vanishes up to the hilt between its shoulders. For an instant, man and animal are joined, then the momentum of the matador carries him out over the horns while the bull jolts and throws its head. If the sword has been placed correctly, the bull is dead on its feet. The matador raises his right hand, walks pace by pace back to the bull, then stands motionless, his hand still aloft as if in farewell. The bull spasms. A few gouts of dark blood emerge from its mouth and nostrils. It thrusts its horns at the matador, tries to take a step forwards, then its legs give way. It sinks to its knees and its head slumps forward on to the sand. The audience erupts in cheers and a host of white handkerchiefs flutter around the bullring. This at least is how a good bullfight should end: 'The bull, as he should be, is dead. The man, as he should be, is alive and with a tendency to smile.'

The ending is not always so pretty: many more bulls are artlessly butchered than are killed with the grace that entitles bullfighting to be called a form of art, and matadors are not always permitted the luxury of smiling in the ring, for if they kill a bull in a cowardly or inept manner they are booed out of it. Sometimes they suffer more than shame, for all are gored several times during their careers, and a few are killed in the sands of the arena. Indeed, the knowledge that matadors *do* die in the ring adds an edge to the spectacle, of which the matadors themselves are only too keenly aware. Manuel Vare Garcia, who fought under the name of Varelito and who was fatally gored at a corrida in 1922, accused his audience of bloodlust as he was being carried out to die: 'This is what you wanted. This is what you wanted, and I've got it. Now you can be happy.'

Sanfermines carry their festival with them into the bullring for the corridas. The bands of the penas take up strategic positions around the arena and attempt to outplay each other in between the tercios, and in between bulls. If a fight is going badly, the attention of the spectators turns from the action in the centre of the ring to each other. Mexican waves convulse the crowd, jets of wine from botas sparkle in the sunlight as they are fired between the tiers of seating. Although 2,000 years separate the contemporary audience from that of a Roman games, the pageant itself is little changed – an amphitheatre, wine in skins, the music of pipes and drums, and for entertainment the spectacle of death.

Taurine contests are not the only diversions available to Sanfermines during the course of the festival. An effigy of San Fermin himself is exhibited, with some ceremony, on the first day of his festival. There are also minor daily parades of the *cabezudos*, people wearing giant papier mâché masks who thrash bystanders, especially children, with inflated pigs' bladders on sticks, and of the *Comparsa de Gigantes* (Company of Giants). The Gigantes consist of four pairs of kings and queens, each 4 metres tall, constructed from cloth stretched over wooden frames which are carried on the shoulders of hidden bearers. They were introduced to the festival as a novelty in the seventeenth century, and have since become a tradition. Indeed, Pamplona has a history of embracing novelties: the chronicles of the seventeenth and eighteenth centuries record – in addition to the clergy's concern over the abuse of drink and the permissiveness of young men and women – the presence of people from other lands who, with their shows, 'made the city more amusing'. A contemporary example of foreigners enlivening proceedings, and coincidentally establishing a new tradition, is provided by statue-diving Australians, who gather during the festival in the Plaza Navarreria to hurl themselves from the top of its stone image of St Cecilia into the arms of the crowd waiting 15 feet below. There are a number of spilled catches and serious injuries each year.

The end of the fiesta takes the form of a midnight vigil by the Church of San Lorenzo, which houses the headless body of San Fermin, the patron of the festival. Sanfermines gather, each with a candle, singing softly and sadly –

> *Pobre de mi,*
> *que se han acabado*
> *Las Fiestas de San Fermin*
> *('Poor me, for the Fiesta of San Fermin has ended')*

At midnight on 14 July, the candles are extinguished and the crowd disperses. Many leave their red neckerchiefs tied to the railings of the church as tokens of thanks to St Fermin for the pleasure his festival has provided. A few diehards, however, unwilling to give up the adrenaline habit, gather the next morning at dawn in front of the corral for the 'running of the bus' in which they re-enact the encierro in front of the number 8 bus whose route approximates that taken by the bulls.

Entertainments that feature animals are common spectacles at festivals, and need not end with the death of the entertainers in order to provide amusement. Events such as agricultural fairs, rodeos and horseraces offer their audience pleasure without bloodshed, by matching animals against their own kind in contests of beauty, strength or speed. In some such spectacles, the animals provide not merely a diversion in themselves, but also serve as excuses for the exercise of other passions. Horseracing, for instance, praised by the Roman emperor Nero as the 'sport of kings . . . practised by ancient leaders, honoured by poets, and sacred to the gods', is usually associated with the pleasures of gambling, and enables its spectators to enjoy, in addition to the races themselves, the prospect of increasing their wealth without effort by placing a successful bet. Indeed, the key purpose of most spectacles involving animals is to provoke their human spectators into a state of excitement, whether by appealing to their sense of aesthetics, or to their primal lust for contest.

A month or so after the Fiesta de San Fermín, an Italian town of similar size to Pamplona celebrates with equal fervour a festival that also features animals. At this latter event, instead of using the creatures in a test of bravery, they are employed to arouse intense states of emotion, and to offer the spectators a licence to behave in an excitable manner. The result is possibly the most intense and corrupt sporting event in the world, which is simultaneously a showcase for medieval pageantry and Italian brio.

CAMERA PRESS

VIII

RIVALS

*The Palio is like a vision of a poem by Ariosto made real! . . .
It is like waking up from a dream of having lived a day in
another era.*

MARGHERITA DI SAVOY, QUEEN OF ITALY, 1860

What better way to solicit the protection of the mother of God than by holding a horse race in her honour? The inhabitants of the Italian city of Siena worship in this way each year during a festival known as the *Palio*, which climaxes in an eponymous horserace around the main square of the city. The contest is a mad gallop that is distinguished by its violence and its brevity. It lasts on average for only ninety seconds – it is quicker than sex – but in this short period it manages to release all the pent-up emotions of the people of Siena. The race and its surrounding festivities act as a kind of pressure valve for the city, which is divided into seventeen districts, called *contrade*, in whose colours each Palio is contested, and who maintain a bitter rivalry with one another. The contrade are no mere municipal divisions, but rather the territories of different tribes, each with its own totems, such as dragons and she-wolves, after which they are named and by which they are distinguished. The Palio gives these tribes the annual opportunity to celebrate their own identities, and their differences with each another, and also serves as a continuing record of their allegiances and enmities, which reach back to the foundation of Siena.

Unlike most horseraces, the Palio is organised not to decide the respective merits of various runners and their jockeys, but rather to allow the contrade to perpetuate long-established feuds. In gambling terms, it is a lottery, for a contrada cannot choose the horse that will wear its colours, but instead must accept that allotted to it by the luck of the draw. Nor is the Palio about the joys of participation, for only the winner is honoured and all the other runners are treated with scorn and derision. In both atmosphere and purpose it is closer to the chariot races of Imperial Rome than the Derby. It is an example of an ancient solution to the pressures of co-existence – let fortune ride on a horse, let people attach their antagonism for one another to it, and as far as is possible, leave the result in the hands of fate.

The Sienese see the arbitrary nature of the Palio as a challenge. Rather than accepting the luck of the draw, the contrade will stop at nothing to hinder their rivals, or advance their own fortunes, including poisoning horses and bribing jockeys. Furthermore, the jockeys bribe one another, even auctioning their favours on the starters' line. There is nothing remotely sporting about the contest – indeed, any attempt at sportsmanship would be ridiculed. Andrea de Cortes, one of the most successful riders of recent times, explained the philosophy of the festival as follows: 'The Palio has two components: the first is fate . . . which you're powerless against, and the second comes from trickery and skill, which counterbalance fate.' Examples of the 'trickery and skill' that Cortes himself employed over more than twenty years as a

Palio rider included bribing a starting official and co-operating in the kidnapping of a rival jockey.

The history of the present event can be traced to 1238, when it was mentioned in a legal document which noted that a jockey was fined because 'running in the Palio and having arrived last, he did not take the pig, the derisory prize assigned by regulation to the most losing of all losers'. At this time, Siena was not so much a city but three interlinked hilltop villages. The villages were already divided into contrade, which seem to have been the basic civic unit. When these combined to form a republic in 1262, after beating off an attack from neighbouring Florence, the Palio was sufficiently well established to be included within their constitution. The context in which it appears in this document is as a defence to murder: any rider in the Palio who caused the death of another would be deemed not guilty of homicide, for in the fury of the race the participants could not be expected to be thinking of anything but victory, and therefore any death had to be accidental. Such early records of the event attest that violent competition was present in its infancy, and that it was from the start a contest where winner takes all.

The early Palio was run in a straight line, from a gate in the walls of Siena to the steps of its newly built cathedral. Its nominal purpose was to honour the Madonna of the Assumption, whose image resided within the cathedral, and the race was an addition to a pre-existing festival in which the Virgin was presented with candles on her feast day. The victor was awarded a banner, or Palio. The word derives from the Latin *pallium*, a cloak; so that the prize has given its name to the race and the festival. Horses were entered and sometimes ridden by noblemen, and were also sponsored by the contrade, which seem to have been born in factionalism. In addition to providing runners for this linear Palio, the contrade kept their rivalry fresh with a number of other races involving pigs, oxen, dwarves and virgins. They further maintained their animosity with spectacles such as *La Pugna*, a bare-knuckle boxing match with hundreds of participants, and the *Elmora*, an event in which they gathered to throw stones at one another.

With the onset of the Renaissance these tribal encounters became a little less violent and very much more aesthetic. The contrade developed giant, allegorical floats – decorated battle-wagons – which they would parade and use as stations from which to fight each other and to kill animals, in a manner reminiscent of the *venationes* of Imperial Rome. It is from these devices that the contrade derived their current names and totems, which are the Dragon, the Snail, the Owl, the Giraffe, the She-wolf, the Goose, the Forest, the Eagle, the Caterpillar, the Porcupine, the Wave, the Ram, the Tower, the Unicorn, the Shell and the Tortoise. While many of these are not suggestive of martial valour to the modern ear, their symbolism was understood by their audiences, so that the goose represented the geese who cackled and raised the Roman legions to the defence of their citadel, thus symbolising watchfulness, and so on.

By the sixteenth century, all the component parts of the Palio were in place: an annual horserace where even murder was permissible in order to win, a tradition of ceremonial fighting between contrade, and civic displays of pageantry and piety. These were united into a single festival after Florence subjugated Siena in 1559, and its republic was brought to an end. Siena became introverted and its inhabitants sought a way in which their identity could be preserved in servitude. In the opening decades of the seventeenth century, an official proposal was made to run a Palio in the Piazza del Campo, a medieval quadrangle in the heart of Siena, with the aim of creating a spectacle that the whole city could watch together. The first documented race in the Campo took place in 1632, and was recorded for posterity in an engraving, which shows bareback jockeys hacking away at one another with whips resembling cat-o'-nine-tails, while members of the contrade fight one another in the background. By 1656 it had become an annual event and had acquired a patroness, the Madonna of Provenzano. This image of the Virgin Mary was selected in preference to the official virgin of the city as a symbol of defiance, for Florence had in its turn been subjugated by Spain, which billeted its troops in Siena, and a number of anti-Spanish miracles had been attributed to La Provenzano.

The circular Palio was a great success, allowing the Sienese an occasion in which to gather and remember their ancient greatness and to renew their eternal rivalries. Some of the present rules – which decree that jockeys must ride bareback and that the horses to be ridden in the race are to be chosen by ballot – were instituted at this point, together with a regulation requiring both the winning jockey and horse to visit the church of Provenzano to give thanks for their victory to their patroness. These modest limitations were soon felt to be insufficient to contain the anarchy that attended the event, for jockeys would attack each other on the starting line, and spectators would assault the horses on their way round the course. In 1721 the regulations that govern the contemporary festival were laid down, and in 1729 the boundaries of the contrade were defined, in order that their members should know precisely where their loyalties lay.

The present-day Palio is run twice a year, on 2 July, in honour of the Madonna of Provenzano, and on 16 August, when it celebrates Our Lady of the Assumption. The second running is a replacement event for the linear Palio, which died out during the nineteenth century, leaving Siena's official patroness uncelebrated. Each race is preceded by an identical sequence of ceremonies, which transform it from a trial of equine speed and human skill into the climax of an elaborate piece of theatre. The initial act of this drama consists of a selection process, in which the contrade that will participate in the race are chosen, for the field is limited to ten horses, against seventeen contrade. The first seven places are filled by those contrade that did not race in the last Palio, so that if a contrada is sidelined in July it will race 'di obbligo' in August, and vice versa. The final three places are determined by lottery. The draw takes place in the Palazzo

Pubblico, the city hall of Siena, an imposing Gothic palace overlooking the Campo where the race will be run, which is filled from wall to wall with anxious Sienese. As each contrada is drawn, its banner is hung on the façade of the Palazzo by a page in medieval garb, to the cheers or groans of the crowd assembled below. However, if a contrada fails to be chosen, its interest in the event is far from over, for it will participate in the pageant that precedes the race, and its members will begin their machinations to ensure that their particular enemies do not win.

The first act sets the scene for the drama to follow. Every contrada is like a stock character in a soap opera, whose singularities and antipathies are well known. The draw determines which of them will be onstage during the forthcoming episode. Selection takes place six weeks before the race itself, and in the intervening period the contrade busy themselves with processions through Siena, visiting its churches in turn to make offerings of candles and to request divine assistance. The interval also serves to allow conspiracies, real or illusory, to develop between the contrade that have been chosen to race. These conspiracies ensure that not only the emotions of the Sienese are engaged by the festival, but also their imaginations.

The next act in the show is the *tratta*, or trial, in which the horses that will run in the Palio are selected. The tratta consists of a series of short races which are held four nights before the start of the Palio. The timing and the moonlight that illuminates them give them a theatrical edge. Seventy or so horses are trialled, from which the ten runners will be chosen. The contrade themselves are prohibited from owning Palio horses, and several schools of breeders have emerged over the centuries, dedicated to providing candidates for the race. Some of the triallists that these supply will have run a Palio before, while others will be novices. The tratta aims to mix veteran mounts with newcomers, and sometimes a horse that has learned the course too well is excluded. A number of these, with several victories in the race to their credit, have appeared over the years, including the immortal

Stornino, who won eighteen Palios in the latter half of the nineteenth century, recording his last win when he was twenty-one years old. Stornino was reputed to be a tranquil creature for most of the year, but as the Palio approached his personality would change into that of a high-spirited charger. His body was embalmed after his death. The Sienese contrast the character of Stornino with that of Gaudenzia, the star horse of the 1950s, who was renowned for her docility and speed. She won several Palios in partnership with a jockey named Vittorino, and when they were separated for the August Palio of 1954, she threw her rider and made after Vittorino's horse. Although he tried to beat his former mount back with his whip, she ran with him side by side to the finish, where she triumphed by a head – for the Palio can be won by a riderless horse.

The day after the last tratta is over and the ten horses have been selected, another draw is held to determine which contrada will ride which horse. The allocation is a public event, held once again in the Palazzo Pubblico. The mayor of Siena draws a horse, then the contrada in whose colours it will run. If the horse is a known quantity, a 'cavallo bono' – a latter-day Stornino – there are cries of joy from the members of the lucky contrada. The creature is collected, smothered with kisses, and is led off in triumph to its stable within the territory of the appropriate faction, serenaded at every step of the way. If, however, a contrada is allocated a bad horse, one perhaps that has never run before, or has competed but without success, it is welcomed at best with silence, and sometimes with jeers and blows. The sorting of horses marks the end of the second act of the Palio. Thus far, the members of the cast who will appear on stage have been chosen, and the others are assumed to be plotting in the wings. The wheel of fortune has spun twice, favouring some contrade with a good horse, and others with the motivation to conspire.

The next part of the performance consists of a mixture of action and reports of offstage intrigues, during which it is assumed that the participants are endeavouring to counterbalance fate with trickery. It begins with identical scenes in all of the contrade that will be involved in the race – the arrival of the horse in its territory and its seclusion, under guard, in a special stable. This vigilance is accounted a common duty: 'Every man, woman, grandparent and child of the contrada watches outside the stable in case traps are set by the enemy.' While such precautions are largely ceremonial, they are nonetheless prudent, for there are no official prohibitions against drugging a rival faction's horse, or for that matter, poisoning it. Curiously there *are* regulations against doping one's own horse, which date back to 1852, when the feverish search for a *beverone* – a performance-enhancing substance that could transform a dud into a winner – led to horses being incapacitated before the race, or uncontrollable when on the course.

Not only the horses are kept under guard, but also the jockeys, who now make their appearance on stage. They are by and large mercenaries, and while they are extremely well paid, they are seldom entirely trusted. Whereas some of the horses that have run in the Palio are remembered with reverence, their riders are usually recalled with mixed feelings, for their role in the festival is that of the villains. Indeed, the Italian for jockey – *fantoni* – is slang for 'untrustworthy' in Siena. Jockeys have performed some sensational betrayals during the history of the race, including for example those of Francisco Gobbo (the 'Hunchback') Saragiolo, a turncoat who raced for fifteen different contrade over a thirty-year career, winning fifteen times. His most spectacular breach of faith occurred in 1855 when, mounted on a favoured horse, he rode straight through the crowd on the first bend of the course and out of the Campo through an open arch. His price, coincidentally, was the same as that of Judas – thirty pieces of silver. The Palio was thrown in a similar style by other jockeys in 1877 and in 1885. Indeed, the majority of rule changes to the Palio over the last 200 years have been instituted to limit the opportunities for a rider to become a traitor. In 1802 they were forbidden from assaulting each other prior to the start, following a number of savage fights which effectively prevented their participants from competing, and in 1907 a rule was instituted that prohibited jockeys who were related to each other from running in the same race, as loyalties of blood had proved thicker than ties to their employers, and relatives had been discovered fixing races in order to pool their winnings. While jockeys are still permitted, indeed are expected to interfere with each other around the course, the Sienese sense of fair play, in so far as this exists, insists that they only do so on the instructions of their paymasters.

Once the heroes and villains, the horses and jockeys have been selected and sequestrated, the chorus – that is the members of each contrada, known as *contradaioli* – appear centre-stage to provide a commentary on the action so far, and to speculate on its future course. The air of Siena is filled with gossip and innuendo. Will old alliances stand firm, or has the combination of factions drawn to race thrown up the potential for new relationships? Has a jockey switched to a different contrada because it has a favoured horse, or has he been bribed by his old employers to do so only in order to hold it back? The business of dreaming up hypothetical conspiracies is accounted by participants to be one of the greatest pleasures of the festival. Every conversation in Siena has the forthcoming Palio as its subject, and while all are tinged with expectation, they are likewise edged by the prickle of suspicion, for conspirators usually suspect everyone else of having the same vice. This orgy of paranoia and fantasy results in sleepless nights for many Sienese, or in dreams with plots of dizzying complexity, populated with totems whose associations run wild and free. Will the Tortoise outpace the Unicorn? Will the Eagle bow before the Snail?

Although many contradaioli no longer live in Siena, there is a gathering of the clans for the Palio. Every contrada possesses a collection of buildings dedicated to the use of its members. These include, in addition to a high-security stable, a chapel where the contradaiolis are baptised, married, and remembered in funeral services, and a museum relating to the past exploits of their faction in the race. The contradaioli born in any one year are baptised en masse on the saint's day of their contrada, and are each given a scarf with their tribal colours at baptism, which are worn with the same reverence as the medicine bags of American Indians. As the Palio draws closer, members of one contrada will not walk through the territory of another on their own, for none are willing to strike their colours, and tension between them escalates to the level of physical violence as the plot advances.

The action now returns to the Campo, where a series of trial races called *provas* are held. The aim of the provas is to accustom the horses to the course, for it is no ordinary track. The Campo is a vast open space, more than 100 yards across, and 330 around its perimeter, enclosed on all sides by medieval buildings. It is dominated by the Palazzo Pubblico, from which soars the Mangia, a slender brick tower at whose summit is a giant bell. The Campo, in plan form, is shaped like a scallop shell, with nine raised ribs that radiate outwards from the foot of the Palazzo. A track of sand 6 inches deep is laid just inside its perimeter and rails are erected on either side of the track, to form the course over which the horses will race. The Campo itself is set on an incline towards the Palazzo, and the course includes two acute-angled corners that must be navigated at a gallop. These are padded with mattresses to protect any riders who overshoot the bend.

Although the Campo is packed for each prova, and the crowd behaves with a fanaticism rarely encountered on a common or garden racecourse, the provas are only teasers – plays within a play. The jockeys do not carry whips, and take great care of their mounts, for the course is dangerous, and if a horse is injured in a prova no substitution can be made for the Palio. After each evening prova the contrade hold banquets, often in spectacular settings, at which the treasures from Palios of centuries past are displayed, old feuds are remembered, and the horses are serenaded. These dinners are refreshed with immense quantities of fine Tuscan wine, renowned since the Renaissance for its

PAINETWORKS

inspirational properties, and acclaimed by Michelangelo as a magical fluid that 'kisses, bites, licks, thrusts, and sings'.

While the provas and dinners are in progress, the captains of each contrada hold meetings with one another, disposing of the money that they have raised from their contradaioli in buying and selling favours with the aim of settling, if they have a good horse, that it will win; if they have a bad horse, which other horses it should impede; and if they are not racing, that their enemies will lose. According to Pierangelo Stanghellini, a former captain of the Tortoise contrada, 'Obstructing the others [in the] race, bribing their jockeys and supporting an allied contrada is nearly as important as winning.' Substantial amounts of money change hands, for the pride of the contrade is at stake, and this is an expensive commodity. These clandestine meetings and secret agreements, known as *partiti*, form the crucial sub-plot, whose complexities will only be unravelled in the final act, when the horses line up for the start of the race.

The day of the Palio itself is occupied with ceremonial. In the morning, the horses are taken from their stables to be blessed. The blessings are performed in the private chapel of each contrada, whose pews are removed before the event so that the horse and its admirers can all squeeze inside. The ceremony is brief. The horse is led to the altar where the priest begs that God might infuse the animal with the Holy Spirit, sprinkles it with Holy Water, delivers it a brief sermon on the merits of not disappointing expectations, and dismisses it with the valediction: 'Go, little horse! And come back a winner!' It is considered to be a good omen if the horse evacuates during the service. The jockeys are also blessed en masse in the Campo at dawn, and each signs a contract binding them to their contrada and the limited rules of the imminent race.

The official start time for the Palio is 7 p.m., although people take their places in the Campo from noon onwards. At 2 p.m. the Mangia bell begins to toll, slowly, rhythmically, sonorously, calling the Sienese to the final act of their festival, and its denouement. It is said that with the wind in the right direction the bell can be heard as far away as Rome. The contradaioli, meanwhile, pack closer and closer within the square, so tightly that the only way to leave is on a stretcher, for they will part for nothing else. There are tiers of seating, crowded to bursting, against the buildings around the Campo, as many people as can fit in each of its balconies and window frames and on its rooftops; and in the centre of the Campo, inside the race track, 50,000 more. The view from the centre is breathtaking. None of the entrances to the square are visible, the horizon is made up on all sides by the outlines of medieval façades, hung with heraldic banners, and it is impossible to tell what exists beyond them, or indeed, which century.

At 4.30 p.m. the entrances to the square are sealed off, so that the crowd are, in effect, locked in the theatre for the final act. This commences with the *Corteo Storico*, literally the 'Historical Cortège', which has been described as 'the most colourful and romantic procession to be seen in the world today'. It is Renaissance in appearance, Gothic in origin, and is the spiritual descendant of the Roman triumphal procession. It is led by the twelve official trumpeters of Siena, each of whose silver trumpet is decorated with the black and white colours of the city. The trumpeters wear tunics and hose, and their stirring fanfare echoes around the Campo. Next comes a horseman clad in armour bearing the civic banner, followed by the flags and uniformed representatives of Siena's ancient tributaries, and those of its historic guilds. This initial section of the parade enacts the antique social order of the city, with each rank marching according to its precedence, and every recognised level of city life above commoner represented. It is followed by the representatives of the people themselves – the *comparsas*, or companies of the seventeen contrade. Each comparsa is preceded by a drummer and two flag-bearers, followed by its captain, dressed in armour and mounted on a charger. These are attended by a body of men-at-arms, pages, more flag-bearers, and finally the jockey riding a parade horse, leading his mount for the Palio on a rein. The contrade enter the Campo in the order in which they were selected to race, followed by those who will not race, and last of all by six knights in armour with their visors down. These are representatives of six extinguished contrade – the Sword, the Bear, the Lion, the Viper, the Oak, and the Cock, which vanished when the boundaries of the present entities were laid down in 1729.

The Corteo Storico is a blast of colour, its vibrant palette showing every combination of rich primary hues in the uniforms of the comparsas – doublets quartered in sapphire and vermilion, decorated with salmon-pink piping and gold braid, - parti-coloured tights of scarlet and sunshine yellow, and red and white chequered caps. It is a reminder of how drab European clothing has become since the end of the Renaissance. As the procession makes its way around the Campo, the trumpets, drums and cheers of the contradaioli mingle with their echoes from the buildings that enclose them. The sound is tumultuous, and breaks over the crowd like an artillery bombardment. Every Sienese in the square voices their admiration and pride for their comparsa, whose members, conscious of the sublime honour of having been chosen to represent their respective urban tribes and to carry their colours and totems, strive to outdo their rivals in display. The leading flag-bearers of each comparsa, known as *sbandierata*, toss their banners high into the air, so that the Campo is filled with heraldic devices, spinning and fluttering above the parade, like 'the painted wings of enormous butterflies'. Every one of these sbandierata aims to surpass himself, their ambition summed up by Alfredo 'Ciappata' Donnini, a veteran of the discipline, as follows: 'If I could I would have hurled [my flag] above the rooftops of Siena, so that everyone could see the purity of the colours that are the image of my contrada.'

PETE MARTIN

The Corteo Storico is like a daylight firework display, a show of pageantry that incites the contradaioli with pride for their emblems, and for the city in which they are united. It is the first scene of the final act and closes with the arrival of the *carroccio*, a genuine medieval battle-wagon, drawn by four snow-white oxen, on which is mounted the Palio itself. The prize, for which all this emotion has been accumulating, is a rectangular silk banner, perhaps three yards long, decorated by a different artist each year with an image of the Virgin, elegant, indeed beautiful in itself, and suitably totemic, like the scarves ladies gave to their champions at the joust to serve as the reward for the fierce and passionate climax that was to follow. The Palio is passed over to the care of the Captain of the Sienese People in a stand at the base of the Palazzo, and the carroccio and the comparsas march out of the Campo.

Once the course is clear, a white flag is raised, and a deafening cannon is sounded to mark the commencement of the final scene. This cannon is brutally loud, as if it were intended to enforce silence, and the ground underfoot vibrates with the aftershock. Next, the ten mounted jockeys emerge from the Palazzo Pubblico and make their way to the starting line. Each has been provided with a bridle to control their horse, and a whip to use upon the other riders. The whips, called *nerbi*, are made from the dried penis of a bull, and in the right hands a nerbo is a vicious weapon.

The jockeys are received with thunderous cheers that drown out the memories of the cannon, the trumpets, the drums, and the tolling of the Mangia bell far overhead. They make their way to the starting line, which consists of a rope held at breast height across the track. There are no stalls, and the horses must line up in an order determined by a secret ballot held minutes before the race, so as to ensure that factions of jockeys cannot box in another rider. However, a last opportunity before the start remains for the riders to try to fix the result: there is only enough room on the line for nine of the ten horses, so that the tenth horse makes a running start, and when it reaches the line, assuming the others are assembled, the race begins.

This running starter, the *rincorsa*, can choose when to begin its gallop, and will wait until its enemies are at a disadvantage.

The start of the Palio is the ultimate in foreplay – it is far, far longer than the race itself, and is invariably preceded by a number of false starts. Just when it seems that the denouement is at hand there is a final procrastination, which increases the tension of the audience to the point that it can only be released by an explosion of emotion. They are on the edge of delirium, in a state known in Siena as *sciabordito*, which has no precise translation. It is a condition in which passion swamps reason. The horses, meanwhile, have been breathing pure adrenaline since their entry with the comparsas into the Campo. They too are close to becoming sciabordito. Their eyes roll, their frames quiver, and froth streaks their flanks. The jockeys, despite the short and dangerous course in front of them, are perhaps the only living creatures in the Campo that can make a show of sang-froid. They are not allowed to use their nerbi on each other until they pass a wrought-iron flag 50 yards down the course, so they keep poker faces, while they argue with and jostle one another, whispering last-minute offers, some of which are bluffs.

At every false start the air is rent with groans and sighs of frustration. A cloud of black smoke from the archaic starting cannon dissipates slowly over the crowd. It is common for an hour to be consumed in false starts, and meanwhile the sun has fallen behind the buildings around the Campo and the course itself has slipped into shadow. Again and again, the riders wheel around one another as they are rearranged in the correct order. The rincorsa, the running starter, retires a few yards behind, its jockey either trying to calm his mount, or maintain its excitement, until he sees an opportunity when the enemies of his colours are suitably compromised, facing the wrong way perhaps, to begin his dash. The line itself is mayhem, with jockeys shouting to and barging against one another, then the rincorsa bounds forwards, the starting cannon fires again: this time the rope drops and they're off!

The course is three laps round the Campo. The race is over in less

PETE MARTIN

than a minute and a half, but this short period of action is so frenzied that the Sienese claim the Palio to be a continuous, ninety-second orgasm. The jockeys cling on with their knees and flog each other with their bull pizzles. Riders and horses crash out of the race. Some career, or are forced into the mattresses at the first turn, where the course descends through a 90-degree bend, while others break through the barriers into the crowd on the next corner. It is not unusual for a horse to end up on its back in the middle of the spectators, all four hooves kicking out in different directions, while its jockey who has landed many yards distant is attacked by outraged members of the contrada whose colours he wears. Even when it is evident that a rider has been knocked from his mount with a blow to the back of his head, and has lost teeth and broken bones as a result of his fall, the suspicion of the crowd is such that they will not rule out the possibility that both blow and fall were staged, for only the accidental is deemed impossible at the Palio.

So fast is the action, which for most of the mass of contradaioli packed into the centre of the Campo is only partially visible, that the race seems to pass in the space of a single breath. When it is over a tumult breaks out that would not disgrace the climax of a Roman chariot race. The winning contrada smothers its horse with kisses, and if it has managed to keep its rider he is lifted shoulder high and carried on a victory circuit. The losers, meanwhile, shower curses and recriminations against their horse, its jockey, their allies among other contrade who clearly deserted them, the evident treachery of their enemies, and some are even known to curse the patroness of the festival for favouring the unjust. Women, children and grown men shed public tears. The race does not offer prizes for coming second or third – indeed, it is the greatest disgrace imaginable to come second, for getting close to victory is a more lamentable failure than never having been in the running.

PETE MARTIN

Meanwhile, the winners besiege the stand where the Palio is held and scream out '*Daccelo!*' – 'Give it to us!' Above them, on the face of the Palazzo, the colours of their contrada, and only their contrada, are unfurled. Once the prize has been presented it is carried to the cathedral of the Madonna of the Assumption, or the Church of Santa Maria di Provenzano, depending on which of the Holy Virgins has been worshipped by the race, and the grateful winners sing a *Te Deum* whose words, whether through excess of emotion or intent, are often very different to the official version. In the nineteenth century their mangling of the hymn so scandalised a visiting abbot that he remarked that it had not contained 'a single healthy word'.

Despite this rough type of worship, ecclesiastical support for the festival is firm, and has been so since more pious ages. In the fourteenth century St Catherine of Siena, the city's medieval mystic, who corresponded with popes, arranged for their return to Rome from exile in Avignon, and who lived off communion wafers, encouraged the race and its rivalry: 'Come, dear children, run this Palio and run it so that only one can possess it.' More recently, Pope John XXIII praised the festival and in 1958, Mario Ismaele Castellano, Archbishop of Siena, observed 'telling the Sienese not to take part in the Palio is like telling fish not to live in the sea'. This matter-of-fact approach shows an astute appreciation on the part of the Church for one of the more frenzied events under its protection. Whereas to the outsider the Palio may appear to be no more than a complex and emotional pageant, to a Sienese it is *High Noon*, *Dangerous Liaisons*, *Ben Hur* and the *Duchess of Malfi* all rolled into one and lived through together in the space of a few days.

For the victors, the afterglow lasts weeks. They promenade their Palio round Siena by day and night, accompanied by the costumed officials of their comparsa. The festival comes to a close with a victory banquet, held within the boundaries of the winning faction, at which the horse is the guest of honour. If it has perished in the interim it is represented by one of its hoofs, mounted in silver. The losing contrade, meanwhile, soon recover heart. As the results of most races are determined by trickery, once the web of deceit has been unravelled there is usually some particularly vile

PETE MARTIN

piece of behaviour that comes to light on which the disaster can be blamed. A starting official is seen driving a new Ferrari, for instance, whereupon it is remembered that the race commenced before the rincorsa crossed the line. Once the conspiracy is solved, the contrade settle back into their traditional animosity. Old enmities are renewed and some new ones are formed. Every contradaiolo believes that next year, justice will be on their side. The justice that they crave is not of the nature that rewards the good and punishes the bad: they desire the Roman version in the shape of the goddess Fortuna, mistress of luck. Besides, they have all the charms of Siena to console them, for the town is renowned as being so beautiful that even the broken-hearted find time to dry their tears and to admire its splendour.

It is easy to envy the Sienese for their beautiful city, their embracing tribalism and their stimulating Palio. They have the comfort of belonging to a 700-year-old tradition of celebration, which licenses them to exercise their emotions at fixed times of the year – to shout, to weep, to indulge in displays of ecstasy and dejection. In contrast, the inhabitants of a new town, or for that matter a new country, must invent their own identities, and devise appropriate ways of enjoying themselves en masse. In most cases, their public ceremonies are commanded into existence by political bodies, in order to commemorate matters deemed of importance to civic unity, such as the anniversary of a revolution. Occasionally, however, new festivals appear spontaneously, and a spectacle created by the people for the people erupts into being like a volcanic island through the surface of an ocean, to stand in accusation against or in celebration of the culture from which it has emerged.

A striking example of just such a festival has materialised in the middle of a desert in the western portion of the United States. A few days after the Sienese have wrung themselves dry of emotion at the August Palio, 30,000 Americans set off for an uninhabitable wilderness with the aim of establishing a temporary city, dedicated to pleasure, where they frolic together for a week. This event, although still only in its teens, is already notorious and its participants have been labelled freaks, nudists, anarchists, fetishists, feminists, sex maniacs, drug addicts, pagans and communists, and their behaviour in their temporary utopia likened to that which flourished in the biblical cities of Sodom and Gomorrah, shortly before God intervened and wiped them from the face of the earth. However, and despite its equivocal reputation, the event is also acknowledged to celebrate a certain type of idealism, and to embody the freedom of expression that Americans so cherish.

THOM VAN OS

IX

THE PURSUIT
OF HAPPINESS

Ah, love! Could thou and I with fate conspire
To grasp this sorry state of things entire
Would we not shatter it to bits – and then
Remould it nearer to the heart's desire!

THE RUBAIYAT OF OMAR KHAYYAM

There is a perceived malaise in American society that travels under the name of atomisation. Atomisation implies that social contact between Americans has been reduced to a series of impersonal transactions – that people only exist in order to consume and to sell each other goods and services for the benefit of a handful of behemoth corporations. Its side effects include the introduction of countless petty rules into the working lives of the country's citizens, which prescribe how they may interact, and which require them to speak to one another using a stilted professional vocabulary from which they are forbidden to deviate. According to the prophets of this evil, the sense of diversity that was once so important to the United States has been destroyed, and its inhabitants have been reduced to a state of passive consumption. Indeed, so desperate has their condition become, that they no longer may be conceived of as individual members of distinct communities, but instead make up a homogeneous mass, divisible by age and income into a range of target markets.

Fortunately, atomisation is encountering resistance. In the style of a comic-book superhero, a festival has arisen to combat the trend. The 'Burning Man' Project, a week-long party staged each August in the Black Rock desert of Nevada, encourages its participants to reject passive consumption, to express their individuality, and to engage with their fellows in any way that their imaginations might suggest to them. Burning Man consists of the creation of a settlement called Black Rock City, a temporary and commerce-free utopia marked out in lines on the surface of the desert, which is occupied for the duration of the festival and then effaced at its conclusion. Within these ephemeral bounds, Americans gather from all over the nation. They come by car, truck and aeroplane, singly and in convoys, carrying everything that they will need for survival or pleasure, for with the exceptions of a coffee shop and an ice-cube stall, it is forbidden to sell or buy anything at the event. The result is a giant adult playground – a cross between a funfair, a beach party, and *Tomorrow's World* – set in a terrain as harsh as a moonscape. Participants attend not only in order to escape the consumer frenzy raging through America, but also to make friends, to find lovers, to entertain and to be entertained, to construct and admire giant works of art, and to participate in a general round of hedonism. After a week of festivities staged in a brand-free environment, Burning Man culminates, as its name suggests, in the incineration of a giant human effigy, the conflagration serving to form a unifying ritual for its disparate participants.

The history of the event is short, and is a tale of unexpected consequences. Burning Man did not begin life as a protest against consumerism, for lost love and its attendant pangs were the true causes of its inception. The festival was born on midsummer's eve in 1985. It was the brainchild of Larry Harvey, a middle-aged carpenter and landscaper who had recently been abandoned by his girlfriend, and who had resolved to construct a wooden likeness of a human and to burn it on San Francisco's Baker Beach in order to heal his wounded psyche. Harvey had intended his actions to be private, but at the moment of conflagration, even as the flames took hold of his offering, the god of mending broken hearts sent a sign that he was listening. According to Harvey, the instant that the effigy was ablaze, 'everybody on that beach, north and south, came running . . . And I looked out at this arc of firelit faces, and before I knew it . . . a hippie with his pants on his head and a guitar . . . materialized out of the murk. And he started singing a song about fire. Now I'm not exactly a hootenanny kind of guy, but it seemed like the thing to do, and we started singing . . . That was the first spontaneous performance, that was the first . . . geometric increase of Burning Man. What we had instantly created was a community.'

The sense of fellowship that had emerged at what was meant to have been a private act of catharsis, not only cured Harvey of his sorrow, but also inspired him to repeat the exercise the following midsummer, when a larger creation went up in flames in front of more people, and every midsummer thereafter until 1990, when a combination of bureaucratic intervention and crowd pressure forced him to cancel his annual sacrifice. The man that he and friends had built to burn that year was 40 feet tall, and the crowd who had gathered to watch its demise was 800 strong. Harvey was busy overseeing the erection of this colossus on the beach when a state official appeared and ordered him to desist, and in no circumstances to set it alight. California had been desiccated by drought and brush-fires were raging through the state, fanned by onshore winds. Unhappily, the waiting crowd were incensed by the prospect of being robbed of their entertainment, and demanded that the image be burned, directing part of their anger at its creator. Harvey found himself trapped between the law and a mob who displayed little of the spirit of community that he had nurtured around the ceremony. 'It was horrible,' he reflected later, 'where had we gone wrong? What had been a communion for us was just a cheap spectacle for them. And you know, our society is largely organized around cheap, and expensive, spectacles . . . spectacles in which you are anonymous, you're passive, you consume a product, you share nothing with anybody, you go away, come back and get some more later when you feel empty again.'

Harvey decided to postpone the burning and to seek out an appropriate place where the ritual might be staged and its spirit of communion revived without being disturbed by civil servants or voyeurs. He enlisted the aid of friends in the San Francisco Cacophony Society, an artists' collective dedicated to anarchy, and together they decided on the Black Rock desert, some 330 miles inland from San Francisco, as a suitable place in which to light a fire, and the Labor Day holiday in the last weekend of August as the appropriate occasion on which to do so.

Both choices proved instrumental to the future development of Burning Man. The venue that they selected is a geological prodigy, belonging to a species of feature known as Alkali deserts, which are notorious for being inhospitable to most forms of life. The example at Black Rock is an ancient lake bed, consisting of 400 square miles of absolutely flat and naked terrain, whose surface is composed of flour-fine alkaline dust. Long, thin and faintly oval in shape, it lies at an altitude of 4,000 feet, and is lined by barren mountains that rise to 9,000 feet on either side. It is prone to dust storms, hurricane-force winds, tornadoes, pelting rain, mirages and meteor showers. Daily temperatures range between −10° and +40° centigrade at any time of year. When the

Harvey party arrived in this untamed environment, in the words of a Cacophonist, 'We all got out of our cars as one member drew a long line on the desert floor, creating what we accepted as a "Zone Gateway" . . . we crossed the line, and knew we were definitely not in Kansas anymore . . . as far as the eye could see it was flat, flat, flat. Some people even claim you can see the curvature of the Earth. Whatever. As one looked out into the desert playa, there may have been nothing there, but there are tons of things to see, one merely has to know where to look.'

Harvey immediately saw the potential of the desert as a site for Burning Man: 'It turns out that in this vast desert space . . . that there are peculiar properties, [a] peculiar magic . . . takes hold. Suddenly we encountered something – it was like the ocean that had backed the Man before . . . a great sweep of nature . . . But this was an ocean you could walk on. This was a great piece of nothing in which anything that was, was more intensely so.'

The man was assembled and incinerated, a decision was taken to return the following year, and attendance at the event began to snowball, as news of the conflagration, its exotic location, and the influence this appeared to have upon people's behaviour was spread by word of mouth. While only eighty men and women were present at the first desert Burning Man, by 2002 upwards of 30,000 had been seized by the pioneer spirit and were making an annual migration to Black Rock. The form of the festival was refined over the intermediate years, with the aim of perpetuating the same sense of community that had appeared around the initial bonfire on Baker Beach. A handful of rules were formulated, some of which were introduced for the safety of participants in the unforgiving climate, while others were intended to shape the conduct of the citizens of Black Rock City. The first of these commandments is No Spectators, whose purpose is to ensure that every person who attends the festival is committed to its underlying philosophy – is ready to embrace hedonism and to renounce the culture of commerce in which they otherwise live and labour. Such a renunciation is considered to be an article of faith amongst Burning Man's celebrants who, singly and collectively, are known as Burners, a label that they wear with pride, as if they were the initiates of a religious sect.

Access to the festival is by road or air, and barring a few hundred people who live in settlements in the vicinity of the Black Rock desert, every one of its participants must undertake what amounts to a pilgrimage in order to reach it. Indeed, the journey can be seen as part of the festival, a ceremony in itself, in which Burners depart the United States for a state of celebration. Most of them come by road from the San Franciso Bay Area, and the first step of their pilgrimage is Freeway 101/80, an eight-lane monster cast from cement blocks that leads inland towards the mountains. The civil engineering that carries it over rivers and canyons is vast and crude, consisting in the main of Meccano style bridges, built out of box girders riveted together, all identical in form and only differing in size. It is as if the highway, the cars and the chunks of infrastructure have been spewed together on to the landscape. Every ten miles or so, exit signs advertise petrol stations and fast-food concessions – Macdonalds, Wendy, Taco Bell, Subway, always the same names, in various combinations, which create a sense of déjà vu, so that the traveller suspects he is driving around a loop, and that the same stretch of road is repeating itself endlessly before his eyes. After Sacramento the traffic thins, the road rises, and conifer forests replace the billboards. The landscape becomes imposing, empty and brutal. Freeway 80 peaks at 7,500 feet where it crosses the Donner pass,[1] then descends and leaves California for Nevada. Hoardings re-appear along its verges advertising gambling opportunities ahead. It continues, four lanes in each direction, right through the centre of the city of Reno, in between multi-storey casinos which are ablaze with neon after dark and seem to drip giant golden

---

1   Named after a party of starving migrants who were trapped nearby one winter, lapsed into cannibalism, and thrived on it, for their well-fed appearance gave their crime away when a search party found them the following spring.

dollars on to the highway, past brothels, a golf course, and on into the empty heart of the American West.

Burners turn off at Highway 447, a two-lane blacktop ribbon with a parallel line of telegraph poles alongside. The road runs through a barren landscape that is dotted with sage-brush, crossed now and then with a straggling line of fenceposts, and bordered by mountains in every direction. After 30 miles it passes Pyramid Lake, a vast and enigmatic body of water whose peerless blue appears like a mirage against the hushed pastel colours of the landscape around. Pyramid Lake is sacred to the Paiute Indians and is contained within their reservation.[2] Once beyond this liquid paragon, Highway 447 skirts the floor of a slender valley, pinched into segments at the points where the fringing mountains come together. A heat haze ripples off its asphalt, so that at times it seems to lead like a runway into the sky. Wildlife en route is limited to the odd raptor overhead and the occasional animal skull on its verges. Seventy miles later, it passes Empire and Gerlach, the last outposts of civilisation, then arrives at the edge of the Black Rock desert, the point of no return.

Thus far, little by little, Burners have left the urban culture of America behind. The hoardings that fleck its landscape promising pleasure if a certain product is purchased have vanished, along with the ugly conglomerations in which such promises may be redeemed. The vista that now confronts them is the absolute antithesis of shopping-mall America – 'Imagine a vast, waveless ocean stricken dead and turned to ashes.' Aside from the tarmac track that skirts the desert's edge, and its accompanying fringe of telegraph poles, mankind has left no

---

2 Interestingly, the Paiutes are also distinguished for introducing a new festival to America – ghost-dancing – a series of rituals that revolved around a communal, hypnotic dance. Ghost-dancing was widely imitated, and its ceremonies were enlarged by other tribes, including the Lakota, who added the promise that ghost-dancing would make its practitioners bullet-proof, a promise found to be untrue when ghost-dancers were massacred by gunfire at the battle of Wounded Knee.

permanent mark upon the landscape. All that is visible to denote the site of the festival is a little cluster of brightly coloured shapes, rendered insignificant by their surroundings, like a handful of confetti resting on a flagstone in the nave of a cathedral, a few brilliant specks set against a field of marble.

Those who decide to take the plunge are greeted as they turn off the highway and on to the desert. Their greeters are in studied states of undress, as befits the gatekeepers to a temporary utopia. Both boys and girls wear leather and lingerie, in combinations that would provoke a riot if worn in a public place in any other city, and all are covered from head to toe in a grey-white dust, which gives them a feral appearance. Their role is equivalent to that of immigration officers. They search vehicles on arrival for stowaways, as Burning Man is a ticket only festival,[3] and test first-time attendees on their knowledge of the rules of the community which they are about to enter. The rules that are emphasised are Self-Sufficiency, No Vending, No Guns, and Piss Clear, the last of which relates to the need for vigilance over kidney function in the arid climate. Burners are next pointed out the conditions of entry, written on their ticket, which include the sombre warning: YOU VOLUNTARILY ASSUME THE RISK OF SERIOUS INJURY OR DEATH BY ATTENDING. Finally, after any novices have been put through a short initiation ceremony, arrivals are allowed inside the city limits.

On paper, Black Rock City is a near-perfect counterfeit of a permanent metropolis, and might appear side by side in a gazetteer with other Nevadan settlements of a similar size. It has its own fire service, police force and media, including Radio Free Burning Man and the *Black Rock Gazette*, published daily. It is equipped with public lavatories, an airport, communications facilities and a central administration. A coherent and rigid set of traffic laws is applied within its boundaries. In substance, however, and in contrast, it consists of little more than a pair of

---

3 Proceeds from ticket sales provide for the infrastructure of Black Rock City, public works of art and insurance – the event is not run for profit.

concentric rings, marked out like crop circles on the surface of the desert. The section of ground between these circles is divided into blocks by radial avenues, within which the Burners set up camp. A third of the city, facing east down the length of the desert is left clear, as is the ground within the inner circle. The Burning Man, the effigy to be incinerated at the conclusion of the festival stands at its centre on a plinth, and resembles a lighthouse rising from a flat sea. From the air, Black Rock City looks like a giant horseshoe, its arms curling round a pinprick. At ground level, it makes an immediate and powerful impression on account of its size, its complexity, and the ingenuity and extravagance of the structures it contains. Most Burners carry far beyond the bare minimum needed to live in a wilderness for a week. Some bring fairground rides, radio masts, tents large enough to stage a circus, carbon-fibre pyramids, geodesic domes built from coloured glass hexagons, dancefloors, sound-systems, railway carriages, industrial strength lasers and their associated 16-ton cooling trucks, swimming pools and the water to fill them, and American government surplus material ranging from NASA discards and VERTOL apparatus to pup tents. Above all this, a myriad of coloured banners and the flags of states and nations are suspended from spires and masts that stretch into the sky.

The Burners themselves are no less eyecatching than the City they have constructed. They dress in accordance with another festival rule: Radical Self-Expression. An astonished consumer-studies expert, sent to investigate Burning Man and to analyse any trends that might arise therefrom, described a cross-section of its population as follows: 'people in intricate costumes, with butterfly wings, helmets, huge hats, strange hats, body armour, leather bondage outfits, historical costumes, alien costumes. Others . . . coloured blue or red or green, . . . nude or covered with glittering particles, or riding in strange vehicles that resemble animals, birds, insects, crustaceans, a Viking ship, a living room, a haunted house, a dragon.' The overall effect of such diversity in appearance has been compared to being trapped in a pornographic science fiction film set on the moon. There are many genitalia on display, of either sex, of every age. Some have been tattooed, others shaved and painted, and a few are artificial, built from skin grafts. Everyone, whether dressed or merely decorated, wears goggles and a dust mask. Dust storms that arrive without warning are every day events on the *playa*, the festival name for the desert. A shadow falls from a mountain, the air beneath it cools and begins to flow, disrupting the complex convection patterns on the desiccated lake bed, resulting in a picture-perfect tornado, a supple column that winds across the playa with the grace of a dancer, tearing at everything that falls in its path.

TONY PLETTS

Once Burners have staked down their camps and decorated their bodies, they are ready to join in the festivities as fully fledged citizens of Black Rock. They are expected to provide their own entertainment, for with the exception of the burning ceremony on the last night of the festival, and the 'Critical Tits' rally of topless bicyclists, now in its eighth year, there are no official rituals. Instead, participants offer a variety of goods and services to each other, for free, and draw their pleasure from sampling their respective offerings. This state of affairs is a result of the No Vending rule, which prohibits the use of money at the festival. Instead of hard cash, the official exchange system of Burning Man is gift giving. A gift is not limited to something tangible – a present of a trinket or a drink. The concept also encompasses actions – the provision of services such as music, lighting, sexual acts and haircuts, or the creation of monumental works of art, such as a 50-foot long motorised rubber duck with a free cocktail bar and a live jazz band in its belly. A gift can be as simple as singing a song, telling a joke, or helping someone stake down their tent when a dust storm threatens. The results of the gift-giving culture in operation at Burning Man are spectacular. Not a single one of the temporary wonders that have been assembled in the desert is a commercial venture. Burners can dance, play and feast all day and night for a week, without having to pay for any of these pleasures, entertained all the while by concerts and fireworks, and inspired by the sculptures and other works of art that are scattered over the playa.

The first day of the festival is usually taken up with an inspection of what gifts have been brought to Black Rock City. This is conducted on foot or by bicycle, for the surface of the playa has the texture of pollen, and any vehicular movement kicks up clouds of blinding choking dust. The preliminary tour is undertaken in the spirit of a Spanish *Paseo* – to look and to be looked at – and the experience that it offers is similar to wandering through a giant bazaar. Black Rock City functions, in metaphor at least, as a market. People bring things to offer – a handful of decorated shells, or perhaps even only themselves. Some build imposing structures that symbolise a part of their identity – generosity, perhaps, or genius, and in return everyone is seeking friends, admirers, lovers and inspiration. People set out their stalls, as a spider sets its web, to catch the attention of passers-by. And the playa, the desert itself, forms the perfect blank space on which to display their wares. It does indeed possess a 'peculiar magic'. Its even surface and vast expanse provide a setting any surrealist would envy. It gives everything the element of surprise – it isolates for scrutiny whatever rests upon its surface, so that even a paper-clip could be fascinating. We are used to looking at things in context – every day, most of us encounter thousands of objects that are more or less invisible in their environment, even though each one may be, in its own way, a tremendous invention, a miracle of technology, or its perfection be the consequence of centuries of refinement. The desert restores the mystery to such things, just as gift giving during Burning Man is intended to revive the pleasures of contact with strangers.

In the course of their Paseo, Burners congregate in the

uninhabited inner circle of Black Rock City, at whose centre stands the Burning Man, a skeletal effigy with its arms by its sides that appears insubstantial from a distance – a few black lines, a few brush strokes against an empty sky. Close up, it is an imposing and elegant piece of art – a wooden-frame Vitruvian man, 40 feet tall, balanced on a plinth of similar height. It is a symbol at the heart of the festival, and its likeness is reproduced in every camp, incorporated into costumes, and is even tattooed on people's skins.

Once Burners have admired their fellows, their city and its centrepiece, they are ready to interact in meaningful, non-commercial ways with one another. The opportunities at their disposal are listed for the most part in the *What When Where?* guide that is issued to all participants upon arrival. It contains hundreds of entries, laid out in columns like lonely hearts advertisements, in which individuals and collectives have set down, in language which satirises advertising copy, the gifts they wish to offer other Burners. A meander through the guide offers a snapshot of how celebrants pass an average day in their festival city. The examples that follow are taken from the 2002 version.

Turning first to morning activities, what better place to start a day in Black Rock City than the Ritual Reincarnation Camp, which offers Burners the opportunity to be

> *reborn to the world of the Playa! Confess your sins (if you have none, we will help you commit some!), serve penance and crawl through our 6 ft vagina to be reborn & receive your personalized rebirth certificate.*

Rebirth is not to everyone's taste, and those accustomed to shaving in the mornings, or feeling burdened by an excess of body hair, might chose instead to pay a visit to the Liver's End Bar whose hosts invite all-comers to

> *stop by for a libation and a shave. We'll supply the drink, razor, shaving cream and water, you supply the woolly or pilose zone . . . Bring your own razor for intimate areas.*

A number of forms of morning exercise are listed for energetic Burners, including yoga classes, an organised run and a nature walk. Those who prefer to stimulate their lungs with a gentle smoke may repair to the Hookah Bar, which urges them to

> join us for the daily ritual of smoking the Hookah pipe. Flavored aromatic tobaccos and sanitary nipples will be provided . . . Tea, too, will be served in a resplendent, luxurious Moroccan atmosphere. Leave the camels and the footwear outside!

Even those industrious souls who believe that the perfect morning involves work will find soulmates on the playa. There are plenty of entries in *What When Where?* seeking volunteers to help fabricate giant works of art, such as *ZE ARC OF HAWAII*:

> participate in the creation of a 240 foot circumference playa earth compass sculpture. You and hands of friends will shape a charted and scaled recreation of one of the volcanoes/craters of the Pacific Rim 'Ring of Fire'.

It is interesting to note that many of the morning activities are mundane – a shave, a cup of tea, a gentle workout – and are not in themselves a reason to spend a week in a toxic desert. It is rather the spirit in which they are offered that makes them special. The residents of Black Rock City live a normal life in an abnormal way. They turn humdrum matters into ceremonies, and make games out of elements of their everyday routines. Burning Man, it seems, serves as an antidote to the 'fatal increase of routine'. It is a celebration of the simple pleasures of life, as they should occur in the ideal metropolis, while simultaneously acting as a protest against modern America, by parodying its banalities.

The pace of hedonism in Black Rock City slows down towards the middle of the day, when temperatures on the playa spike upwards, and convection from its surface creates flowing shadows that are reminiscent of the ripple patterns thrown by

sunlight off water. Many encampments provide covered spaces where Burners can while away the daily heatwave engaged in such useful pursuits as whistle-making, penis-moulding, Japanese bondage sessions and distilling vodka, or where they may enjoy some passive form of entertainment, such as listening to a Dr Seuss story or watching a film:

> *Enjoy a break from the heat and weather in our 50' x 50' carpeted enclosure. Today's program: The Wicker Man, Carnival of Souls, Surrealist & Dadaist shorts, Nazi porn (time permitting).*

The late afternoon, when the air starts to cool, is usually dedicated to personal contacts of a more intimate nature. Burners offer services to each other intended to improve their feelings of well-being (*'Bring us your tired toes, your poor feet, your huddled cuticle masses yearning to be pampered! You will receive a professional grade pedicure, be lavished with a luxuriant foot massage, and/or decorated with a gloriously hued Rembrandt for your toes'*), or to enhance their appearance (*'Make some fairy wings to wear on the playa. Helper fairies guaranteed from 1–4 pm'*). These activities, best categorised as ritual grooming, have a particular resonance at Burning Man, where, as a class, they form the greater part of the gifts that Burners wish to offer one another. Grooming, from the point of view of a biologist, is a fundamental part of human behaviour, and remains the principal social activity of our nearest animal relative, the chimpanzee. When chimps are bent on reconciliation, for instance, 'they circle each other tensely, shriek and embrace, then formalise the truce by mutual grooming'. Clearly, Burners feel that there is not enough grooming in the world in general and seek to redress the imbalance at their festival.

Grooming is often a preliminary to sex, which is available in a considerable variety of styles at Burning Man. Most Burners are aged between twenty and fifty, and very few bring their children to the festival. As a consequence, there is a distinct bias towards adult forms of entertainment. Amongst other opportunities listed in *What When Where?* are

THE GREAT CANADIAN BEAVER EATING CONTEST MANGER TROIS. This is about the lovely act of pleasing a woman by going down on her . . . CRITERIA: Artistic Merit & Presentation, Athleticism, Enthusiasm, Perversion, hairstyles . . . Bring your towel, paper towels, tissues, baby wipes, costumes, fetish gear and an open mind.

and

DAMNED HAPPY HOUR 'Leave your soul at the door, to get it back, be a whore'. Enjoy a couple of hours of beats, Damned Martinis and the constant entertainment of suckers (like you) whoring themselves in our Amsterdam style brothel window, or doing whatever we ask in order to win back their souls.

Explicit invitations to perform sexual acts with strangers are a common feature of the festival. Any form of sex that is legal between consenting adults (in private) is permitted in public in Black Rock City. This tolerance enables many of the people who attend to enjoy a freedom of expression that is denied to them in their everyday lives, thereby adding to the general air of celebration that prevails at Burning Man. Indeed, the host of opportunities for communication and interaction available at the festival are renowned as being conducive to forming friendships, and sometimes more, for if a day of sharing, giving, grooming and sex has led to greater things, and promises have been exchanged, Burners may avail themselves of the Black Rock City Wedding Chapel where they can marry *'in the splendor of a Moroccan-style bazaar'* and consummate their legal union in the civic *'Pleasure Nook'*.

Perhaps the perfect end to a perfect day at Burning Man is a sunset cruise around the playa in a mutant vehicle. Mutant vehicles are mobile works of art, licensed by the city authorities to roam its environs.[4] Vehicle mutation at Burning Man focuses on decoration, or outright transformation, rather than speed, and the results are always enchanting, and often are intended to appeal to the sense of the fantastic, or absurd: a giant mobile shark built on a truck-bed, fitted out inside with a bar and an amplified band, and provided with tow-ropes for outriders on roller-blades . . . a rickshaw drawn by a pair of robot legs . . . a cabin cruiser on wheels with a jacuzzi on its foredeck and a crew of nudes. Many of these vehicles offer not only pleasure cruises but more complex forms of entertainment. Returning to *What When Where?* 2002 for an example, the *SS Ark of the Nereids*, a two-masted boat the size of a train carriage, mounted on wheels, shaped like a fish, and equipped with a narwhale's horn for a bowsprit and a 20-foot tail, invited all-comers aboard for a spot of *'Tuvalese throat singing,*

---

4 *Per curiam*, the playa once played host to the ultimate mutant vehicle, *Thrust* – the world land speed record holder (763mph), the first and as yet only wheeled vehicle to travel faster than sound.

Middle Ages singing, acrobatics, and many other forms of self-expression', so that they might *'engage in a short, improvised opera'* whenever the vessel hove too. Mutant vehicles are clearly a wistful celebration of a key feature of American life – the automobile – and are intended to reinvest this form of transport with some of the magic that it has lost.

The playa changes character at night. Its horizons appear to contract in some directions while expanding in others. Whereas the mountains to the north and south of the desert seem to creep inwards, and squeeze Black Rock City between them after dark, the empty eastern horizon expands as stars rise over its edge, and the view in that direction can be measured in light years. Black Rock City is full of noise and motion after sundown. Generators, acoustic and amplified music, explosions close and distant, and a rumbling undertone of drums form the background sound, while cycles whirr by and mutant vehicles roll around the desert, illuminated from top to bottom, blasting out music, live and direct. The nocturnal activities on offer at Burning Man are as numerous as those available during the day, and are likewise characterised by idealism. No licensing laws are in force, nor are closing times imposed. There is dancing in every part of the city, and there are a hundred dancefloors to chose from.

Darkness also reveals the technology that underwrites Burning Man, which makes it possible for its participants to spend a week in an environment that is officially classified as uninhabitable. Technology is present not only to work but also to entertain, and the festival presents many instances of serious machines being put to frivolous uses. Here, is an example of the technophilia that characterises the event:

> The *Ship to Ship* crew are . . . two hardware engineers, several software engineers, a tech writer, and a masseuse, who have built a device where you can, at last, send a message to intelligent folks on distant planets. The device converts speech into light that is then beamed to any one of a choice of fifty stars, including the Pleiades, Betelgeuse, and Orion. Conversion is accomplished by modified xenon/mercury arc bulbs, which have been set to work in an entirely innovatory way. Transmission to the cosmos is via industrial scale equipment: a tracking mount from SETI that can handle a 3,000 pound satellite dish. 'It's this incredibly heavy industrial thing totally built for the playa' according to one of the device's inventors. *Ship to Ship* are comfortable that the messages they send will be intelligible to extra terrestrials, for 'Advanced alien cultures should be able to translate' English.

The predominant technology on display after dark at Burning Man is fire. Fire-dancing, fire-juggling, fire-eating and flame-throwing abound. Many mutant vehicles breathe fire, or shoot sheets of flame towards the stars. Pyres are located at strategic points throughout the city, so that any Burner seized by the urge to incinerate something has the means at their disposal. And there is artificial fire – from Tesla coils spitting out static electricity like lightning bolts, from lasers weaving grids overhead, and pulsing inside light sculptures on the playa.

The principal ritual of Burning Man, the sacrifice of the effigy to the flames, takes place on its last night. The conflagration is presented as a mere spectacle, a ritual without any specific purpose beyond delight. According to Larry Harvey: 'Originally, the core ritual around the man was the raising and the burning. That required that people act together, perform a co-operative action that had enormous expressive quality. But essentially we didn't have to assign any meaning to it . . . We did it because it was fun.' Harvey believes that the sole function of the conflagration is as a reference point that serves to bring all the Burners together, and that that is all – 'It's an experience, a mystery, an initiation. People are free to extract from that experience any belief which satisfies them.'

The burning ceremony, even after a week in America's most exciting city, is spectacular. The entire community gathers in the open ground at the centre of Black Rock for the event, and this is the only occasion during the festival when they see themselves en masse. A circle is marked out by a light rope around the effigy at a radius of 100 yards, and the ceremony commences with the entry of mutant vehicles mounting flame-throwers within its bounds. These pump fire into the sky, and each eruption is accompanied by a *whump!* and a rush of air. Some vehicles rely on volume for effect and mount a single powerful weapon, others on pattern of discharge and carry five or six smaller devices. The parade of flame-throwing mutant vehicles is followed by a procession of welded braziers on wheels, vomiting coloured flames, their surfaces incised with patterns and symbols that glow from the inferno within. These latter are the devices that will be used to light the effigy. The initial stage of the burning ceremony concludes with the entry of hundreds of fire-dancers into the ring, twirling poles with a swab of flame on each end, juggling flaming torches and cracking burning whips.

Meanwhile, an atmosphere of expectation develops among the

GABE KIRCHEIMER

Burners. For a week the effigy has stood alone in an empty space in the heart of their city. They have become familiar with its presence, and now it is about to leave. Noise around the ring dies down. Despite the absence of an official purpose for the ritual, Burners are nonetheless encouraged to make an act of transference during the forthcoming fire, that is to concentrate on anything they would like to eliminate from their lives and imagine that it also perishes in the flames. If their hearts have been broken, for instance, they should bid farewell to lost love, and interpret the blaze as an act of catharsis. Burners are also invited to meditate on their hopes, in particular on any specific thing they might wish to achieve, and imagine it as a phoenix emerging from the ashes. These acts of reflection are reminiscent of rituals practised at the summer solstice fire festivals held across Spain and Portugal under the auspices of St John the Baptist, at which participants make lists of the good and the bad in their lives and throw the lists of the bad into the fire. They suggest that Burners *do* attach significance to the burning, and that the effigy, bearing the sins of the community in the form of wishes and resolutions, is sacrificed to the flames as an act of purification.

The final part of the ritual commences when the arms of the effigy, which hitherto had rested at its sides, are raised into the air. Its frame is illuminated within by a network of blue neon tubes, resembling veins, that lend it the illusion of life. As emotion mounts in the crowd, and cries of 'Burn Him!' pass around the ring, a display of fireworks commences. These seem modest at first in the desert against the star-filled sky, but grow in intensity, each wave of rockets more spectacular than the last. Meanwhile, the many drummers around the circle synchronise their beat until the sound of their drums is like rainfall advancing with thunder across the surface of the ocean. All of a sudden, white fire wells up and gushes out of the pedestal on which the effigy is mounted, as if a fountain of light had been tapped under the desert floor. The tempo of the fireworks increases and fills the sky overhead with new and intricate constellations. Finally, the effigy is set on fire. Smoke billows from the pedestal, thick and turbulent like hurricane clouds. Flames take hold of the skeletal figure from top to bottom and form into a pillar, which begins to revolve, creating a whirlpool of fire stretching between the earth and sky. It is like being present in a scene from the Old Testament, when God reaches down from heaven and stirs up a maelstrom with a fingertip. It is biblical.

The conflagration is so fierce that it is over within an hour. As the flames subside, the curious convection patterns of the playa make twisters from the column of smoke rising from the ashes, and these spin off through the crowd and race away into the desert. When all that remains is a bed of glowing coals, fire-dancing commences. A wheel of Burners revolves slowly around the embers, and those who have been inspired by the conflagration dash out and dance upon the remains of the pyre. Others meanwhile give their pyromania its head by casting their works of art on to the municipal braziers, creating minor spectacles at various points in Black Rock City.

The following morning the exodus from Black Rock begins. The final commandment of Burning Man is Leave No Trace – Burners comb the desert prior to departure, collecting cigarette butts, glitter flakes, even stray human hairs so that they leave no more evidence of their presence than tyre tracks and footprints, and these are soon erased by the dust storms, cloud bursts and all the other violent natural convulsions that grace the desert.

Although the festival appears a curious exercise – build a city in a wasteland, equip it with laws and essential services, occupy it for a week, then dismantle and remove it entirely – it nonetheless has historical precedents. Burning Man is not the first occasion on which Americans have rushed off into wildernesses, with the aim of establishing a utopia, or of purifying themselves. Indeed, many of the English colonies established in America in the seventeenth century were founded with the aim of creating ideal societies, and thus in general terms prefigure the sentiment behind the event. More specifically, the two religious revivals, termed Great Awakenings, which occurred in the 1740s and at the turn of the nineteenth century, featured open-air meetings, held at some distance from civilisation, which were intended to arouse the faithful, and to turn their minds from the blandishments of society towards communication with the Almighty. Preachers would encourage their congregations at these gatherings to fling their rings, wigs and other vanities on to bonfires, and express their piety through dances, seizures and by speaking in tongues. Whilst the aim of these camp-meetings was primarily evangelical, hedonism seems to have crept into some, and there were complaints that 'More souls are begot than saved there.'

It is interesting to note the further parallels, probably accidental, between Burning Man and fundamental Christianity. The festival was founded by a carpenter, found its inspiration in a desert, is dismissive of commerce – one thinks of Jesus ejecting the moneylenders from the temple – offers a simple set of commandments to its followers, and a ritual of absolution, and it has as its motif the figure of a man with his arms and legs outstretched – as if he had been crucified in the manner of St Andrew.

However, the appearance and behaviour of its participants

suggest that Burning Man is rather a celebration of secular America, and that its attendees are patriots, vigilantes of the spirit of the Declaration of Independence, whose opening lines enshrine as self-evident 'Life, Liberty and the Pursuit of Happiness'. The pursuit of happiness was an unusual aim to include in a such a document. France, which attempted republicanism not ten years after America, did not offer happiness to its citizens. The phrase can be traced to the Roman emperor Hadrian, who broke with numismatic tradition and had the words *Libertas*, *Vida* and *Felicitas* (Liberty, Life, Happiness) inscribed on the coins of his reign, instead of the customary declarations of valour and strength. Thomas Jefferson repeated the combination when he wrote the *Declaration of Independence*, intending it to stand in contrast to the English formula 'Life, Liberty, and the ownership of property'. The pursuit of happiness has stood centre-stage in the American conscience ever since. Burners therefore do no more than their duty to their country when they assemble in Black Rock City and attempt to extend the limits of bliss.

TONY PLETTS

The idealism, the self-sufficiency and the explicit rejection of consumerism that together characterise Burning Man, likewise form the motives for a festival staged in barren terrain in West Africa. A fortnight or so after Burners have put away their fairy wings and recreational vehicles for another year, an isolated patch of semi-desert near an oasis town on an ancient caravan trail comes alive with celebration. However, the participants at this latter event do not return to their houses and jobs after the close of play — no suits, titles or salaries await them in the world beyond. The self-sufficiency they commemorate is a way of life, as opposed to a week of hedonism; their idealism a rigid and ancient moral code; and their rejection of consumerism is incidental — a consequence of choosing to live beyond its reach. Indeed, the two events are more notable for their differences than their similarities. Whereas Burning Man is staged within the territory of the wealthiest nation in the world, and is only possible through technology, the African festival occurs in one of the poorest countries on earth where the marvels of science seldom intrude. The matter it celebrates, however, whilst capable of improvement by scientific means, is accounted to be at its most compelling when it is the result of nature alone.

CAROL BECKWITH

X

AN IDEAL
FATHER

Beauty is the mother of lust, and lust, according to Plato, is 'the fiercest and most despotic' of all urges, driving men 'most powerfully to all kinds of lunacy'. The power of beauty to disturb is universally acknowledged, and as a consequence many cultures have evolved philosophies to reduce its influence, usually by depicting it as decorative and thereby intrinsically worthless. In certain societies, however, beauty is accepted as something wonderful in itself and is celebrated accordingly. The Wodaabe, a tribe of West African nomads, belong to this latter category, and value mortal beauty so highly that its recognition and praise form an important part of their rituals. Every year they gather together to identify the most attractive of their youth, and to acclaim their good looks in a festival known as *Gerewol*.[1] Gerewol takes the

---

1 While Gerewol is used as a generic term for the annual gatherings of the Wodaabe, strictly speaking it refers to a specific dance ceremony that is rarely performed authentically, and then away from the eyes of outsiders.

form of a series of dances, in which young Wodaabe men parade their beauty before the women of the tribe, who select the most appealing, judging them on their looks alone. The winners are rewarded with a night of love with the judges, and honour amongst the rest of their kindred.

While it may seem unusual that the men are the contestants at the Gerewol displays and the women are the judges, it is not unnatural, for biologically mate choice is usually a female affair. Not only peacocks, but the males of countless other species have evolved ornamental features to seduce the opposite sex. While humans do not possess the more flamboyant motifs of some of their near relatives in the animal kingdom, such as the electric blue testicles of vervet monkeys, their morphology nonetheless implies that men are built to compete for the attention of women, and this presumption is supported by a plethora of cultural evidence, ranging from the medieval concept of courtly love, to the obsessive vanity of the male characters depicted in *Saturday Night Fever*.

The Wodaabe have developed a complex ethos that justifies their worship of beauty, encourages their young to revel in their charms, and teaches them how to cultivate these from an early age. The beauty that they celebrate is a tribal ideal, although it includes certain traits that are universally considered to be enchanting, such as symmetry of features, and youth. According to the Wodaabe, the perfect man should be tall, slim yet well muscled, he should be able to dress in style and to dance well. He must be creative in the manner in which he decorates himself, and his stamina be beyond criticism. The features of his face should be symmetrical, his eyes large and round, his nose fine and long, and his teeth white and even. These are the attributes that are tested at the Gerewol festival, and which the youth of the tribe are encouraged to cultivate, as far as is possible, from the cradle. This ideal has evolved, at least in part, as a consequence of the differences in physical appearance between the Wodaabe and the other African tribes through whose territory they pass, and the desire of the Wodaabe to maintain their visual identity.

The tribe is nomadic and its members wander the savannah of West Africa in small family groups with their herds of long-horned zebu cattle for which, incidentally, they also hold beauty contests. The Wodaabe are a sub-group of the Fulani people, who themselves are the largest nomadic tribe in the world, scattered in a belt that girdles Africa between Senegal and Sudan. The Fulani as a whole trace their origin to Constantinople, the eastern capital of the Roman empire, a derivation supported by their appearance, for they are taller, more delicate of features and paler than the majority of sub-Saharan Africans. These physical differences have led to elaborate speculation among anthropologists as to their extraction and the Fulani/Wodaabe have been credited as being of Hindu, Jewish, Berber and even Malayo-Polynesian stock. History, however, locates them firmly in West Africa, where they have been documented as a distinct unit since AD 872, and archaeological evidence, in the form of cave paintings, suggests that they have been present in the region for over 6,000 years. Originally animists, they were converted to Islam in the seventeenth century, and in the following two centuries initiated a jihad that subdued the Hausa kingdoms in northern Nigeria, so that by 1830 they were masters of a considerable African empire. Many of them settled upon conquest, governing the agricultural peoples they had subjugated.

The Wodaabe played an important role in the jihad, and were rewarded with many slaves, whom they placed in villages to grow food or manufacture clothing and weapons for them – for according to their moral code, any occupation other than raising cattle was undignified. Despite the elevation of their Fulani brethren from outcasts to masters, and the augmentation of their own possessions by numerous vassals, the Wodaabe continued to live as nomads, albeit maintaining loyalty to and placing themselves under the protection of their static cousins. These ties were renewed at annual gatherings during the rainy season, in which the place of the Wodaabe in the Fulani constellation was confirmed, gifts were exchanged, and ceremonial beauty contests were staged.

The Fulani empire was gradually dismembered. In some parts

their influence decayed, in others they were supplanted by native tribes, and latterly by European imperialists. The French were the first white men to try their guns on the Fulani, and noted their discipline under fire and their bravery. The last of their dominions was subjugated by the British in 1904, who abolished slavery, superimposed a protectorate on the existing Fulani political structures, and required the nomadic sections of the group, including the Wodaabe, to pay taxes to the new administration.

After a brief stasis under colonial rule, during which period their existence was acknowledged and their interests were protected, the condition of the Wodaabe took a turn for the worse when independence was granted to the nations through which they wandered. Clumsy attempts were made to settle them in villages, they became the incidental victims of civil wars and insurrections, and recurrent droughts in the final quarter of the last century deprived many of them of their cattle, forcing them into cities to find work. In order to ensure their integrity, indeed their continuation, the Wodaabe were compelled to fall back on their ancestral moral code, which provided them with a model for survival in adversity.

The Wodaabe ancestral code in the most part is austere, making virtues out of necessities, as befits a people who live on the move and who have few assets beyond their herds. At the heart of its philosophy is the concept of *Laawol Pulaaku* – 'the Wodaabe Way' – which may be summed up as a cross between stoicism and chivalry. Pulaaku encompasses a number of virtues, including *semteende*, which governs etiquette, and requires the Wodaabe to exhibit reserve, to be formal and distant in their behaviour; *munyal*, which is patience and fortitude; and *hakkillo*, which denotes wisdom, foresight and prudence. Hakkillo is a pragmatic virtue that extends to cattle as well as humans, so that the ideal Wodaabe should always have the welfare of his herd in mind.

While the Wodaabe interpretation of Pulaaku is akin to Zen in its emphasis on self-sufficiency, simplicity and fortitude, it is more extravagant when it comes to human aesthetics. Whereas the Wodaabe would consider it ill mannered to address their own parents by name, they are happy to admit that they are the most beautiful people in the world, and that this beauty finds its perfect expression in the physical appearance of their men. Their term for beauty under the code of Pulaaku is *wodde*. Wodde does not merely imply that Wodaabe men are attractive and models of integrity, but rather that they are irresistible. This confidence-building doctrine is supplemented by the reputation that the tribe possesses for concocting love potions, whose ingredients include their own sweat, and which are said to be so effective that they will enable any man to draw the woman of his choice to his feet and to satisfy her in a manner she had previously thought impossible.

Unsurprisingly, the tribe are anxious to protect their reputation as sexual paragons, and to perpetuate their physical perfection. This latter quality is in the main secured via arranged marriages between close relatives, preferably first cousins. Couples are betrothed in their infancy, and are wedded shortly after the bride has begun to menstruate. Inter-clan marriages also serve to preserve the integrity of the tribe's beloved cattle herds. However, even the most perfect bloodlines can become corrupt, and to avoid the magnification of faults as well as virtues, the Wodaabe have established supplementary ways of forming alliances to preserve their good looks. These include polygamy, so that after a first arranged marriage, a man may take up to three more wives. These wives may be supplemented by concubines, but only so long as a husband is capable of giving sexual satisfaction to all his spouses. If he refuses a wife intercourse, then she is justified in leaving him, indeed is expected to do so. In addition to polygamy, the Wodaabe also permit a number of other types of relationships, whose purpose is to enable their women a degree of sexual freedom and choice of partner that would have them stoned to death in some Islamic societies.

Wodaabe women are free to run off at any time with any man they find attractive, and to stay with them for as long as is mutually desirable. When this state of affairs occurs it is known as a *deetuki* marriage. A woman may make as many successive deetuki marriages as she wishes. Further, if a woman finds her husband ugly, she is permitted to sleep with and to be impregnated by a man more handsome than him. These deetuki and stud arrangements allow the all important criteria of female choice to operate in a closed society without damaging its stability. Women usually return to their official husbands after a spot of deetuki, for the ownership of property (i.e., cattle) principally devolves in the male line, and as the Wodaabe proverb runs, 'a woman marries where she can get milk'.

Having glanced at the methods by which the tribe perpetuate their all important beauty, it is time to turn to the manner in which this is encouraged and developed. The central importance of good looks is literally impressed upon the Wodaabe while they are still children. Mothers massage the facial features of their babies, with the aim of moulding them closer to the tribal ideal. Infants are instructed in the use of hand mirrors – to recognise their reflection and to alter their appearance by reference to it – while still in their first year. As soon as a child can walk, it is subjected to a beauty regime that teaches it how to protect and to cultivate its appearance. It will learn, for instance, to allow the cool morning milk to warm up before drinking, lest the enamel of its teeth is put at risk. Diet is also an important factor in the Wodaabe quest for excellence. The tribe lives almost exclusively off cows' milk, augmented by butter and millet. They are extremely reluctant to slaughter or otherwise to part with their cattle, and eat meat only on the occasion of a feast, which usually is linked to a betrothal or baptismal ceremony. In addition to maintaining strict beauty and dietary regimes, the tribe also follow, albeit inadvertently, a stringent programme of exercise. The arduous nature of the nomadic life keeps them slim and fit. Both sexes cover many miles and expend much energy every day, the men in leading their cattle to pasture and drawing water for them, the women in milking and carrying the heavy calabashes of milk through the camp.

All this intricate preparation is directed ultimately at Gerewol, the annual festival of beauty, where the results of years of training and of generations of breeding will be judged. Wodaabe of both sexes begin to learn the special skills that they will need for Gerewol in their teenage years. The boys are given training in the science of make-up and the manufacture of love potions; the girls are taught the arts of tattooing and embroidery. All attend the *hirde*, the evening gatherings of the youth of the tribe in the bush, where younger members are instructed by their elder brothers and sisters in the songs and the dance steps that are employed at the festival. Whenever sufficient members of a clan are gathered in one place, a fire is lit away from the tribal encampment, in the vicinity of which the young men arrange themselves in a circle, leaning against one another, and sing their polyphonic songs, swaying and clapping in time. The girls meanwhile form another circle and also sing, letting their voices mingle with those of their clan brothers. Visitors who have been privileged to witness these gatherings have found them exhilarating – the powerful yet harmonious music in the still desert nights, at the edge of the firelight, overlooked by the African stars, and distant from any settlement, for 'Only in the immense savannah, far away from the eyes of strangers, do these eternal wanderers give themselves to celebration.'

These desert celebrations usually end in embraces, for unmarried Wodaabe of either sex enjoy an even greater sexual licence than their elders. During the course of the circular dances, which spin slowly in an anti-clockwise direction, the inner circle of boys moves faster than that of the girls, and if a girl is attracted to one of the men as he passes, she will stroke him softly on the back, to signify her desire. A tryst is then arranged with eye and hand signals, indicating the point in the savannah where they should meet to pass the night. Although such freedom of liaison is at odds with Islam, the nominal faith of the tribe, it would have won the approval of Socrates, who considered premarital sex to be an essential safety valve whose purpose was to release the 'pressures of lust'. Its functions in Wodaabe society appear to be to reinforce bonds between its members and to provide a sensual reward for their efforts in the cause of beauty.

The Wodaabe spend the greater part of the year moving
between water supplies, travelling from well to well across the
arid savannah. Throughout this period their contact with other
clans of their tribe, or indeed any other people at all, is limited to
chance meetings in the bush, or occasional visits to villages that
lie in the path of their migrations. When the rains commence they
follow the clouds, leading their herds to where shoots have
emerged and puddles have collected. The brief rainy season,
encompassing July and August, is a time of plenty, during which
their cattle will regain the weight and form they lost during the
harsh dry months. It is also the period for reunions between the
clans, for betrothals and for Gerewol. The approach of the festival
is eagerly anticipated by young and old alike. For the youth of the
tribe it is an opportunity to parade their beauty and win honour,
the young belles look forward to being seduced, married women
who are bored meditate on the chance for some deetuki, and
every member of every generation anticipates the pleasures of
company after a year of wandering.

One of the principal September gatherings of Wodaabe, and
celebrations of Gerewol, takes place in the vicinity of InGall, an
oasis town in a semi-desert zone that forms the gateway to the
Sahara. InGall is a conglomeration of mud houses, whose
gardens, in contrast to the barren landscape in which the town is
set, are filled with fruit trees and vegetable patches. It is
dominated by its mosque, whose pyramidal tower, built from
mud and stones and spiked with the projecting ends of wooden
beams, is the tallest building for a thousand miles around. InGall
is encircled by saline terrain, hence its attraction to several clans
of Wodaabe who bring their cattle to feast on the salt-enriched
grasses that springs up in the rainy season, and thus replenish
their reserves of this vital chemical.

There is an audience of non-Wodaabe at InGall during
Gerewol, for the Tuareg, a Berber tribe of nomads, also gather
around the oasis at the same time of year, likewise attracted by its

salty grazing. The government of Niger takes advantage of this concentration of its wandering subjects and sends officials to broadcast health messages over a tannoy, which encourage the members of the various tribes to wash their food before eating it, to vaccinate their children, and to beware of the AIDS risk posed by casual sex. As a consequence of all these converging people, InGall becomes a party town for the month of September. The masses of nomads in exotic clothing, the long-horned cattle of the Wodaabe, the thoroughbred camels of the Tuareg, and the health and other government officials are supplemented by the Landcruisers and Land-Rovers of foreign spectators and also, finally, by the inhabitants of the town itself, who live a life more lonely than their visitors, marooned in their oasis on the edge of the Sahara.

The Wodaabe travel to InGall in clans. Each of these forms a column of herds, interspersed with tribes-people mounted on camels and donkeys, or on foot. Their arrival is usually heralded by a gang of charging camels, whose riders sit high up and cross-legged on their mounts, swathed in robes and cloaks that mask them entirely barring their mouths and noses. This advance party of men of a fighting age is followed by the women, leading pack oxen which are laden with their precious calabashes, any children not able to walk, and the occasional kid or calf which cannot maintain the pace of the herd. Young boys keep the animals in good order, walking or running alongside their charges, armed with wands which they use to redirect strays back into the column with gentle and indeed respectful blows.

The Wodaabe dress predominantly in indigo, or black, and their preference for sombre clothing has given them a dark reputation amongst the settled tribes through whose territory they pass. This reputation is compounded by their unusual markings and their hairstyles. Wodaabe women wear their hair in a bun on their foreheads, the men in long braids that resemble pigtails. Both sexes use make-up in their day to day wanderings: indeed a man would not consider appearing before his cattle without first applying mascara. Each Wodaabe man carries a short sword and a *malafaare*, a broad-brimmed straw hat when on the move. In contrast to the rest of their everyday clothing, the malafaares are exuberant creations, bursting with colour and decoration, and crowned with ostrich feathers and a button that represents the mythical 'Mount of the World'. Their fashions change each year, like the hats at Royal Ascot, and a Wodaabe man will do his best to ensure that his malafaare is *à la mode*, even undertaking special missions into villages to enlist the aid of their craftsmen in customising his headpiece.

The Wodaabe lay out their camps to a formula. The notional front of each faces west. The camping ground is divided according to clan, and within these divisions into families. The most senior families camp at the front of the section of ground occupied by their clan, to the south-west. Each family takes a circular pitch, perhaps 15 yards in diameter, that they divide across the middle with a calf rope, made of plaited leather to which the unweaned calves are tethered. In front of the rope are the corral and the men's quarters. Women occupy the semi-circle of the camp beyond the calf rope, and the family's few possessions are stored in their section. These consist in the main of nesting sets of milk calabashes, festival-going clothes, and in the case of each married woman, a travelling version of a four-poster bed. The beds have canopies of bark over their sleeping platforms, and form the principal type of shelter used by the tribe, as the Wodaabe seldom erect huts. A married man will visit the beds of each of his wives in rotation on successive nights for his evening meal of milk, and to perform his conjugal duties. Unmarried members of the tribe sleep on bark mats under the stars, which they cover with boughs should it rain.

While Pulaaku forbids explicit displays of excitement, there is a mounting sense of anticipation as the various kin groups assemble around InGall and set up camp. In some years up to 1,000 members of the tribe can gather for Gerewol. The Gerewol festival is an inter-clan affair, in which women of two separate lineages will judge the beauty of the men from opposite clans, and everyone is curious to sneak a look at the competition before the celebrations commence. There is much to-ing and fro-ing around the camps, in excess of the necessary formalities attendant upon an annual reunion.

The forthcoming festivities consist of competitive dances which serve as beauty contests, supplemented by cattle-judging events (the *beefootirki*), and displays by the married women of the tribe of their milk calabashes and other prized possessions. There are strict limitations on who may appear in the dance contests. Gerewol is an initiation ceremony for the young, and once a man has married and bred, he cuts his hair, grows a beard, and refrains from competition. In limiting participants by age, the festival acknowledges tacitly that beauty is a quality enjoyed only by youth, and one that cannot be replaced by artifice once it has passed.

At the break of dawn on the day that has been fixed for the festival to commence, a woman sings out in the Wodaabe encampment, encouraging the young to rise in readiness for the dancing ahead: 'The morning star has arisen! Beautiful girls! Handsome boys! Get up before the day begins!' The young men commence their beauty preparations at once, while the girls enquire of one another 'Where will the sun rise today?': a veiled reference to which of the men will be chosen as the most attractive at the forthcoming contest. The principal competitive dance performed at the festival is called the *yaake*. A yaake is intended to allow its participants to demonstrate their overall physical presence, their poise and sense of rhythm, and the particular beauty of their facial features. As a spectacle, it is a cross between opera, ballet and a drag show, performed without props in the middle of a semi-desert.

The young men who will participate in the yaake spend hours at their toilet. They shave their hairline to elongate their foreheads, and make up their faces with the aid of a hand mirror, the indispensable accessory of a Wodaabe male. They begin with the application of a yellow foundation to their entire face, whose purpose is to isolate it against their darker bodies. Next, they outline their eyes and lips in black, to emphasise through contrast the milky whiteness of their eyes and teeth. A single white line is drawn on their forehead, nose and chin to divide their faces perpendicularly, and a circle composed of white dots, like a daisy, is created on each cheek. These circles are a tribal pattern and represent *suura*, or camps. The preparations are communal: members of each clan assist one another with their toilet, and share cosmetics amongst themselves. Both the foundation and the lipstick worn at the festival are composed of rare ingredients that are considered to have magical properties. The face powder, for example, is only to be found beside a special mountain near Jongooria in central Niger, and some clans of Wodaabe must undertake a 1,400-kilometre round trip on foot in order to secure a supply.

Once their faces are ready the participants tie amulet bags, necklaces and crosses around their necks, then dress in tunics that hang to their ankles, the fronts of which are embroidered with coloured beads and thread in linear patterns – slender trails of scarlet, of canary yellow and of emerald, interspersed with cowrie shells. Their heads are wrapped in white turbans, surmounted with a single ostrich feather. The overall effect is startling, not to say ambiguous, for the yaake look is very feminine. In many other cultures the participants would be accused of cross-dressing. Although the overall form of costume is traditional, competitors are happy to augment their decorations with any new technology to hand, and will include zips in their embroidery, whose steel is burnished until it gleams, or hang plastic watches on their necklaces. Invention in ornamentation is valued by the tribe, who believe that it demonstrates a creative spirit in its wearer. Each candidate for the yaake is a perfectionist in his preparations, and searches to find the precise arrangement and balance of decoration he believes will highlight his beauty to its best effect. It is as if instinct has given every youth an ideal pattern to interpret and reproduce. The finishing touches are provided by a splash of perfume – a favourite brand is 'Bint-el-Sudan' – and a few drops of magic potion, whereupon the contestant is ready to show his charms to the world.

While the participants are absorbed with their meticulous beauty regime, the only other preparation necessary for the event is the selection of a suitable piece of open ground on which the ceremonies will take place. The Wodaabe do not require a formal stage for their festival, nor props, bunting, sideshows, or any of the other paraphernalia that tends to accumulate around public spectacles. Gerewol is conducted with nomadic self-sufficiency, and all that is needed for its celebration is a patch of savannah, and the presence and enthusiasm of its participants. There are no illusions on show, only people and their voices, and the festival is created in its entirety with these uncomplicated yet persuasive components. It is beautifully simple.

The yaake begins in the heat of the day, which is usually well over 100° Fahrenheit. It opens with a call, a single sustained note, and the competitors drift towards the vicinity of the singer and assemble in a line, divided into their respective clans by a space in the middle. Together, they create a startling visual effect, as if an elegant rank of warriors had sprung up from the dust, the tall and slender body of each emphasised by the single ostrich plume quivering in their headbands. They are all beautiful, and their looks are complemented by their poise and their grace. They take up the note and a song develops – rhythmic, call and answer. They sway from side to side as they sing and once they are underway the clans gather in a semi-circle in front of them, men to the right, women and children to the left, the leaders in a cluster in the middle. The young men on show develop their chant, while the backing singers weave emotion into the music, so that at times it is tender, at others forceful. Its polyphonies are interspersed with dancing. The performers raise themselves on tip-toe to emphasise their height, advance a pace or so, then retreat. Sweat streaks their bodies, and their voices and their movements blend together. The display takes on a cyclical form as the participants pass from music to dance and back again. Although each man is aiming to demonstrate individual perfection, collectively they present a harmonious unit that gives great power to the spectacle.

The yaake is as much about function as of form. It celebrates the vital beauty that cannot be frozen by a camera to adorn a magazine cover. Not only are good looks required of its participants, but also movement and stamina. Rather than leaving this last virtue to be implied from appearance, by striking up poses, it must be demonstrated. The dance lasts for five or six hours, for every minute of which the dancers are expected to remain both sprightly and enchanting. This is rather like requiring the participants in a conventional beauty contest to run a marathon in their make-up. The importance of both endurance and style in dancing to the Wodaabe is summed up in one of their proverbs: 'The bad dancer deserves neither food nor drink.'

The yaake contest also focuses on facial beauty and the charm with which it is expressed. Not content to let their cosmetic skills bring out their best features, the competitors animate these with a variety of expressions intended to highlight their perfections. The line of young men presents a truly hallucinogenic vision: they cross their eyes and roll them around in their sockets, thus confirming the ample expanse of white that these possess; and their even and flawless teeth are demonstrated through comically exaggerated smiles which are timed to coincide with their eye movements. A man who can roll one eye and grin simultaneously is considered especially captivating. These manoeuvres are augmented by other facial contortions: the dancers pout their lips, puff out their cheeks, vibrate their throats, and produce clicking sounds, all of which are calculated to throw the female part of their audience into raptures of desire.

The use of artificial stimulants amongst contestants is permitted, indeed is universal. Before lining up for a yaake, the young men will drink a cocktail that contains a psychoactive bark, which will assist them to put on their best face, make their most

CAROL BECKWITH

elegant moves, and to stay on their feet all night.[2] This laissez-faire attitude towards performance-enhancing substances, pace Mr Universe contests, is yet another point of difference between the festival and the common or garden beauty pageant. The competitors in a yaake do not have the luxury of announcing themselves by name, nor of providing a résumé of any skills or ambitions that they may possess. Instead, they must project their beauty and their personality through presence alone, and against the considerable charms of their peers who are ranged alongside. Furthermore, they must maintain their composure in the face of antagonism, for when a youth advances on tip-toe from the rank of dancers, he will often give a surreptitious shove

2 Interesting parallels exist between the yaake dance and the Saturday night celebrations of the young men of Newcastle.

to the man beside him to throw him off balance or destroy his harmony of movement. According to the Wodaabe, *Fijjo kamma habre* – 'Dance is war' – and foul as well as fair means are employed to gain victory in the contest.

The use of magic during play is also sanctioned. The Wodaabe have a very real fear of its powers, and to many of the contestants the air about them is filled with a crossfire of spells, any one of which might make them stumble or paint a frown upon their faces. The amulet bags they wear around their necks are intended to counter this fusillade and to drive away any curses that their opponents may have launched to make them appear ugly or clumsy. Indeed, every ingredient of their make-up has defensive as well as decorative properties. Their magic black lipstick, for example, which is manufactured from the charred bones of a cattle egret, is believed not only to enable the wearer to vibrate their lips in an irresistible manner, but also to protect these from being hexed into paralysis.

The two groups of dancers in the yaake contest are judged separately by a jury of three young women of the opposing lineage. Only one winner is chosen from each group. The selection process is identical in each case, and is as follows. Once the contestants have been allowed to build up a head of steam, a process that takes many hours, the first jury makes a hesitant entrance into the open semi-circle of space between the crowd and the dancers, and kneels down. Their heads are lowered, their eyes downcast, and they are pictures of modesty. Wodaabe women are every bit as beautiful as the men. They are slender, with sparkling eyes, delicate features and are similarly graceful in their movements. While they wear less make-up than the boys, they adorn themselves with equal care. Their necks are encircled with bead necklaces and amulet bags, their wrists with a dozen or so coloured bracelets. Their ears are pierced with large hoops of silver or gold. Those who are traditionalists will have thick brass bangles around their ankles, intended to give them a 'cow-like' step – a prized virtue in their cattle culture.

CAROL BECKWITH

The arrival of the objects of their desire in front of them arouses the young men to greater efforts. If they prove themselves beautiful enough, they will be rewarded with beauty, and will have their pick of all the watching women. This magnificent equilibrium between participants and prizes illustrates the purity of ethos behind Gerewol, and confirms that the greatest incentive that can be offered to the beautiful is the prospect of provoking longing in the heart of someone who attracts them.

Once the jury have made their entry into the arena and have sunk to their knees, a hush comes over the spectators. Their attention has wandered between the dancers and each other during the long course of the spectacle. The old have whiled away the hours in reminiscence, the young in fantasising. They watch in silence as the three girls are raised to their feet one by one by a tribal elder, after which they proceed in single file towards the line of competitors, their eyes still downcast, hands cupped in front of their faces. Their movements are unhurried and ceremonial, and are followed by the spectators with breathless anticipation. The jury passes slowly along the grimacing rank of suitors, every one of whom is doing his best to make himself irresistible. But even the beautiful can be graded – it is as if we carry some ideal standard within us and search for its closest match in the flesh.

The moment of selection is one of the few occasions on which the straitjacket of Pulaaku is laid aside. The jury of girls announces its verdict by stopping in front of one of the participants, indicating in the most casual way – a slight inclination of the shoulders of the lead girl – that *he* is the most desirable, and the entire tribe breaks out in shouts of praise. To be Wodaabe is to be beautiful, so the selection of a paragon is a celebration of not just an aesthetic, but also of a tribal ideal. The victor of the contest will be remembered for generations and commemorated in song. He can expect as many wives as his wealth will afford and as many lovers as his stamina permits.

The process is then repeated with the second jury choosing its champion from the opposing clan, and the dance closes amid scenes of jubilation. However, the exertions of the dancers do not end when the yaake finishes, for every participant will have caught the eye of several women in the crowd, and will be the subject of many discreet approaches. However, in order to be sure of the favours of their admirers, the young men are expected to demonstrate gallantry and wit in keeping with their elegant performance in the dance. According to Wodaabe theory, these will be every bit as compelling as their exteriors, for beauty is considered to be indicative of underlying virtue. This belief manifests itself in tribal proverbs, in particular those relating to the nose, the shape of which is thought to be the key to facial beauty, and therefore also, in a manner reminiscent of Pinocchio, probity. *Raara kine nana gikku*, for example ('See the nose, understand the character'), is a common Wodaabe saying, and should a member of the tribe suffer a setback, they will be described as having been 'struck on the nose'. The participants, therefore, will be required to live up to their noses, even after hours of exertion under the glare of the blazing sun.

In addition to presenting an enchanting spectacle, the festival also provides opportunities for women to elope, or to spy out a potential partner in the crowd whose good looks will justify an affair. Since beauty is accepted as an end in itself, and vital to tribal identity, infidelity in the cause of aesthetics is not so much an indiscretion as an established custom, sanctioned by precedent. Furthermore, since beauty also implies virtue, a quest for beauty, for the ideal father, can only be virtuous. Besides, Gerewol festivals would have less attractive competitors if they were all the results of arranged marriages between first cousins.

Married Wodaabe men are also on the lookout for a new lover in the audience. The festival is notorious as an occasion during which *kordotas*, or wife thieves, are on the prowl. Kordotas rely on charisma rather than violence or sleight of hand to abduct the women of other men, and their victims are invariably willing. However, a ceremonial fuss is made should a wife be stolen, and the thief will bring honour to his clan. The knowledge that kordotas are operating adds an air of danger to the celebrations, and allows an otherwise permissive society to enjoy the frisson of scandal.

The arid environs of InGall witness a surprising concentration of beauty contests during September. While the Wodaabe are celebrating their own good looks, the Tuareg tribe who have gathered in the same place at the same time stage tournaments between their camels. There are contests for the fastest, the best behaved and the most attractive camel, with substantial money prizes in each category. It seems that once the urge to discriminate amongst living things on aesthetic grounds is given its head, there is no creature alive, excepting perhaps such prodigies of ugliness as the Javan Warty Pig, that cannot be ranked as to individual beauty.

The innocent pleasure of differentiating by appearance is out of fashion in the first world, indeed in some countries it is grounds

CAROL BECKWITH

for litigation. As a consequence beauty concourses – Miss Worlds and Mr Universes – are debased versions of the genre. The female contest is compromised by its insistence that participants must give evidence of ambitions beyond being celebrated merely for their looks, and the examples of male excellence on display at Mr Universe are considered by the women for whom they should be competing to be gross caricatures of their desires. Gerewol, in contrast, focuses on the superficial, and the ability of good looks to provoke lust in the opposite sex. Moreover, the beauty that the festival celebrates is considered to be short lived: it is a gift confined to the young and is left to them to parade for the delectation of all.

A hunger to be beautiful and a thirst for attention are perhaps the greatest self-indulgences of the nomadic Wodaabe, who otherwise make a virtue out of asceticism. They do not generate the surpluses of the settled cultures that they scorn, and have little interest in and few opportunities for gluttony or drunkenness. The rare occasions on which they slaughter a heifer – to commemorate a betrothal for example – are ceremonial events as opposed to simple exercises in self-gratification.

In contrast, agricultural societies celebrate the bounty that they gather from the fertile earth with feasting and excess. The same moon that foretells the end of the rains in Niger announces the arrival of the harvest in northern Europe, a season of abundance. It is a time to indulge in the pleasures of eating and drinking, and to enjoy the fruits of patient months of cultivation. Its arrival puts a spring in the step of every epicure, great numbers of whom hasten to a major German city where delight in appetite and its satisfaction are celebrated at the largest festival in the world. This event, staged in a vast, artificial Arcadia, encourages feats of endurance in consumption, and not merely of the raw produce of field, orchard and forest, but also and in particular, of a refined foodstuff that leaves its consumers inspired as well as sated.

REUTERS/MICHAELA REHLE

XI

THE FAT OF
THE LAND

Beer is proof that God loves us and wants us to he happy
BENJAMIN FRANKLIN

A current theory in archaeology holds that mankind cultivated grain not to bake bread, but to brew beer, and that this useful fluid is the original 'Staff of Life'. The contribution made by beer to human nourishment and happiness is acknowledged and celebrated, by drinking it in immense quantities over a sixteen-day festival held in Munich, the capital of the German province of Bavaria. The *Oktoberfest*, as this event is known, in addition to offering beer galore, presents its participants with the opportunity to feast on a variety of animals that have been fattened up for their delectation, and also provides a giant funfair to assist them with their digestion. It is held on a dedicated piece of ground within Munich, forming a city within a city for its duration. Vast crowds, many dressed in traditional costume, gather in its brightly coloured beer tents to drink, to sing and to gorge themselves. This simple formula of entertainment has led to the Oktoberfest becoming the most popular annual festival on the planet. Around 6 million people visit it each year, and indulge in a frenzy of feasting, which in turn generates an orgy of statistics. At the millennial event, for example, 6.2 million litres of beer, 750,000 chickens, 300,000 sausages, 81,000 pork knuckles and 73 oxen, all of them fat, vanished down the throats of celebrants.

Strictly speaking, the Oktoberfest commemorates neither beer nor gluttony, but rather the wedding anniversary of a prince and a princess long since dead, of a principality that now forms part of a republic. It was first celebrated on 17 October 1810, on the occasion of the marriage of Prince Ludwig I of Bavaria to Princess Therese von Sachsen-Hildburghausen. The royal couple wished to make a spectacle of their nuptials, so a horserace was organised to draw the crowds, refreshments were laid on, and 30,000 out of Munich's total population of 40,683 attended. Prince Ludwig's subjects elected to show their gratitude by celebrating his first wedding anniversary in a similar fashion, adding a livestock show to the festivities. They repeated their displays of loyalty in subsequent years, and continued to do so after the abdication of Ludwig I following a scandalous affair with a dancer.[1] Despite this setback, the Oktoberfest retained its royal patronage, for in the intervening years it had grown to become much more than the celebration of a failed marriage, having absorbed various aspects of Bavarian culture, to the extent that it had come to be perceived of as its showcase. The festival continued to fulfil this role over

---

1 The infamous Lola Montez, an Irish woman born in India who pretended to be Spanish, and who caught Ludwig's eye by exposing her breasts to him during a private audience.

subsequent decades, acquiring a parade of traditional dress, another of brewers, and a third of oompah bands. Tents were erected to sell refreshments, and the automata which grace Bavarian cathedrals appeared on their façades. These *Festhallen*— became ever larger and more elaborate over time and their interiors, capable of seating thousands, were decorated with another Bavarian motif – the forest and its animals. Moreover, the Bavarian tradition for music, both high and low, became attached to the Oktoberfest. Bands were installed in its Festhallen, and popular music was composed in its honour. The meadow in which the event was held was named the Theresienwiese, or Wiesn, in honour of Princess Therese, the royal bride, and set aside for its sole use. Finally, an immense bronze statue of a semi-naked woman, representing Bavaria, was cast and seated on a plinth to overlook the annual revels.

Despite all this Bavarianness, the Oktoberfest became famous and was imitated abroad, not for its wurst, oompah music and *Lederhosen*, but rather for the fervent consumption of beer by its participants. It has been copied in many countries: towns in America, Japan and even French Canada have instituted Oktoberfests of their own, some of which have already celebrated centenaries. All of these reproductions have been founded on the assumption that beer is the essence of the original festival, indeed that beer is the soul of Bavaria, and the rest of the Oktoberfest is no more than a collection of decorative rituals intended to enliven beer drinking. While the festival is certainly more complex than the wassail in fancy dress suggested by its mimics, tippling does indeed form its core ritual, and a sketch of the history of beer will provide an indication of why this is such a pleasant and compelling pastime.

Beer, a drink made from brewed, fermented and flavoured cereals, has long and illustrious associations with Munich, and indeed mankind. Evidence of brewing has been discovered amid the debris of our most ancient cities, and the remains of the world's oldest brewery, founded in Hierakonopolis in Egypt c.5600 BC, are testament to the importance of beer in the diet of early domesticators, for the brewery was capable of producing up to 300 gallons of beer per day for a population of only 200. The drink that it manufactured was very different from the 'amber nectar' of the present age. It was a cloudy liquid, low in alcoholic strength, that still contained the husks of the grain from which it had been made, and had to be drunk through straws. The ancient Egyptians used beer as a currency – indeed, their word for beer, *kash*, is still in use as a term for money. Beer had spread to Europe by c. 3000 BC – residues in drinking vessels dating from this period have been discovered in the Neolithic village of Skara Brae in the Orkney Islands, and it is likely that its consumption in Germany commenced during the same era. The earliest archaeological evidence of beer in Bavaria dates to 800 BC, when pots of it were included amongst the grave goods of a fallen warrior. Its persistence was documented by the Romans, who reached Germany seven and a half centuries later, and recorded of its inhabitants that, 'for their drink, they draw a liquor from barley or other grain; and ferment the same so as to make it resemble wine'. The Romans also observed that the Germans did not merely drink beer to assuage their thirsts, but also for the joy of intoxication, and that drunkenness was obligatory whenever any matter of importance was to be debated amongst themselves, such as the election of a new ruler, or whether or not to go to war. Such compulsory inebriation was justified on the grounds that 'at no season is the soul more open to thoughts that are artless and upright, or more fired with such as are great and bold'.

After Germany fell under the sway of Rome, the vine and bread were introduced, but neither of these staples of Classical civilisation supplanted beer in German affections, despite a tie to the imperial power that lasted for over 400 years. When the tie was severed in the fifth century AD, the present region of Bavaria was settled by a confederation of tribes called the Baiuoarii, from whom its name derives, and who brought with them a mythology built around brewing, tree worship and war. Several centuries later, when Bavaria was visited by Christian missionaries from Ireland and England, beer drinking and the worship of sacred groves were considered to be the principal obstacles to the conversion of the Bavarians. The missionaries struggled manfully and, if their biographers are to be believed, had some successes – notably against the trees. Saint Boniface, an Englishman né Wynfrith martyred by the Frisians in AD 754, is recorded as having destroyed a mighty oak dedicated to the pagan god of thunder with a prayer, a penknife and a single cut. Beer, however, was harder to displace and so was absorbed instead. Monasteries appeared in Bavaria and opened breweries, for both the good of their flocks and the sustenance of their monks. This latter class considered it a godsend, for their calendar was littered with fasts, and it was permissible to drink beer while on a diet of bread and water. Monks were, however, limited to a daily allowance of five litres per head.

By the eleventh century there were over 300 monastic breweries in Bavaria, one of which, founded by the Benedictine order in the eighth century, occupied the site of present-day Munich. It was settled on as the location for a new town by King Henry the Lion in 1138, and named after the monks – Munichen. The town was gifted a salt monopoly and flourished: it lay at the crossroads of Europe and became a centre of transcontinental trade. Its breweries and monasteries multiplied. The former were in particular demand with the onset of the 'little ice age' (1300–1900), when the nutritional properties of beer, and the warming sensation created by the alcohol it contained were highly valued. Beer was the ideal bulwark against long, dark winters and frozen landscapes. It was also a fine method of storing cereals. Indeed, its consumption was considered so important in that cold and cruel age, that it became the subject of a popular German saying: 'drink beer and become fat, drink water and die'. It must be noted that throughout this period the production and consumption of beer was unisexual. Brew-kettles, and the knowledge of how to use them, were considered to be an essential part of any bride's dowry. There were brew-nuns, known as *brewsters*, as well as brew-monks, one of whom, Hildegard von Bingen, was the first to advocate the use of hops in beer, on account of their medicinal value. However, whether produced by brewsters or brewers, medieval beer resembled soup. It was a thick, dark liquid, with chunks of its ingredients, including grains and herbs such as bog myrtle present in every mouthful. No two pints could ever be the same, in flavour, alcoholic strength, or even texture. Despite this inconsistency, it was considered indispensable, and its production was a lucrative business.

Beer became something of a political football in Germany in the late Middle Ages, with the Church, the feudal lords and the new class of merchants fighting for the rights to brew or to tax it. While all three powers suffered triumphs and reverses, control of the breweries slowly moved into the hands of the commercial class, albeit with strict controls on who might brew and where their product could be sold. Such controls had beneficial side effects for drinkers, for in addition to enacting a series of revenue protection laws, known collectively as *Bierzwang* ('beer coercion'), which limited consumers to locally brewed and taxed products, many German principalities also introduced quality-related legislation. In Munich, for example, brewers were only allowed to work between St Michael's Day (29 September) and St George's Day (23 April), and their product was subject to the *Reinheitsgebot*, introduced in 1516, which stipulated that beer could only be made from brewed water, malt, hops and yeast, and which is still observed.[2] The imposition of a brewing season, intended to prevent bad beer being produced in the hot summer months, had two important consequences for Munich. First, by

---

2 The Reinheitsgebot was declared illegal by the European Union in 1987 as being in restraint of free trade, in order that Bavarians might have access to beer with chemical additives. The brewers of Munich, however, continue to follow the old rules.

limiting brewing to cold weather, the regulators effectively restricted the type of beer that could be produced in the town to lager, as ale yeasts (as a general rule) do not work at low temperatures. Second, at the commencement of each new brewing season there was an excess of last year's product to clear, and hence a tradition of drinking large quantities of beer in late September was established centuries before the first Oktoberfest.

Quality controls and brewing seasons resulted in great improvements in the general standard of beer. The bog myrtle and the unidentifiable lumps of floating matter vanished from the average brew. However, and despite the onset of the age of enlightenment, the process by which beer became alcoholic was not yet understood, and as befits a mystery, the best and strongest beer was still brewed by Catholic monks, in particular by the obscure Paulist sect, whose monastery was located just outside Munich. This order had the little known St Francis of Paola as its patron, and to commemorate his saint's day on 2 April, they manufactured a super-strong beer named *Heilig-Vater-Bier* ('Holy Father beer'), which was later abbreviated to 'Salvator'. This was distributed to the needy who gathered at the gates of the monastery every year, and the annual act of charity metamorphosed into Munich's other beer festival, the *Starkbierfest*, which is still celebrated in April – although the production of Salvator has long since passed into the hands of laymen.

The ecclesiastical production of beer in Munich was terminated in the first decade of the nineteenth century as a consequence of the Napoleonic wars. The French occupied parts of Germany, forced Bavaria into an alliance, and set about rearranging Europe's frontiers, laws, roads and social institutions. The monasteries were dissolved and their breweries were taken over by merchants. In addition to removing the production of beer from the hands of churchmen, Napoleon was also indirectly responsible for the birth of the Oktoberfest. He promoted the feudal rulers of Bavaria from the status of Herzog, or duke, to that of king, and these responded with an increase in pomp, hence the public extravaganza surrounding the royal wedding in 1810.

Science and industry began to intrude upon the art of brewing from the middle of the nineteenth century onwards, resulting in significant changes to the appearance and character of beer. In 1851, an Australian named James Harrison constructed a refrigeration device for a brewery in Sydney, with the aim of achieving control over the temperature of the fermentation of its product. A few years later a 'cold machine', the forerunner of the modern refrigerator, was installed in the Spaten brewery in Munich. After temperature control, which assisted brewers in producing a consistent brew, came an even greater breakthrough. In 1868 Louis Pasteur published *Etudes sur la bière*, which explained the process of fermentation, and which enabled brewers, for the first time in history, to understand why beer was alcoholic. These twin advances, together with the development of the beer filter shortly afterwards, resulted in the production of a clear, refreshing and stimulating fluid, that could be relied upon to taste the same from glass to glass – in other words, modern beer.

Having glanced at the roots of the cult of beer, and the firm hold they have taken in Bavaria, the importance of the substance to the Oktoberfest is unsurprising. A festival surrounding beer carries the most awesome associations in the Bavarian mind, for the Bavarians, indeed most Germans, have preserved as valid every one of the historical reasons that have been employed to justify its consumption. It is still considered to be food in Germany: nursing mothers are encouraged to drink some every day to help them to make milk, and men involved in the manual trades breakfast on it. Beer is also still in use as a tool for decision-making – the role it served in Roman times. It has been a part of the German identity for nearly 3,000 years, and under strict quality control for almost 500 years. Brewing beer has strong associations with the various powers that have ruled over German territory. The Catholic Church, its feudal princes and the emergent class of merchants have all added something to its allure and history. Finally, it has inspired German artists in every medium to celebrate it in their works. There are Germanic odes, paintings, choral works, fairytales, sculptures, and even philosophies dedicated to beer drinking. Such is the pedigree of the substance on sale to all-comers at the Oktoberfest.

Although the quality of the beer served at the festival improved steadily over its first seventy years, and has remained consistently excellent ever since, the event itself has experienced considerable fluctuations in popularity. Its opening decades were ones of continuous growth – in 1835 the Oktoberfest was recorded as having become so extravagant a spectacle that it 'exceeded anything that might have been seen before in Germany'. Not only was its expansion rapid, it also enjoyed a soaring reputation as an ideal kind of entertainment for the masses. The Oktoberfest came to be seen as a model form of popular celebration, and in 1850 an attempt was made to revive the ancient Olympic Games (which had not been commemorated since AD 393), with the aim of making them part of its festivities. It seems, however, that competitive athletics were incompatible with rampant epicureanism, and the Olympics had to wait another forty-six years before they were restored to the calendar of celebration.

By the turn of the twentieth century, however, the Oktoberfest had begun to attract criticism as well as praise. In 1910, Thomas Mann described the festival as a 'monstrous' event, 'where a defiant people corrupted by modern mass movements, celebrate their Saturnalia'. When the masses were sent into the trenches in World War I the festival was cancelled, lest it tempted them to reflect on the potential of good fellowship between strangers. It was revived in 1920, but cancelled again in 1923, when Germany was in the grip of hyper-inflation and there were few who could afford to pay the asking price of 21 million marks per litre of beer.

The Oktoberfest recovered quickly from this low point and within five years it had regained its reputation as an event where the masses might both indulge and express themselves. The author Thomas Wolfe paid a visit in 1928 and left a picture of proceedings:

> The beer tents are absolutely enormous and alarming – in one single tent there are four to five thousand people in one spot – you can hardly breathe or move. A Bavarian band with 40 players is producing a horrendous noise. The noise is fantastic – you could cut the air with a knife – and in these [tents] you discover the heart of Germany, not the heart of the poet and the thinker, but its real heart, which is really nothing but a monstrous stomach. They eat and drink and breathe themselves into a frenzy of animal-like apathy – the whole tent becomes a screaming roaring beast, and when the music plays one of their drinking songs, they all jump onto the tables, climb onto chairs, and sway arm in arm.

Unfortunately, such concentrated excitement led to the festival, and the culture that it represented of mass inebriation and an idealistic view of the past, being appropriated for more sinister ends. Although himself a teetotaller, Adolf Hitler was inspired by the potential commensal drinkers offered as an audience and attempted his first *Putsch* in a Munich beer cellar in 1932. The damages bill for this failed coup of 143 steins, ninety-eight stools, two music stands, all of them smashed, and 148 stolen sets of cutlery, remains unpaid. Upon attaining power, Hitler made Munich the headquarters of the Nazi party, endowing it with the Haus der Kunst, a museum dedicated to Nazi art, and Dachau concentration camp in the countryside nearby. The Oktoberfest was forced into service as a showpiece of Aryan culture until the outbreak of the World War II, whereupon it was labelled as decadent and prohibited. It was not revived until 1949.

When the festival was restarted it was intended that it would

serve as a recreation of Bavarian life before it had been blighted by the horrors of fascism – to be the sort of event that might be found in a fairytale and enjoyed by anyone, whatever their creed, as an exercise in the picturesque. Since then, it has grown at a rapid pace, borne forwards by Germany's swift economic progress and the *Fresswelle* – the 'wave of guzzling' – that swept through the country in the 1950s and 1960s. Although it continues to attract occasional criticism – in 1985, for example, to mark its

175th anniversary, the Munich City Museum arranged a
commemorative exhibition entitled 'The Bavarian National
Drunken Frenzy' – its popularity amongst people of all nations
increases every year, and the Oktoberfest has transcended the
darker moments in its past to become an event of universal
appeal.

Munich, the home city of the festival, is a *mélange* of concrete,
Gothic and Baroque buildings, set along broad roads and
interspersed with parks, trees and fountains. It prides itself on the
quality of life it offers, indeed according to opinion polls it is the
city that most Germans would prefer to live in if they left their
own, and a transfer to Munich is considered to be a ticket to
paradise. It is known as the *Millionendorf* – the village of a million
souls, on account of its reputation for friendliness. Its principal
annual festival commences on the penultimate weekend of
September, when autumn is in full progress – the Linden trees
drip golden leaves, bright as petals, that strew its pavements and
flash upon the surface of its river. The city has grown to surround
the Wiesn, so that the festival grounds which once were outside
its walls are now enclosed by the metropolis on all sides. The
Wiesn are at their most striking when viewed from the sky,
especially at night, when they form a great golden rectangle of
lights, beside which the floodlit stadium of Bayern Munich
nearby is insignificant – like a little blue swimming pool attached
to a palace.

The festival opens with a morning procession of Munich's
brewers through the city to the Wiesn. Vestiges of the influence
of Bierzwang persist – only six local breweries are allowed to
take part in the parade and to sell their products at the
Oktoberfest. All six trace their roots to the monasteries,
merchants or the feudal houses of the Middle Ages. In order of
age they are: Augustiner – which as the name suggests was
founded by Augustinian monks in 1328; Spaten, by Benedictines
in 1397, Löwenbräu (1383), Hacker-Pschorr (1417), Hofbräuhaus,

once the court brewery of the Wittelbachs (1561), and Paulaner, by the Paulists in 1634.

The parade of brewers is led by the Munich coat of arms, mounted on a beer dray, which is followed by the town's mayor, in a coach, and a half-mile long procession of horse-drawn carts and floats, manned by several thousand adults, dressed in what appears to be school uniform. The horses are low, rotund, draught animals with shaggy hoofs. Their tack is encrusted with silver and they wear little lace bonnets covering their ears and the crowns of their heads. Some of the floats are equipped with oompah bands which pump out happy music and the crowds lining the route of the cavalcade sing along as they pass by. The spectacle is in the style of a harvest procession, in which the fruits of nature, represented by beer casks, are carried in a triumphal parade to the place where they will be consumed. The casks themselves are antiques rather than the steel kegs that will be used during the festival – small wooden barrels bound in brass and garlanded with hop vines.

The parade is but a foretaste of the fantasia on offer in the Wiesn. Although no initiation rites are in force at the Oktoberfest, the visitor must nonetheless make a mental adjustment before entering its bounds, for the immediate impression they will receive is that they have wandered into a paradise for children. Everything within the field of vision has been simplified, as if it were a sketch in crayons, composed of elementary shapes and bright colours. Everything too is of a giant size, as though a nursery had been reproportioned in order to please the adult imagination.

The brewers' procession reaches this wonderland at 11 a.m. sharp. The mayor disembarks from his coach and proceeds to the Schottenhamel Festhalle, where a keg of beer is waiting on a podium. A cannon fires twelve thundering blasts, the mayor drives a spigot into the keg, pours himself a stein, raises it to his lips and announces '*Ozapft ist!*' ('It's tapped!'), and that, as far as formal ritual goes, is that. No prayers are made, no speeches are

given, neither blessings nor sacrifices are offered. The royal wedding of 1810 is not even mentioned, let alone commemorated. Once the beer has arrived and a barrel has been spiked, it is time for the feast to begin.

The principal attractions of the festival are its fourteen festhallen, the largest of which is the size of a football pitch and holds 10,000 people. The festhallen are erected from scratch each year, a process that takes a month, and are dismantled and stored after the festival ends. They are laid out along four broad avenues, and are interspersed with carnival rides and food stalls. It is often difficult to distinguish the façades of the beer tents from the adjacent fairground attractions, for they are fronted by equally extravagant ornamentation. The Spatenbräu Festhalle Ochsenbraterei, for instance, sports a bowed façade, suggestive of a giant's head with a gaping mouth in which an enormous replica ox is turned on a spit by four life-sized mannequins, while metal flames ascend towards and retire from its carcass. This mechanical display includes a hint of titillation: at a crucial point in the ox-turning cycle, the girl on the right's hoop dress tilts up and bares her legs. Some tents have towers in front of them that are crowned by automata. The Paulaner Brauerei Festhalle, for instance, displays an immense foaming stein that spins slow, hypnotic circles atop a 50-foot pillar, and the Löwenbräu Festhalle sports a giant lion with a beer mug in its hand that is mounted on a column shaped like a lighthouse. A mechanical lion also figures on the façade of the same tent. Every time a new keg is tapped inside, the lion raises a mug to its mouth, its lower jaw sags and it emits a truly ridiculous roar. When the festival is in full swing, and kegs are being tapped one after the other the lion roars continually, its jaw quivering all the while. There is a certain wonder in these things. They are toys, but their size and audacity are pleasing nonetheless. Collectively, they present a single message to the Oktoberfest-goer: suspend disbelief, all those who enter here.

The pattern of oversized ornamentation is repeated inside the beer tents. It is as if a Munich Bierkeller had been taken as a design and amplified a hundred times, and its decorations proportionally, so that only the clientele appear out of scale, and resemble dolls in bright costumes with thumb-sized glasses, seated at miniature tables scattered around the floor of a normal room. Many of the festhallen take the forest and its creatures as their decorative theme. Antlered stags, wild boar, the snarling masks of wolves, and eagles' talons appear as devices on banners or as giant replicas stuck to their walls. Pillars are cased in bark and twined with creepers and flowers. The decor is pure Bavariana, and its pedigree is ancient. The Romans remarked on the reverence that the people of the region held for trees – 'They consecrate whole woods and groves, and by the names of the Gods they call these recesses; divinities these' – and felled a number of them. Christian missionaries such as St Boniface

BEN GLADSTONE

waged war against them, but to judge by the interiors of the beer tents, the Bavarian veneration of the forest has survived intact millennia of persecution.

The festhallen are not merely striking for what they contain, but also for what they omit. There is nothing on display to suggest the twentieth century has passed, which is incongruous, for Munich is a modern city – more than half of it was bombed to dust during World War II, and while its ancient monuments have been rebuilt, it also has examples of modernism, of minimalism, of 'cool', in both its architecture and interiors, none of which have been accommodated within the beer tents. The retro styling of the festhallen is reinforced by the appearance of the people that they contain. While Munich is home to the German fashion industry, and is the national capital of *Schick* ('chic'), most of the clothing on display is decidedly un-schick. At least half the clientele are in traditional dress, which at its simplest consists of embroidered leather britches, called lederhosen, for the men, and a bodice-skirt-apron combination known as a *Dirndl* for the women. For ornament, both sexes wear gingerbread and icing sugar hearts the size of dictionaries on strings around their necks.

The traditional dress on show at the Oktoberfest is not, strictly speaking, traditional, and its pedigree does not match that of the beer. To take lederhosen as an example, there is conflicting evidence as to when trousers of any sort were introduced to Germany. The body of a man discovered in the Austrian Alps who perished c. 1850 BC, was found to be dressed in buckskin chaps which are recognisably the precursors of lederhosen, but whether or not any Austrians succeeded in getting these to Germany during the Bronze Age is not known. In any event, it appears their use had been lost by the time the Romans made contact. Plutarch records German warriors sledging naked down the Alps on their shields to attack Roman territory, and Tacitus described the wardrobe of a German male as consisting of little more than a cloak, 'fastened with a clasp or, for want of it, with a thorn. As far as this reaches not they are naked.' Indeed, it seems

BEN GLADSTONE

that the true ancestors of the traditional costumes paraded with
such pride at the Oktoberfest did not appear until the middle of
the eighteenth century, and that their design owes more to
nineteenth-century imaginations than pre-existing traditions. Just
as the Viking theme of Up Helly Aa was conjured out of the mists
of romanticism, so the dress on display at the Oktoberfest is not
salvage, but invention. Much of it was the fruit of a surging
nationalism in the late nineteenth century, when Germany was an
idea, but not yet a country, and the roots of *Volkstrachtenverein* or
'peasant uniform preservation' can be traced to the various clubs
of that period founded by bourgeois Bavarians, who wanted to
idealise their history and their nation.

Interestingly, the dirndl, the traditional dress of women at the

Oktoberfest, has a better claim to antiquity. Tacitus noted that German women were 'orderly attired in linen . . . and use no sleeves, so that all their arms are bare. The upper part of their breast is withal exposed.' While sleeves have appeared, the upper breasts remain uncovered to the present day, and dirndls gather, elevate and present them to the eyes for admiration. Dirndls are kind to their wearers for they are a true costume, rendering all attractive, while hiding their age and concealing their shape. Even the formidable barmaids of the festhallen – who sometimes bear more than a passing resemblance to the female athletes of East Germany in its sporting hey-day, and who can carry up to twelve litres of beer weighing a total of more than 20 kilogrammes in their fists – look fetching in dirndls.[3]

Each festhalle has a reputation for attracting a different type of clientele. The Löwenbräu tent, for example, is a favourite amongst visitors from the southern hemisphere. Australians, New Zealanders and South Africans gather in its mock Arcadian confines to observe the antipodean ritual of a 'cleansing ale' in which beer is employed as an emetic. The Schottenhamel Festhalle, in contrast, is reckoned to be the most traditional of the Oktoberfest's tents. A majority of its clientele are Bavarian and do their drinking in volkstrachten. Bench sharing is the operative etiquette at all the festhallen, for communal eating and drinking is customary in Bavaria. Restaurants in Munich are as likely to sport benches as chairs, and diners prefer to join on to tables that are already colonised, rather than open up new territory. This philosophy is encapsulated in a Bavarian saying, 'Nur ein Schwein drinkt Allein' – 'Only a pig drinks alone' – and newcomers to a bench at the Oktoberfest are welcomed on arrival, are addressed

---

3 Interestingly, the barmaids of the Oktoberfest have a mythological precedent in the form of the Valkyries, the female helpers of the Teutonic god of war, who influenced the outcome of battles, then conducted the slain to heaven, where they served them roast pork and beer.

BEN GLADSTONE

as *'Herr Nachbar'* ('Dear Neighbour') and are encouraged to
contribute to the revelry in progress.

The ambition of the commensal drinkers at the festival is to
achieve a particular state of mind known as *Gemütlichkeit* which
the dictionary translates as 'comfortable, snug, cosy, pleasant'.
Their weapon of choice is a beer called *Märzen*, so named because
it is brewed in March, and matured for six months before the
festival commences. Märzen is cool, amber in colour, and very
delicately flavoured, blending an initial bitterness with a sweet
finish. Its bubbles are soft and it foams like champagne. Its aroma
is a hundred faint scents mingled – like those of a spring meadow.
It is reputed not to cause a hangover, a reputation that it does not
deserve. Märzen is drunk by the *Mas*, or stein, whose official
measure is a litre, although a good quarter of its volume may be
taken up by the beer's head. Upon the arrival of a fresh glass it is
customary to toast one's neighbours on the bench with song:

Ein Prosit, Ein Prosit
Der Gemütlichkeit
(repeat twice)

Although Märzen is only 5.5% ABV (alcohol by volume), that is nonetheless 5.5cl of pure alcohol per glass, and while alcohol taken daily in small quantities has been proven to prolong the human lifespan, its effect in large doses over a short period of time is not so beneficial. The heartbeat begins to speed, the senses to blur, co-ordination vanishes, and emotions become unstable. Alcohol switches off that part of the brain that controls judgement, and hence its consumption makes its drinkers uninhibited. This can result in uncontrollable rages, unrestrained self-pity, or overwhelming friendliness. The usual form of uninhibited behaviour on display at the Oktoberfest is of the amicable kind, Gemütlichkeit, in a word. Life, in the drinker's mind, is pleasant and uncomplicated, and these properties, once perceived, are worthy of articulation and repetition. It is also the type of drunkenness that handicaps the tongue, so that such splendid sentiments are hard to express, and dissipate themselves like the froth of bubbles on a head of beer. Should festival goers be overcome by Gemütlichkeit, they may avail themselves of the *Bierleichenzelt* ('beer-corpse-tent'), located to the rear of the festhalle, which acts as a sanctuary for fallen drinkers.

Inebriation is not the only repercussion of volume beer drinking. The body processes Märzen very quickly and the metabolic consequences have been anticipated and provided for at the Oktoberfest. Between them, the beer tents offer over half a mile of urinal space which is connected to a formidably efficient drainage system, so that their faux rural interiors are not compromised by farmyard odours.

Gemütlichkeit is perfected by music. The benches of each festhalle are arranged in ranks around a central bandstand, and when the band comes on, people respond at once to its melodies, singing along to their favourite tunes and swaying or waving their steins if they cannot remember their lyrics. While Munich has an enviable reputation in the world of classical music – Mozart premiered *Idomeneo* in its opera house, Wagner was patronised by King Ludwig II of Bavaria and his operas were first performed in the city, and Strauss, Liszt, Bach and Beethoven all played, visited and composed there – the music produced by the festhalle bands does not reflect this rich tradition. Instead of complex pieces, they rely on simple tunes with strong rhythms and memorable choruses. Song lyrics are always a good source of information about festivals – the matters they celebrate or denigrate illuminate the state of mind of the participants. The subjects of the lyrics of Oktoberfest songs ('*Stimmungsmusik*') fall into three broad categories, which are the pleasures of drinking in company, the bittersweet nature of love, and stirring marches. The few protests they register concern the ephemeral qualities of pleasure. According to Stimmungsmusik, life is sweet, and this sweetness derives from good fellowship, affection and enthusiasm:

> *There, where the blue Isar flows,*
> *Where everyone greats you with 'God bless you!'*
> *There is my beautiful city of Munich,*
> *The likes of which you've never seen.*
> *Water is cheap, pure and good,*
> *But it thins our blood.*
> *Far better is a drop of golden wine,*
> *But the best of all is this:*

> *In Munich is the Hoffbrau pub!*
> *One, two, drink up!*
> *Where the kegs are everflowing*
> *One, two, drink up!*
> *There is always some brave man,*
> *One, two, drink up!*
> *Who wants to show how much he can drink:*

You find him starting early in the morning,
and coming out late in the evening –
Ah! The beautiful Hofbräu pub!
One, two, drink up!

It is customary, in between bouts of singing and drinking, to take some solids. The food on offer, and its manner of presentation, mark the Oktoberfest as the modern equivalent of a hunter-gatherer feast, the probable forerunner of all celebration. The virtue of a feast is that there is enough for everyone to eat, no need to scrabble over bones, and therefore the normal laws of society and precedent are relaxed. Food is presented at the Oktoberfest to convey the impression of superabundance. Every stall, both inside and outside the beer tents, emphasises plenty – countless thousands of fattened creatures turn slowly on spits, dribbling grease and juices, whole pigs and oxen are stripped to their ribcages as flesh is hacked away and portioned out. 'We have 30,000 fat *Hendl* (chickens) for you' is a typical notice to find on a stall. Menus confirm that every animal has been plumped up before its slaughter – one imagines smiling pigs, gobbling themselves into obesity for the agreeable duty of feeding humans. The depiction of food animals as fat and happy rather than dead and cut into pieces is, perhaps, a kind of seduction, intended to encourage overconsumption. This convention holds true at even the most bloodthirsty of contemporary feasts. The posters that advertise the pig-killing festival of Campillo de Arenas in Spain, for instance, *do* show pigs being strapped to pig-killing tables and being gutted, but the pigs wear monocles and are smiling.

After a bite to eat – and there are many local delicacies to appreciate such as cow udder tripe and veal-lung sausages – many Oktoberfest-goers take a tour of the fairground rides. These share the retrospective theme of the rest of the festival. The majority are antique and rely on their beauty for effect, rather than an ability to scare their users. There are a few, however, that are thoroughly modern and which generate sufficient g-forces to dislodge the most solid of lunches. Perhaps the most testing of the attractions of the festival is its flea circus, which features these diminutive parasites hitched to tiny wagons, or forced with a needle off 3-inch high gangplanks, and whose performers are very hard to see at all after several Märzens.

The Oktoberfest has a reputation for being child-friendly – its artificial marvels appeal to young eyes as well as old. There are special children's days, during which rides on the amusements are offered at discounted prices, and many of the festival's participants attend in family groups. However, children under the age of six are prohibited in the festhallen after eight in the evening, largely for their own safety, for should the table dancing get out of hand, or an impromptu human pyramid collapse, there is a genuine risk of injury from flying bodies. The festival is also popular amongst pensioners, and most benches in its festhallen feature an octogenarian or two nursing a stein and leading the singing of a sentimental favourite.

A sense of calm pervades the Oktoberfest. There is of course excitement and anticipation, but the crowds are in general tranquil, as if enjoying the presentiment that their wishes will be fulfilled – that there will be plenty to eat and drink, and the pleasure of the company of hundreds of thousands of like-minded people. Indeed, the festival functions as a very gentle form of mass sedation. There is no central spectacle or climax towards which the passions of its participants can build, nor any single event that defines the celebrations. Instead, it offers good fellowship and abundance twelve hours a day, for sixteen successive days. It has the further attraction of egalitarianism. A brace of parades aside, no one sets out to draw attention to themselves or to their creations. There are no castes, nor festival hierarchies. Except in the matter of dress, there is no discrimination between the sexes.

In addition to offering simplicity and equality to its participants, the Oktoberfest also provides an environment that is surprisingly familiar to many of the foreign beer lovers who attend, for Bavarian iconography is well known to non-Bavarians. For nearly

200 years, Bavarian fairytales, illustrated with Bavarian peasants and forest scenes, have been a staple of children's reading in the west. For example, in 1880 Mark Twain had sufficient confidence that his readers would possess a stereotype of the people of the region to use it as a kind of shorthand when describing the meeting of a group of rural councillors: 'They were men of fifty or sixty years of age, with grave, good natured faces, and were all dressed in the costume made familiar to us by the Black Forest stories: broad, round topped black felt hats with the brims curled up all around; long red waistcoats with large metal buttons; black alpaca coats with the waists up between the shoulders. There were not speeches, there was but little talk, there were no frivolities; the council filled themselves gradually, steadily, but surely with beer.'

MUNICH TOURIST OFFICE

Since Twain's time, Bavarian culture has been disseminated further through the medium of cartoons. Its fairy tales have been the inspiration for several feature films including *Snow White* and *Sleeping Beauty*, and even the Bavarian landscape has been mined for inspiration – the Magic Castle of Disneyworld, for example, is modelled on Neuschwanstein Castle, built by King Ludwig II, the grandson of the founder of the Oktoberfest. Indeed, and especially for those in thrall to Gemütlichkeit, the festhallen interiors are reminiscent of the scenery in a Disney feature, and since these have happy associations with childhood for so many people, it is easy to understand the charm that the festival possesses, in addition to its promise of the fat of the land.

A month after the last 'Auf Wiedersehen' has rung out in the festhallen at the Oktoberfest, the seasons spin into winter in northern Europe, and the landscape begins to die. The nights draw in, the frosts arrive, and the exuberant vegetation that sprung up over summer withers to its roots. The sentiments and traditions attached to the approach of winter tend towards the melancholy – the year is visibly fading, and with it any hopes that were entertained for achieving triumphs within its course. The feeling of resignation was captured by Rainer Maria Rilke, writing of Munich:

> He'll not build now, who has no house awaiting.
> Who's now alone, for long will so remain:
> sit late, read, write long letters, and again
> return to restlessly perambulating
> the avenues of parks where leaves downrain.

The absence of public celebrations, too, marks the period as one of despondency. A gap appears like a no-man's land in the calendar of festivals. After the excitement that attended the harvest, and the agreeable duty of acquiring fat as a bulwark against the winter ahead, a period of calm ensues, during which nature literally falls apart.

However, the years do not die in so spectacular a manner in less cruel climates. While Bavarians are building fires against the cold, and mourning the decline of daylight, in Mexico, the crops, drenched in sunshine, have grown tall and ripe. Their harvest coincides with a festival that draws its inspiration from both Europe and the Americas, and its participants from a place that claims dominion over both.

JOSÉ GUADALUPE POSADA

XII

THE MEXICAN
WAY OF DEATH

The word death is not pronounced in New York, in Paris, in London, because it burns the lips. The Mexican, in contrast, is familiar with death, jokes about it, caresses it, sleeps with it, celebrates it: it is one of his favourite toys and his most steadfast love.

OCTAVIO PAZ, THE LABYRINTH OF SOLITUDE

At first sight, it may appear an exercise in futility to include dead people on the invitation list to a party. Not only is it unlikely that they will attend, but it is also impossible to predict their condition should they do so. One tends to remember the dead in their prime, rather than when imprisoned by age or disease, or as they appeared after a fatal accident, and there is no guarantee that they might not return in a less than pristine state. While such uncertainties would stay the writing hands of most hosts and hostesses, in some cultures a neat solution has been discovered to this problem of etiquette, which enables the dead to be included in the festivities of the living.

Imagine if, like Faust, it were possible to summon Helen of Troy back to life. Imagine inviting a dead relative, whose company was once treasured, to return for a feast in their honour. These are the possibilities that inspire a festival celebrated throughout Mexico, *Los Dias de Muertos* – the Days of the Dead – which, as its name suggests, is dedicated to the entertainment of those who have passed away. While such an event might be expected to be sombre, like those usually associated with the dead such as funerals, it is instead a blaze of colour, and rather than assuming that the returning departed have lost both their sense of fun and their sense of taste, the Days of the Dead are filled with sensual treats, with fine food, sweet incense, stirring sounds, spirited dancing and serious drinking.

The festival is held over the days that surround the Catholic feasts of All Saints (1 November) and All Souls (2 November), and usually commences on 28 October. Like Hallowe'en in the United States, with which it overlaps, it is celebrated to some degree by most of the population of Mexico, and similarly, rather than being a single public event, it consists of a multitude of private celebrations. Although its rituals vary across the country, they usually take the form of a three-day ceremony, during which the dead are welcomed back to their family homes where they are offered food, flowers, incense, alcohol and other gifts, and are assumed to enjoy circulating among their descendants. Los Dias de Muertos is also a time for gift giving between the living – people present their children with little sugar skulls with their names inscribed on them, and purchase skeletons and other *memento mori* for their friends. These private celebrations are augmented by public festivities. There are parades and pyrotechnic displays in villages and towns throughout the nation. Plays are enacted with death as their subject and competitions are held for the most attractive offerings. Skeletons appear in the newspapers, in shop windows and on television, indeed death becomes a theme for all of Mexico. The country is proud of Los Dias de Muertos. The festival is perceived of as being uniquely Mexican, a fusion of pre-Columbian beliefs and Catholicism. Its celebration is encouraged by the government, explained in schools, and occasionally is subsidised. The newspapers trumpet its virtues: *'Los festejos tienen como finalidad fortalecer las traditions y costumbres de nuestra Mexicanidad'* ('The ultimate purpose of the celebrations is to reinforce the traditions and customs of our Mexican-ness').

From a historical perspective, it is not surprising that Mexicans have seized on death to foster their sense of identity, for premature or violent death has been a common occurrence for much of the country's recorded past. The Aztecs, who ruled in Mexico before the arrival of the Europeans, considered human sacrifice to be essential to the health of the cosmos, and murdered tens of thousands of innocents every year in the name of prudent government. When the Spanish subjugated the Aztecs in the sixteenth century, they replaced their regime with one that was even more bloody. On the eve of the Spanish conquest in 1519, the population of Mexico was estimated to be 16 million. Fifty years later it had fallen below 1.5 million. While epidemics played their part in this holocaust, the majority of deaths were the result of systematic cruelty.

An official report, written in 1555, noted that the Spanish conquistadores had got through Indians at such a rate by working them to death in their mines and on their farms that they had brought the economy to the point of collapse. The Indians themselves were accused of having a hand in their own depopulation by resorting to the sin of suicide and also by refusing to breed, for 'they did not want to have children who would suffer as they had suffered'. Amongst specific acts of cruelty cited in the report is the example of a conquistador engaged to march labourers to the mines, who dropped his dagger in a swamp just as dusk was approaching, so that the chances of finding it were faint. Fortunately, the nearest porter was a woman nursing an infant and the conquistador took the child from its mother and left it on the spot as a marker, so that its screams, or vultures, would enable him to locate his lost dagger the following day. Another sixteenth-century Spanish commentator, Bartolome de Las Casas, in addition to recording a seemingly endless list of massacres, noted that one Spaniard had established a human abattoir which he operated under the auspices of the King of Spain, 'where he himself would preside over the slaughter and grilling of children and where grown men were butchered for the sake of their hands and feet which were generally held to be the best cuts'.

The Spanish conquest of Mexico was genocide as much as empire building. An entire culture was all but washed away, and its few remnants accumulated, like debris lodged in a plughole, around the various Christian feasts introduced by the conquerors. Among the Christian holy days that found their way to Mexico were the feasts of All Saints and All Souls. Both festivals originated in Europe in the Dark Ages, the former to commemorate the dead who were assumed to have reached heaven, the latter to assist via prayer those who were passing time in purgatory en route. Interestingly, both owed their place in the calendar to the older Celtic festival of *Samhain*, with which they had been positioned to coincide and thereby make legitimate. Samhein, meaning 'summer's end', had marked the close of the Celtic year, and the beginning of winter, when cattle were brought down from their upland pastures. It was a time when evil spirits were thought to walk the earth and witches were believed to fly through the air on broomsticks, or to gallop round the countryside mounted on giant coal-black cats, and these baneful apparitions were either appeased or driven away with charms as part of the celebrations. Much of the iconography of the present day festival of Hallowe'en, including jack-o'-lanterns[1] and the habit of trick-or-treating, derive from Samhain.

All Saints and All Souls had a particular appeal to the Mexicans, who had possessed under the Aztecs a complex set of beliefs and rituals relating to the dead, which they were eager to preserve, as being their last links to all that had been lost. They began to employ the Christian feasts as Trojan horses, within which their old rites were concealed. The existence of two adjacent festivals for different types of dead was particularly useful, for, according to Aztec theology, and in contrast to Christian belief, the fate of an individual in the thereafter was not determined by how they had lived, but rather by the manner in which they had died. Warriors who had perished in battle and women who had died in childbirth assumed the forms of butterflies or hummingbirds, and followed the sun along its course through the sky. Dead children had their own heaven where they were nourished with milk that dripped from the branches of a divine tree. People who had expired by drowning, from dropsy, or any other form of water-related death had a special paradise named Tlalocan where they enjoyed an afterlife of ease. Finally, those who died of natural causes went to Mictlan, a cold and gloomy place, devoid of any form of comfort or entertainment, where they passed most of their time in a state of suspended animation.

Each class of dead was honoured with a dedicated festival, at which the souls of the departed were assumed to return to earth to reacquaint themselves, for a short spell, with the pleasures of the flesh. The principal Aztec dead-fest, for the majority who had died of natural causes, was a lively affair featuring ritual

---

1 Originally made with turnips before the discovery of the New World and pumpkins.

drunkenness, human sacrifice, and cannibalism, for after the
hearts of sacrificial victims had been offered to the gods, their
bodies were served up to the public either barbecued or stewed.
While the Mexicans found it impossible to incorporate the more
carnal aspects of their old rites into the feasts of All Saints and All
Souls, they nonetheless managed to smuggle some of their
customs under the cloak of the Christian ceremonies. The resultant
mélange was christened Los Dias de Muertos, and eventually
acquired the blessing of the Catholic Church.

The most important of the pre-Columbian convictions to
have been preserved within Los Dias de Muertos is its central
tenet – that the dead are capable of returning to the world of the
living. In retrospect this was a surprising triumph, for the
concept of the dead coming back to earth for any reason bar
attendance at the Last Judgement is utterly alien to Christian
doctrine. Whereas Christians might tend the graves of their
ancestors out of a sense of filial duty, they would not consider
cooking food or mixing drinks for their occupants. *Requiescat in
pace* – 'rest in peace' – is all that is expected or desired of the
deceased.[2]

In addition to serving as the guardian of a number of heretical
indigenous beliefs, Los Dias de Muertos also came to function as
a vehicle for political expression. This role commenced in the
nineteenth century, during which, amongst other vicissitudes,

---

2 Interestingly, a belief that the dead returned to earth and required
entertainment when they did so was common not only in Aztec Mexico but
throughout the Americas. In what is now the state of Missouri, for instance, the
Mandan Indians would hold daily conversations with the skulls of their
ancestors, offering these their food to taste, or blowing tobacco smoke through
their eye sockets; and in the present day, the Guarani tribe of Paraguay go a step
further, sharing not only their pipes but also their bodies with their ancestors.
Every year, they welcome the dead into their houses for a drinking bout, then
lend them their persons so that they may live out any fantasies they cherished,
but were unable to realise when alive. The resulting orgy is blamed on the dead
and enhances their glory.

Mexico won its independence, lost nearly half its territory, participated in a number of civil and foreign wars and endured a thirty-year dictatorship. Amid this disorder, the festival was used as an occasion on which the people of Mexico might air their grievances by satirising their rulers in public works of art, which ostensibly were dedicated to mourning the departed. The element of protest that became attached to the festival is best exemplified by the works of Jose Guadalupe Posada (1852–1913), an illustrator for various periodicals of the period. Posada produced topical and satirical etchings, which drew on the iconography of the festival by substituting skeletons for people, thereby emphasising the common mortality of his subjects, be they the powerful or the oppressed. His work gave Los Dias de Muertos a popularity and a public image that it had never before enjoyed, and once the festival had been established in the national conscience, it became not merely an exercise in superstition, to be tolerated among the rural poor, but a secular entertainment that a well-to-do city dweller might associate with and be proud of. The transcendental appeal of Los Dias de Muertos lay in the fact that it was distinctively Mexican. It was new, like the independent nation, yet also boasted antiquity in both its Christian and Aztec pedigrees. It was a harmonious mixture of Spanish and pre-Columbian customs, which possessed the best virtues of both its parents – devotion, a creative urge, a pride in the past, stoicism, and humour even, in the face of death.

The contemporary festival of Los Dias de Muertos has two aspects: the family celebrations that take place in houses and graveyards across Mexico; and the various public events and works of art that the theme of the event inspires. Turning first to the family celebrations, their core rituals are the production of an offering for the dead, known as the *ofrenda*, comprised of food, drink, flowers and small personal gifts such as cigarettes, which are assembled on an altar in the home or on the tomb of the deceased; and a reception, at which the dead mingle with the living and enjoy the refreshments that have been prepared in their honour.

The ofrenda has both Catholic and Aztec influences, and could be said to lend a functional aspect to the festival, based on the concept of a reciprocity existing between the living and the dead. Both creeds promote the activity of petitioning the dead on the grounds that these are capable of evoking the sympathy of higher powers in favour of their flesh and blood supplicants. In the case of Catholicism, petitions are limited to prayers and sometimes candles, whereas according to Aztec doctrine, they were understood to extend to tangible gifts, such as food, clothing and drinks. The Aztec blood is dominant in the present-day ofrendas: indeed, the dead are said to have become rather demanding – they 'come back to visit us and to ask for bread, fruit, salt, water, and, while they're at it, for aguardiente, tequila, pulque, mole with rice, tamales, little sugar skulls, chocolates, and candied pumpkin'.

The term ofrenda encompasses both the gifts for the visiting dead and the structure on which they are laid out. This latter is a makeshift, or permanent altar, which is set up in the houses of the hosts of the deceased. The appearance of these shrines is reminiscent of the profusely decorated pasos of the Madonnas at Semana Santa, and they often dominate the rooms in which they have been assembled. They are arranged in ascending tiers, which taper as they rise from floor to ceiling, and culminate in crucifixes and postcards of the Catholic saints dressed in fluorescent robes. Each tier is laden with a cornucopia of fruits, and arrayed with flowers, snapshots of the departed, stone tripod incense burners, candles, a washbasin where the dead may freshen up after their journey from their usual abode, and personal gifts – the favourite things of the deceased. Ofrendas are arranged with a careful eye for effect, to evoke all the sensations and pleasures of the world for someone who has not seen it for a year.

The materials included within an ofrenda are accumulated long in advance of the festival – indeed, many poor families budget for them throughout the year and there are cautionary Mexican tales in the style of *A Christmas Carol* that warn of the dire consequences of making an inadequate offering. One such tells of an agnostic who scorned his wife's entreaties for money to prepare an ofrenda, telling her that should his dead ancestors wish to or indeed be capable of returning to earth they could eat his shit. Sure enough, on the last night of the fiesta, this sceptic observed a procession of happy spirits returning to their graves, laden with the gifts their children had collected for them, and at the tail of the procession, looking miserable, were his own parents, with nothing to show for their journey to the world of the living but a plate of their son's faeces. The tale concludes with the impoverishment and death of the disrespectful offspring.

The luxury of ofrendas varies in accordance with the means of the people who make them. There are, however, certain gifts common to them all, including bread, salt and something to drink. The presentation of bread is a vestige of the Aztec harvest festival, with which Los Dias de Muertos coincides, and some of whose rituals it preserves. The Aztecs celebrated their harvest by baking special types of loaves in honour of the maize goddess, Chicomecohuatl, and by slaughtering various innocents. While the traditional conclusion to this event – the sacrifice of a little girl, whose blood was splattered over the harvest offerings, after which her body was flayed, a priest squeezed into the bloody skin, and a parade held around the temple, 'all of them dancing to the tuck of a drum, while he acted as fugleman, skipping and posturing at the head of the procession as briskly as he could be expected to do, incommoded as he was by the tight and clammy skin of the girl' – has not survived, allusions to the sacrifices the Aztecs thought necessary to encourage crops still appear in the shapes of the *pan de muertos*, 'the bread of the dead', which is prepared for the present-day festival. This serves as an allegorical substitute for human victims, and is produced in anthropomorphic shapes or with coloured heads emerging from its surface as if these were bursting forth from tombs. The importance of including bread in an ofrenda also shows Spanish blood, for it is customary in Spain to eat baked goods adorned with the iconography of death on the festival of All Saints. In Seville, for example, parents buy their children *huesos del santos* ('saints' bones'), a type of pastry shaped to resemble bones, although unlike the pan de muertos, the huesos are intended solely for the living to consume.

In addition to accumulating presents for the dead, Mexicans also purchase gifts for their living relatives and friends. For weeks before the festival commences the market stalls of towns and villages throughout the country are piled high with sugar skulls and confectionery coffins in bright colours, which are stacked in tiers so as to resemble a charnel house of pygmies. The skulls, made by pouring sugar water into a mould, are sometimes labelled with names and arranged alphabetically – Alfonso, Anna, Jesus, Jose, Maria, Paloma, Xavier . . . At night, under a string of naked bulbs, the crystals and flaws glitter inside them like flecks of silver in a vein of quartz. These sweets are bought as presents by parents for their children, and by children for each other. The market stalls also sell miniature plaster of Paris or papier mâché sculptures, known as *calacas*, which depict skeletons performing various mundane tasks such as typing letters, driving cars and extracting teeth. Calacas serve as gifts between friends and are also included in ofrendas as reminders to the dead of their former occupations.

As a final preliminary to the festival, the cemeteries of Mexico are spruced up. Graves are cleaned, repaired and repainted, and the ground around them cleared. This work is undertaken in the spirit of a family outing. Children run and play between the tombs, adults salute their friends, and any of their relatives who have arrived early to share the work, for Los Dias de Muertos functions as a family reunion for the living as well as the dead. Mexicans aim to return to their native pueblo to celebrate the festival, and many people who meet in the graveyard will not have seen each other in the past year. Mexican graves tend to be elaborate structures built of concrete, ranging in size from dog kennels to garden sheds, and painted in vibrant colours such as coral pink, solar yellow, deep purple and ultramarine. Once they have been refreshed, the graveyards resemble toyshops filled with brightly coloured dolls' houses, each topped with a cross. As activity increases in the days leading up to the festival, Mexico's cemeteries, which are usually located on the edges of its towns, become the social hubs for its population. Vendors set up their carts alongside their walls. Street urchins haunt their gates, in order to hire themselves out to carry water or assist with the weeding. Lovers wander hand in hand amongst the vibrant sepulchres. The atmosphere is one of happy expectation – the preparation of a haunted dancefloor for an extravagant party.

Once the preliminaries of assembling an ofrenda and cleaning graves have been completed, families make ready a homecoming dinner, usually based around a *mole*, a piquant stew that, like the festival, is renowned for being typically Mexican. By the evening of 28 October, everything should be in place in readiness for Los Dias de Muertos to commence, and the hosts settle back to await their visitors. This anticipatory period is a relaxed affair, which lacks the tension that characterises the parties at which flesh and blood guests are expected. Following the Aztec tradition, the dead are categorised, and are invited to arrive in a set order according to the manner in which they perished. First up are the spirits of those who suffered a violent, solitary or tragic death; next come those who died as children; and last of all dead adults. Each category is received and entertained within fixed periods during the course of the festival.

The hour at which the first guests are invited varies from town to town, as does their place of reception. On the lake island of Janitzio in the province of Michoacan, for example, where they are received in a cemetery, they are not anticipated until dawn on the first day of the festival, and decoration of their graves with flowers and candles does not begin before 1 or 2 a.m. The vigil at Janitzio is renowned for being somewhat austere. Its participants pass their time in prayer or in chanting, rather than treating it as a social occasion for the living. However, in much of Mexico, the first guests arrive from midnight onwards in the very houses in which they used to live and they are welcomed home with church bells, firecrackers, brass bands and gunfire.

An example of the traditional order of events is provided by Totolapan, a village of almost 9,000 souls situated in the province of Morelos, whose Dias de Muertos festivities commence after sunset on 28 October with the arrival of the spirits of all who died violent deaths. This is called *El dia de los matados* ('The day of the killed').[3] These spirits are followed on the 29th by the *Chicititos* – the dead children – and on 1 November by the remainder of Totolapan's former residents. Proceedings for entertaining the various classes of guests are broadly similar, and are typified by those of 1 November, the feast of All Saints. The invitation for the dead expected on this day is fixed for any time from 12 noon onwards, and everyone is considered to be present by 3 p.m. Throughout this period the church bells of Totolapan peal out, summoning people back to their former habitations. The dead are awaited in the homes of their relatives. To help them find their way to their receptions, trails of marigold blossoms are laid along the streets, and through the open doors of family homes to the waiting ofrendas. These trails terminate in crosses marked with petals on the floor, over which the dead must pass in order to get to their presents.

Many Mexicans claim to be able to detect the arrival of their guests, either by sensory perception or through intuition. The experience of encountering the massed spirits of the departed as they arise from their tombs and return to the world has been described by the Mexican novelist, Juan Rulfo: 'I saw that there was no one, although I kept hearing what sounded like the murmur of many people in a market. A constant buzz without rhyme or reason, similar to that which is made by the wind rustling the branches of a tree in the night, when neither the tree nor the branches can be seen though their whispers can be heard. I didn't dare take another step. I began to feel that the murmuring was getting closer and circling me like a swarm until I was able to make out a few words, almost void of sound: "Pray to God for us." That's what I heard them telling me.'

The first few hours of the receptions in Totolapan, when the dead are reunited with the living, are limited to family and close

---

3 This category is surprisingly prolific, on account of the numerous judicial murders carried out in the area by the Mexican army.

friends. Candles are lit on the ofrendas, one for each of the deceased, the rooms are purified with incense, and the dead are presumed to enjoy the feasts that have been prepared for them. They are believed to consume only the flavours, and some of the aromas of food, although their thirst is said to result in more tangible demonstrations of their presence, as glasses of spirits left out for them are often discovered empty. While the guests are assumed to be eating and drinking, they are briefed on events that have passed in the world during their absence. Once this private period is over, and the living have made a start on the leftovers, the younger generations of Totolapans take to the streets, and celebrate as if to wake the dead. From 10 p.m. onwards they don masks and disguises, form into bands known as *ofrenderos*, and make a tour of all the houses that are marked by a path of petals to their front doors, where they view the ofrendas, and sing *coplas*, a form of Spanish verse, in which they request refreshments in return for performing dances:

> *Poor little dead thing!*
> *Your head already hurts.*
> *If you would like us to dance,*
> *You must give us some beer,*
> *And for dinner prepare*
> *Cinnamon flavoured pastries.*

This preliminary tour leads to a second, more intense bout of circulating and drinking. In the words of a visiting anthropologist: 'In the Second Phase (1:00 AM à 3:00 AM), the ingestion of alcohol results in a state of hilarity amongst the celebrants and constitutes their principal motivation for continuing their circuit.' By the end of the second phase, '75% of the ofrenderos find themselves in a state of complete and absolute inebriation'. Their ritual drunkenness is perhaps another vestige of the Aztec harvest festival when liberal consumption of alcohol was an essential element of the celebrations, and participants were expected to become as befuddled as the *Centzontotochtin* – the 400 moon-rabbit gods of pulque. During this period, and indeed throughout the night the principal church of the town acts as a kind of buffet lounge to which tired revellers may retreat for refreshments and to legitimise their paganism with prayer. The celebrations break up at about 4 a.m.

Festivities recommence on 2 November from noon onwards, when families make their way to Totolapan's graveyard. They bring the candles, the decorations and the incense from the ofrendas with them. Graves are given a final polish and adorned with an abundance of flowers, in particular *cempoaxochitl*, a type of marigold, which served to commemorate the dead amongst the Aztecs and is known as *flor de Muertos* in much of Mexico. At 4 p.m. a mass for the souls of the departed is celebrated, and when this is over, a mariachi band, contracted by the town council, plays sentimental Mexican favourites. While the close ranks of graves inhibit lively dancing, people nonetheless take partners and execute a few steps as a gesture towards one of life's great pleasures.

The purpose of these graveyard celebrations is to entertain the dead in public, and to bid them farewell for another year. Those people who are the hosts of more pacific spirits bring radios and televisions to help them while away the hours together, glasses of tequila are passed from hand to hand, and troubadours stroll from grave to grave, offering to serenade the deceased for a small sum. Streamers and fairy lights are strung between the trees of the cemetery, and as dusk descends candles are lit around the tombs, illuminating the faces of a throng of people, some seated at the graveside, others taking a paseo around the graves. The flickering light casts dancing shadows across the tombs, which seem to augment the quantity of celebrants present, and the graveyard scene resembles an evening garden party, whose numbers are fleshed out with shadows. It has all the enchantment that dusk, candlelight, soft music, the scent of incense, and the company of relatives and friends can offer. As night approaches the living say their farewells and toast the departure of their guests with a final glass of tequila. By 10 p.m. the dead have returned to the afterlife, and their hosts make their way back to their houses, for this is vampire bat country, and it is unwise to sleep out of doors unprotected after night has fallen.

From the perspective of a settlement such as Totolapan, Los Dias de Muertos is above all a festival of continuity, during which Totolapans reaffirm their sense of community and perform their duties according to ancestral values. They perceive the dead as those 'who gave us life and who don't want to be forgotten'. The festival is neither a sentimental nor a melancholy occasion, but rather a matter of fact reception for old friends, whose tastes and interests are assumed not to have changed in their absence. The dead are invited back to a world that is to all intents and purposes the same as that which they left behind. In addition to being fêted, they are also reacquainted with the hardships of living: the tools and the calacas that are usually included in ofrendas, as symbols of the trades that they used to follow are *memento vidae* – reminders that life was not all cempoaxochitl.

In the larger towns of Mexico the public, as opposed to family, aspects of Los Dias de Muertos come to the fore. Ever since the festival has been nurtured as an expression of national identity, it has been used by its celebrants as an opportunity for comment on the nation. Each 2 November, Mexican newspapers carry mock obituaries of politicians and other public figures, in which the deceased are recorded as having performed acts of philanthropy entirely out of keeping with their present behaviour. A governor renowned for corruption, for instance, will be eulogised as having undergone a Damascene conversion prior to death, and to have distributed every last peso of his wealth to the needy. In addition to such satires, ofrendas are composed for political purposes, to draw attention to matters such as the plight of the victims of

CAMERA PRESS

industrial accidents, or to the working conditions of prostitutes, and are laid out in public places. Two-thirds of the space in the principal square of Mexico City is taken up with ofrendas during Los Dias de Muertos. Public ofrendas are also made to important historical figures. Leon Trotsky, for example, receives an ofrenda every year in the house in Coyoacan (the 'City of the Coyote'), where he was murdered with an ice-pick in 1940. This ofrenda always includes a bottle of the Godfather of Bolshevism's favourite whisky. The role of such ofrendas is not to cement the links between individuals and their ancestors but rather to protest against the authorities, or to celebrate, in the form of a dead idealist, an ideal.

In addition to mock obituaries and public ofrendas there is an outpouring of creativity during the course of the festival. The newspapers carry columns of poems and illustrations on the subject of mortality, and even advertisements enter into the spirit of the occasion, decorating their messages with skeletons and tombs. Life insurance companies, in particular, take advantage of the coincidental links between the theme of the festival and the usefulness of their product. As a consequence of this political, cultural and commercial activity, Los Dias de Muertos has become a festival dedicated not only to the dead, in the sense of a multitude of deceased individuals, but also to Death, the principal actor in the drama. The Mexican identity for death does not consist of a single emblematic figure like the grim reaper, but rather of a multitude of deaths, represented as skeletons in every conceivable guise – the death waiting inside all of us:

> *Como te ves me vi*
> *Y como me ves te veras*
>
> *As you look I looked*
> *And as I look you will look*
>
> *(copla engraved on a sugar skull)*

The dancing skeleton, with its fixed, fleshless grin is the symbol of the festival. Its ubiquity encourages Mexicans to 'see the skull beneath the skin'. Its cheerful aspect and the manic poses in which it is portrayed enable the living to mock, with death, the ephemeral vanities and trivial employments that occupy their lives. The cities of Mexico are literally overrun with skeletons for the duration of the festival. If this skeletal death is a man, he is sharply dressed – the James Bond of the supernatural world with a licence to kill; if death is a woman, she is depicted as slim and irresistible. *Catrinas*, as these latter are called, are among the most popular representations of death, and can be found depicted in all the fashions current over the last hundred years, ranging from an Edwardian-style temptress with bonnet and bustle, to a contemporary femme fatale dressed in a mini-skirt with red fingernails painted on to her bones.

This latter-day cult of death is nowhere more in evidence than in the town of Mixquic, just to the south of Mexico City. The population of Mixquic swells from 20,000 to over a million during the course of Los Dias de Muertos, and it is perceived as the stylistic home of the festival, in the same manner as the Semana Santa celebrations in Seville take pride of place amongst those that are held throughout Spain. The people of Mixquic prepare ofrendas and hold a candlelit vigil in their graveyard in a similar manner to those of Totolapan, but in Mixquic the private rituals are augmented by plays, films, exhibitions and other displays with death as their theme. The city functions as a showcase, in which both the Mexican-ness and the creativity of the festival are displayed. Moreover, it serves as an example of how Los Dias de Muertos has become not just a cultural, but also a commercial event.

Merchants of death, in the sense of souvenir stalls, crowd the streets of Mixquic. These sell death as a brand that can be applied to any ornament, however trivial. Many of their goods are designed with foreign buyers in mind and have been loaded with clues as to their place-of-origin: plaster-of-Paris skeletons wearing wide-brimmed sombreros and ponchos, strumming guitars, mounted on skeletal mules, and so on. It is rare to see death depicted in so sentimental a manner. In other nations, it is usually represented as grim – as a destroying angel with a flaming sword and an aspect of vengeance, or as a fanged, foul-breathed and ravenous monster – not the sort of thing one would want as a mascot on a keyring. During Los Dias de Muertos, however, death and its victims are reproduced in vast quantities, just like the merchandising that accompanies the launch of a new film for children. These souvenirs serve to take the sting out of death. Ubiquity breeds familiarity, and when a matter becomes familiar it loses its power to shock – indeed, we rather become endeared to it.

The pleasure of spending Los Dias de Muertos in Mixquic derives from viewing the sheer variety and ingenuity of the ways in which mortality is expressed. It is as if the purpose of this overload is to reveal the omnipresence of death by depicting it on

every street and in every possible situation. As a consequence, the Dias de Muertos celebrations in Mixquic have an appeal which is recognised beyond Mexico. The town is not just a fairground, but also a place that people visit in order to gain spiritual benefits. Despite the overcrowding in its cemetery, where tourists outnumber the locals and their guests, and where the scene on 2 November is said to resemble a medieval *danse macabre*, with spectators tripping over tombstones and one another, or engaged in unsightly struggles to decorate neglected graves, while flashbulbs drown the candlelight, many visitors claim to feel inspired to a more profound understanding of the human condition, and its inevitable end. Indeed, Mixquic does not just draw tourists, but also pilgrims and even hedonists, who derive pleasure from the contemplation of their own mortality. This libertine streak has a long pedigree in European thought. The philosophy of death that Spain exported to the New World was phrased in the language of pleasure. St Teresa of Jesus, for example, lamented her life as no more than a period of frustrated lust for death:

> *Which causes me such fiery pain,*
> *That I die, because I cannot die.*

Even amongst the lay population, death was the climax, the release from a life that was at best a dream:

> *How if our waking life, like that of sleep,*
> *Be all a dream in that eternal life*
> *To which we wake not till we sleep in death?*

This neo-stoic approach found a close match in the pre-Columbian philosophy of life and death. 'We come only to sleep, only to dream' mourned Netzahualcoyotl, the poet-king of Texcoco, in the fifteenth century, and the fusion of the parallel beliefs of Mexico's very different parents has resulted in a philosophy of death and an accompanying iconography that is both striking and compelling.

The Mexican cult of the dead and death shows signs of spreading beyond its borders. Although Mexicans agonise over the colonisation of Los Dias de Muertos by Hallowe'en, with which it coincides, lamenting that their children, instead of begging pesos for a sugar skull in accordance with tradition, have taken up trick-or-treating, and that the appearance of witch-masks and jack-o'-lanterns is a warning that Los Dias de Muertos is losing its meaning and becoming a wholly commercial occasion, there are indications that the trend is running the other way, that ritual is proving more potent than commerce. Many American schools teach their children how to make ofrendas. The iconography of the festival has been dispersed throughout the USA by bands such as the Grateful Dead, and regular exhibitions of the artistic works associated with the festival are held in American museums and cultural centres.

While the penetration of Los Dias de Muertos is at present limited to its decorative aspects, its philosophy is likely to follow. After all, the central premise of the festival, that the souls of the departed can and do return to earth, and the deduction that their return should be celebrated, together form an attractive notion, and one that robs death of its finality – dying need not mean a farewell to hedonism. One can imagine oneself coming back in the same fashion to be fêted by those to whom one gave life, and to enjoy once more some of the pleasures and the vices that may have hastened one's end.

Just as the dead are required to return to the afterlife upon the conclusion of the festival of Los Dias de Muertos, so must its living celebrants go back to a different world – to the conventions and occupations that fill the rest of their time. They will return to rising and retiring at regular hours, to working for fixed periods for agreed wages, and will eschew strange behaviour until the next fiesta arrives. Indeed, the end of any festival, just like its beginning, is a transitional stage during which its participants must readjust their conduct, resign themselves to certain conventions of dress and yield to restrictions on their behaviour. They will no longer find themselves at liberty to sing, to dance until their legs give way, to drink to excess, to start fires and let off fireworks, or to shoot pistols into the air. They may be mocked if they burst into tears or wear too much make-up, and besides, they may feel themselves in no condition to tussle over a ball in an icy river, or take on a fighting bull in a trial of speed.

Fortunately, festival-goers usually make an easy passage back to the identities under which they live and labour. They consider their periodic excesses to be sanctioned by custom, and they do not feel remorse for their behaviour during the course of the revels. As a consequence, the closing scenes of a festival rarely consist of crowds hanging their heads in shame. And if an event has served its purpose well, if it has enabled its celebrants to exercise a passion they must otherwise restrain, and granted them relief thereby, it should leave them satiated until its next performance the following year.

Notwithstanding the useful roles that festivals serve in acting as a vent for the more savage urges to which humanity is prone, the surroundings in which they have been staged are seldom pretty after their conclusion. People will have stored up energy to release in celebration, and the damage occasioned by the resulting explosion of hedonism can last far longer than the pleasures that were its catalyst. Although disorder may only rule for a few hours, it can require weeks to put right. However, while the aftermath of vigorous revelry often presents unpleasant sights and smells – empty bottles, discarded underwear, the earth trodden into a mire by the dancers of last night, crutches thrown away in the belief of a miracle cure, puddles of liquid of uncertain origin and disagreeable scent – there is yet a poignancy in the disorder. It resembles the mess generated by children at play , which is a reminder of their excitement as much as their lack of co-ordination – the inevitable side-effects of pleasure and of innocence.

Rather than ending, metaphorically speaking, this voyage of celebration amidst the ashes and detritus that attend a festival's demise, and abandoning the traveller in a gutter with an empty bottle and a new best friend while a wonderland is dismantled piece by piece around them, we shall meditate instead on the plethora of spectacles that await another journey. We are fortunate to live in an age when diversity is encouraged, for we are now aware that it is vulnerable, and that unless it is protected it will perish. Just as we clean and care for dinosaur bones when they are unearthed, instead of cursing them as evidence of the devil's work and causing them to be destroyed, so we encourage the preservation of rituals, some of which our ancestors did their level best to exterminate, whatever their culture. As a result, the state of global celebration is in rude good health, and every year old festivals are revived and new ones are invented, so that the travelling hedonist would find it impossible to exhaust the entertainments on offer around the world in the space of a single lifetime. Indeed, their principal problem would not be a lack of opportunities, but rather the need to choose between a mass of conflicting and equally appealing fixtures.

While the juggernauts are rolling in Puri, tens of thousands of people are gathering in the Spanish town of Bunol, in order to bombard each other with ripe tomatoes; and on the same day that San Fermin is honoured in Pamplona, Canadians celebrate their mastery over animals with a giant rodeo, chicken racing, and the consumption of lashings of Kinky Poo Joy Juice. Meanwhile in Kandy, Sri Lanka, at about the same time, a priest of the Temple of the Tooth will be taking a cut at a river with his sword, to mark the coming of the rains, before leading a procession of elephants and dancing troupes on a ritual circuit of the town. And in addition to such giant spectacles, there is a host of more intimate events, some the last vestiges of abandoned religions, of forgotten superstitions, which no longer draw the masses for whose entertainment they were formulated, and others which serve no greater purpose than to honour that perfect excuse for celebration – the joy of existence.

NOTES

I ANY EXCUSE FOR A PARTY

9 'brilliant, resplendent and popular, with the utmost display':
Beacham, Richard C., *Spectacle Entertainments of Early Imperial Rome*,
Yale University Press, 1999, p. 4.

II NORTHERN LIGHTS

17 'preferred their calendar': quoted in Ewing Duncan, David, *The
Calendar*, Fourth Estate, London, 1998, p. 307.

18 'popery is favourable to ceremony': Johnson, Samuel, *A Journey to
the Western Isles of Scotland*, project Gutenberg e-text.

19 'Here we are, a troop of some sixty or seventy': Brown, Callum G.,
Up Helly Aa, Custom, Culture & Community in Shetland, Manchester
University Press, 1998, p. 87.

20 'poor looking place': Scott, Walter, *The Voyage of the Pharos, Walter
Scott's Cruise around Scotland in 1814*, Scottish Literary Association,
p.14.

20 'upwards of 40 Special Constables': quoted in Brown, p. 98.

23 'we have made Italy': Hobsbawm, Eric, and Ranger, Terence,
(eds.), *The Invention of Tradition*, Cambridge University Press,
1992, p. 267.

26 'Bear thine own Devil thyself': *The Orkneyinga Saga*.

29 Up Helly Aa song written by J. J. Haldane Burgess.

30 'A powerful, fearful wind began to blow': Smyser, 'Ibn Faldan's
Account of the Rus with Some Commentary and Some Allusions to
Beowulf', in J. B. Bessinger and R. P. Creed (eds.), *Franciplegius:
Medieval and Linguistic Studies in Honor of Francis Peabody Magoun,
Jr.*, New York, 1965, pp. 92–119.

III WE KINDA PEOPLE

37   'Can you hear a distant drum / Bouncing on the laughter of a melody'
      Rudder, Dave, *Calypso Music*.

38   'the history of a common people's struggle for freedom': Hill, Erroll,
      The Trinidad Carnival, University of Texas Press, Austin and London,
      1972, p. 49.

40   'a festival in which, in point of fact, is not given to the people': from
      Goethe, *The Roman Carnival*, quoted in Falassi, Alessandro, ed., *Time
      out of Time, Essays on the Festival*, University of New Mexico Press,
      1987, p. 15.

41   'a wretched buffoonery': from *Port of Spain Gazette*, 1838, quoted in
      Hill, p. 17.

43   'Jerningham the governor': quoted in Hill, p. 59.

45   'They were soaked with sweat': McDonald, Ian, *The Hummingbird
      Tree*, Heinemann, 1969, quoted in Mason, Peter, *Bacchanal, The
      Carnival Culture of Trinidad*, Latin American Bureau (Research and
      Action) Ltd, London, 1998, p 61.

50   'The mud, cold against warm skin in the early morning': *Express
      Carnival Magazine*, p. 25.

54   'Mas is dancing sculpture': *Express Carnival Magazine*, p. 40.

59   'Man, de song so sweet': from the Keith Smith column, *Trinidad
      Express*, 2002.

IV A FRIENDLY KIND OF FIGHT

65   'cross between Rugby': Lidz, Franz 'Wild in the streets' in *Sports
      Illustrated*, 18 March 2002.

67   'A round ball and a square goal': quoted in Walvin, James, *The
      People's Game, The History of Football Revisited*, Mainstream
      Publishing, Edinburgh, 1994, p. 11.

67   'first ball that ever was made to Nausicaa': Burton, Robert, *The
      Anatomy of Melancholy*, New York Review Books edition ii, p. 72.

68   'for as much as there is great noise': quoted in Holt, Richard, *Sport
      and the British*, Clarendon Press, Oxford, 1989, p. 29.

69   'any exercise which withdraweth us from godliness': quoted in
      Walvin, *The People's Game*, p. 22.

70   'a match of futtball was Cried at Kettering': quoted in Walvin, p. 26.

71   'it becomes our painful duty to record the death': quoted in
      Vorspan, R., 'Popular Urban Leisure in Victorian England', *McGill
      Law Journal*, 2000, p. 891.

72   'You will do away with the courage and pluck': quoted in Walvin,
      p. 43.

76 'There's a game that bears a well known name': quoted in Porter, Lindsay, *Shrovetide Football and the Ashbourne Game*, Landmark Publishing, Ashbourne, 2002, p. 206.

82 'a new factor arose when Mrs Mugglestone jumped in': quoted in Frost, Carol, 'Girlpower Milestone', *Ashbourne Telegraph*, 5 March 2003.

84 'a wonderfully hard and vigorous game': quoted in Porter.

85 'I have got seven children': *Ashbourne Telegraph*, 3 March 2003.

V THE AGONY AND THE ECSTASY

89 'busy in cutting up several beasts': Burton, Robert, *The Anatomy of Melancholy*, edition ii, p. 107.

94 'so large that those who see it shall think': quoted in Evans, Sarah Jane, *Seville*, Sinclair-Stevenson, London, 1991, p. 28.

97 'Believe, proclaim and defend to the point of bloodshed': see the website of the brotherhood – www.elsilencio.com

109 'Abrir las puertas carceleros': gracias a Roccio Olid Fiances.

110 'If you have seen Semana Santa you can say': Machado, Manuel, *Estampas Sevillanas*, quoted in *Sevilla Penitente*, IMAN producciones, Seville, Vol. II, p. 310 (author's translation).

VI CHARIOTS OF THE GODS

113 'naked as a turtle's back': Dimmit, Cornelia and van Buitenen, J. A. B., (translators and editors), *Classical Hindu Mythology, A Reader in the Sanskrit Puranas*, Temple University Press, Philadelphia, 1978, p. 42.

114 'many . . . who have come to this feast cast themselves': quoted in Yule, H., editor, *Hobson Jobson – A Glossary of Anglo-Indian Words and Phrases*, London, 1886, available on www.bibliomania.com.

115 'They voluntarily offer up their wretched lives': quoted in Lewis, Norman, *A Goddess in the Stones*, Jonathan Cape, London, 1991, p. 165.

115 'truth, forgiveness, control of senses': quoted in Gupta, Subhadra Sen, *Puri, Lord Jagannatha's Dhaam*, Rupa & Co., New Delhi, 2002, p. 2.

117 'O Forgetful mind, why do you forget?': Panchaska Poets, translated by Sarbeswar Das, *Orissa Review*, Vol. LVIII No. 12, July, 2002, p. 4.

118 'This country is no fit subject for conquest': quoted in *Orissa Review*, p. 13.

119 'A thousand pilgrims strain': Southey, Robert, *The Curse of Kehama*, 1810, XIV. p. 5.

122   'appearance He had while killing a crocodile in order to save an elephant': Padhi, Jagabandhu, *Sri Jagannatha at Puri*, S.N.G. Publications, Puri, 2000, p. 128.

123   'sufficient to procure inestimable blessings': Dubois, Abbe J. A., *Hindu Manners, Customs and Ceremonies*, translated by Henry K. Beauchamp (1906), Rupa & Co., New Dehli, 1992, p. 810.

128   'O Lord of the Gods! Take away from me all attachment': *Jagannathastakam*, translated by Subas Pani, *Orissa Review*, p. 3.

129   'Why do you, O mad mind': translated by Sarbeswar Das, *Orissa Review*, p. 4.

130   'applaud them heartily and regard them': Dubois, p. 676.

130   'spectacular, although non-fatal results': Lewis, p. 166.

130   'Decency and modesty are at a discount': Dubois, p. 683.

131   'The sight here beggars all description': quoted in *Hobson Jobson*.

131   'lulled to their last sleep by the roar of the eternal ocean': Wilson Hunter, Sir William, *Orissa: Or the Vicissitudes of an Indian Province under Native and British Rule*, quoted in *Orissa Review*, p. 14.

134   'sublime visions, strengthened transcendental consciousness': Lewis, p. 164.

134   'What is important is not the object worshipped': Gupta, p. 32.

135   'He who kills the cow of a Brahmin will go after death to hell': Dubois, p. 630.

VII THE PLEASURES OF THE CHASE

140   'If I am drowned in blood, what a pleasant death!': Gibbon, Edward, *The Decline and Fall of the Roman Empire*, Everyman Edition, 1993, Vol. VI, p. 636.

144   'an ordeal by noise and wine': Tynan, Kenneth, *Bull Fever*, Longmans, Green & Co Ltd, London, 1966, p. 2.

145   'the fiesta had really started': Hemmingway, Ernest, *Fiesta, The Sun Also Rises*, Arrow Books (Random House) London, 1994, p. 136.

153   'What do I want with exercise, Hombre?': Hemmingway, Ernest, *Death in the Afternoon*, Arrow Books, London, 1994, p. 138.

154   'when I feel the horn go in': Tynan, p. 37.

155   'Without valour, bullfighting is like the sky without the sun': quoted in Tynan, p. 159.

157   'The bull, as he should be, is dead': Hemmingway, *Death in the Afternoon*, p. 249.

157   'This is what you wanted': Hemmingway, *Death in the Afternoon*, p. 224.

VIII RIVALS

162 'The Palio has two components': quoted in 'Speedy Snail Wins Palio', *Corriere Della Sera*, 17 August 2003.

163 'running in the Palio': quoted in *Palio: The Colors of Siena*, etext on www.commune.siena.it.

168 'Every man, woman, grandparent and child': quoted in Jessi, Carlotta, 'The Palio, A War of Dirty Tricks', www.venere.com.

172 'Go little horse! And come back a winner!': Morton, H V, *A Traveller in Italy*, Methuen, London, 2001 p. 253.

173 'the most colourful and romantic procession': Morton, p. 259.

174 'the painted wings of enormous butterflies': Huxley, Aldous, 'The Siena Palio', in *Along the Road*, Chatto & Windus, London, 1974, p. 92.

174 'If I could I would have hurled': quoted in *Palio: the Colors of Siena*.

IX THE PURSUIT OF HAPPINESS

185 'everybody on that beach, north and south came running': Harvey, Larry, speech at Burning Man 1997, *Burning Man Archives*, www.burningman.com.

186 'It was horrible': Harvey, Larry, speech at Burning Man 1997.

187 'We all got out of our cars': Brill, Louis M, 'The First Year in the Desert', *Burning Man Archives*.

187 'It turns out in this vast desert space': Harvey, Larry, speech at Burning Man 1997.

189 'Imagine a vast, waveless ocean': Twain, Mark, *Roughing It*, Penguin Classics, London, 1988, p. 163.

191 'people in intricate costumes': Kozinets, Robert V, 'Can consumers escape the market? Emancipatory illuminations from Burning Man', *Journal of Consumer Research*, 29 June 2002, pp. 20–38.

198 'they circle each other tensely, shriek': Etcoff, Nancy, *Survival of the Prettiest, The Science of Beauty*, Abacus, London, 2000, p. 98.

201 'The Ship to Ship crew are': *Black Rock Gazette*, 27 August 2002.

202 'Originally, the core ritual around the man was the raising': Harvey, Larry, 1994, *Burning Man Archives*.

205 'More souls are begot': quoted in Johnson, Paul, *A History of the American People*, Phoenix, London, 1998, p. 303.

X AN IDEAL FATHER

214 'a woman marries where she can get milk': Stenning, Derrick, *Savannah Nomads, A Study of the Wodaabe Pastoral Fulani of Western Bornu Province, Northern region, Nigeria*, International African Institute, London, 1959, p. 55.

215 'Only in the immense savannah': Brandt, Henry, *Nomads du Soleil*, e-text on www.pulaaku.net (author's translation).

219 'The morning star has arisen!': Brandt, (author's translation).

222 'The bad dancer deserves': Bovin, Mette, *Nomads who Cultivate Beauty, Wodaabe Dances and visual Arts in Niger*, Nordiska Afrikainstitutet, Uppsala, Sweden, 2001, p. 40.

224 '*Fijjo kamma habre* – 'dance is war'': Bovin, p. 69.

226 '*Raara kine nana gikku*': Bovin, p. 56.

226 'struck on the nose': Stenning, p. 57.

XI THE FAT OF THE LAND

234 'for their drink, they draw a liquor from barley': Tacitus, *Germania*, Project Gutenberg e-text.

234 'at no season is the soul more open': Tacitus.

235 'drink beer and become fat': Barr, Andrew, *Drink, A Social History*, Pimlico, London, 1998, p. 270.

239 'exceeded anything that might have been seen before': Bauer, Karl, *The Oktoberfest, Portrait of a Fair*, Verlag Georg D. W. Callwey, Munich, 1970, p. 28.

240 'The beer tents are absolutely enormous and alarming': Mann, Thomas, letter to Aline Bernstein, 4 October 1928, (translated by 1st Transnational).

246 'They consecrate whole woods': Tacitus.

255 'They were men of fifty or sixty years of age': Twain, Mark, *A Tramp Abroad*, Penguin Classics, London, p. 140.

XII THE MEXICAN WAY OF DEATH

257 'He'll not build now who has no house awaiting': Rilke, Rainer Maria, 'Autumn Day', translated by J. B. Leishman, Penguin, London, 1964.

259 'The word death is not pronounced in New York': Paz, Octavio, *The Labyrinth of Solitude*, translated by Lysander Kemp, Penguin Books, London, 1985, p. 57.

261 'The ultimate purpose of the celebrations is to re-inforce': quoted in Garciagodoy, Juanita, *Digging the Days of the Dead*, University Press of Colorado, 1998, p. 68.

261 'they did not want to have children': Zurita, Alonso, *The Brief and Summary Relation of the Lords of New Spain*, translated Benjamin Keene, Rutgers University Press, 1963, p. 89.

262 'where he himself would preside over the slaughter': las Casas, Bartolome de, *A Short Account of the Destruction of the Indies*, translated by A. P. Griffin, Penguin Classics, London, 1992, p. 31.

266 'come back to visit us and to ask for bread': *Cronicas y Leyendas (de esta Noble, Leal y Meftica Cuidad de Mexico)*, pamphlet, Colectiva memoria y Vida Cotidiana A.C., Mexico, 2002, (author's translation).

268 'all of them dancing to the tuck of a drum': Frazer, Sir James, *The Golden Bough*, Wordsworth Editions, London, 1993, p. 591.

272 'Poor little dead thing!': Arroyo Sámano, Alfonso R., *Estudio sobre el Dia de Muertos de Totolapan* (author's translation).

272 'In the Second Phase': Arroyo Sámano, (author's translation).

276 '*Como te ves, mi vi*': Garciagodoy, p. 14.

279 'How if our waking life, like that of sleep': de la Barca, Calderón, *Life is a Dream*, Project Gutenberg e-text.